IMAGES
of America

LINDEN
NEW JERSEY

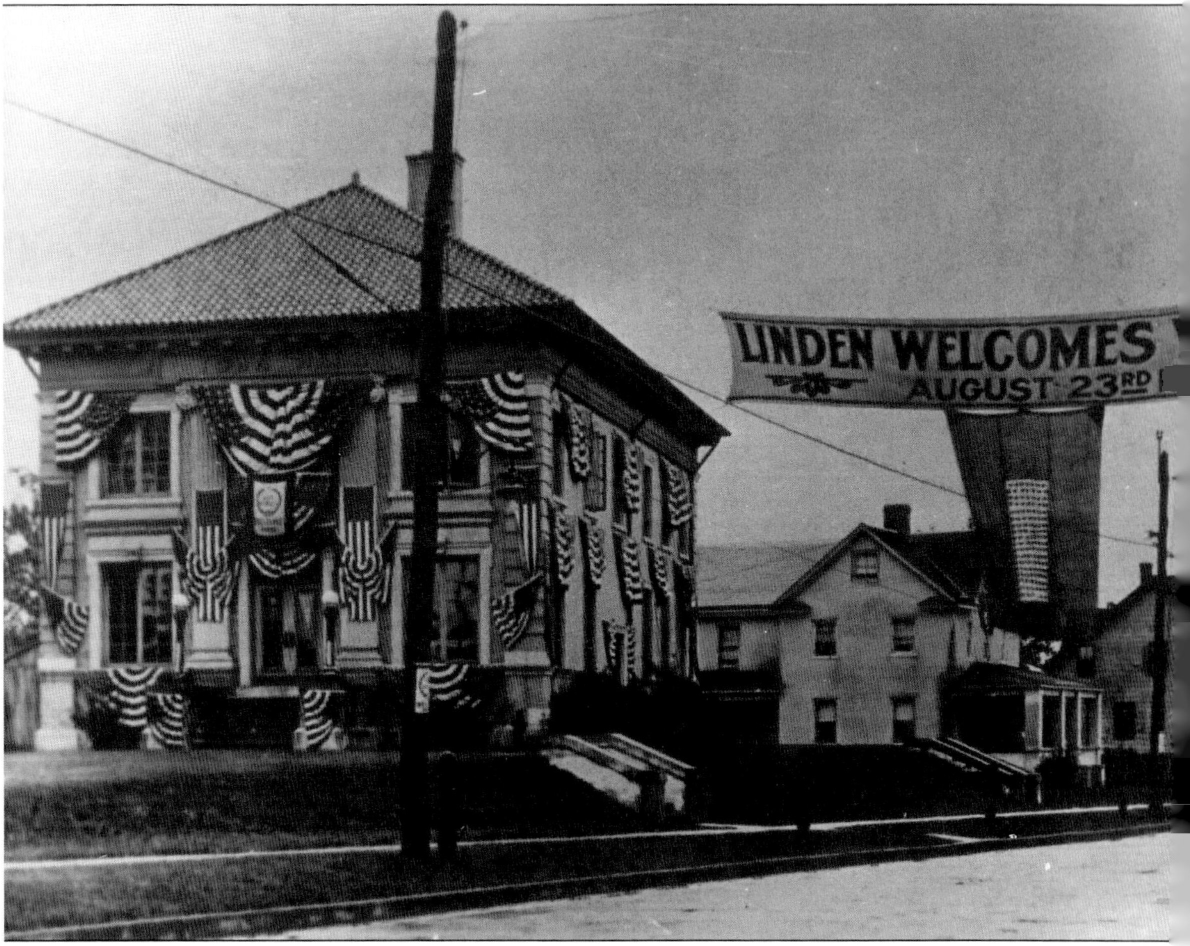

Welcome to Linden, New Jersey! Linden is a very active community whose citizens take pride in their city and its history. Shown here is the town hall (now referred to as the Old City Hall) in 1919, dressed up to honor and welcome the returning veterans at the end of World War I.

This book is dedicated in honor of the unique past of the city of Linden and in appreciation of the people of Linden of the past, present, and future. Also in loving memory of my favorite storyteller, my father, Michael Pancurak.

IMAGES
of America

LINDEN
NEW JERSEY

Lauren Pancurak Yeats

ARCADIA
PUBLISHING

ISBN 978-0-7385-6326-8

Published by Arcadia Publishing
Charleston, South Carolina

Printed in the United States of America

Library of Congress Catalog Card Number: 2008927253

For all general information contact Arcadia Publishing at:
Telephone 843-853-2070
Fax 843-853-0044
E-mail sales@arcadiapublishing.com
For customer service and orders:
Toll-Free 1-888-313-2665

Visit us on the Internet at www.arcadiapublishing.com

"We celebrate the past to awaken the future."
—John Fitzgerald Kennedy, August 14, 1960.

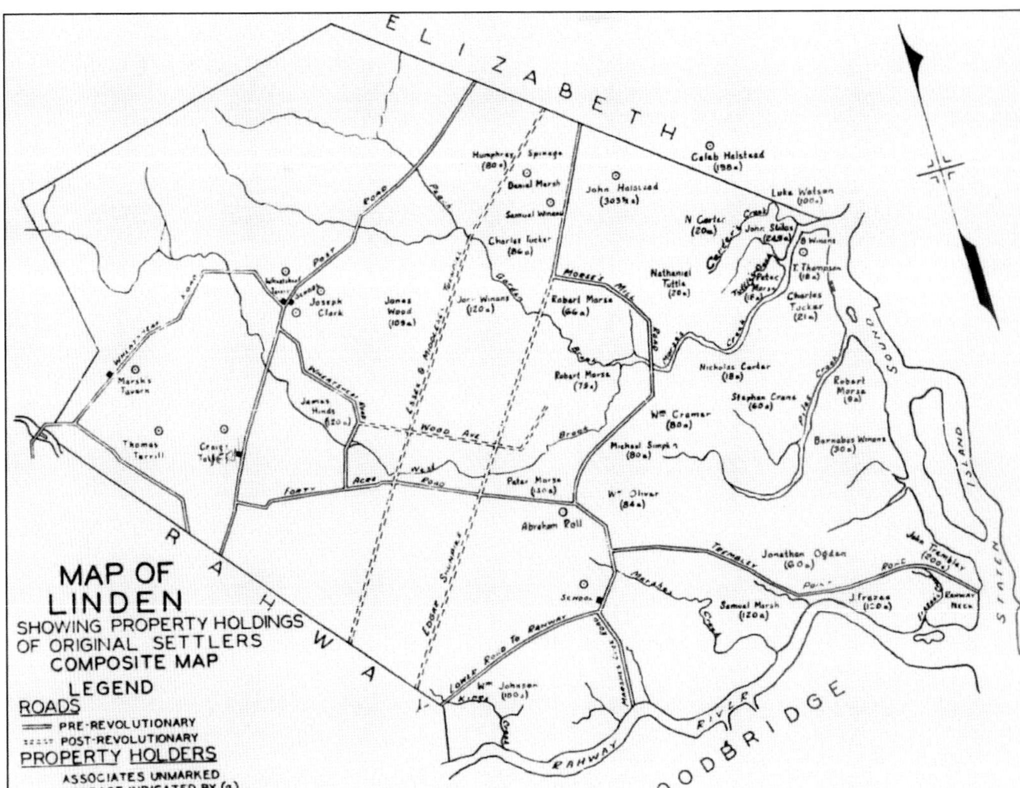

Map showing the shape of Linden in 1862, depicting the locations of the original settlers. Forty Acre Road is Stiles Street; Old Post Road is St. George Avenue. The Edgar Shunpike is Edgar Road. The Essex and Middlesex Turnpike is now the railroad.

Contents

Acknowledgments

Every effort was made to provide interesting images as well as informative text for this book. I enjoyed meeting so many folks that are interested in preserving and sharing memories of Linden. This project was like a big jigsaw puzzle and many sources were sought to locate missing pieces of the past. I wish that I could have fit every image into one book. A second volume may soon be created to include things that couldn't fit or weren't available at the time of this printing. The support of everyone listed below has kept my enthusiasm strong. To everyone who contributed in some way, I thank you from the bottom of my heart:

To Mayor John T. Gregorio, for welcoming the concept of a book of this format about Linden, and for supporting my efforts, allowing me access to request images from city departments, and announcing my project to the City Council; to George Milkowsky and the City Council members for allowing me to speak at their respective Ward meetings: Virginia Graziano, Robert Bunk, Anthony Orlando, Ralph Strano, William Niemeck, Albert Youngblood, Derek Armstead, and Richard Gerbounka; to Councilman Edwin F. Schulhafer, also for lending me Linden Fire Dept. images; to Councilman Charles Crane, also for images of his family and the Sixth Ward including J. Wheeler Park and early parades; to Louis Di Leo Esquire for legal advice; to Myles Hergert for historic information; to Morton Weitzman for history, locations, and excellent help in reaching numerous people; to Nina Sadry for her support; to Linden Recreation Department Director Alfred A. Volpe, for the front page image of town hall; to Joan Mastowski, for aid with the parade photographs; to City Engineer John Ziemian, for inviting me to the engineering office; to Jeffrey Sias for verification of images; to George Vircik for much help while reviewing the photographs of the city; to Roberta Canavan, Director of the Linden Public Library, for permitting me to borrow numerous images from their archives and for inviting me to speak at the Kiwanis luncheon; to Michael Bono, for having me to speak to the Economic Development Corporation; to Captain Frank Kuczinski for an image of Highway Patrol Car #1; to John Venditto for his support ; to Joseph Stigliano for an image of Sanitation Truck #3; to John Chabak for identifying people in some photographs; to Stephen Hoptay for the history of Tremley Point; to Lawrence Lukenda for fire department images and his community study; to Francine Lopez for images of the blacksmith and Linden Police Department.; to Paul Werkmeister for a photograph of George Sweet and Mayor Hurst; to Ted Efaw for locating the Kennedy quote; to Joseph Clarke Jr., Superintendent of Schools, for his support and notifying the school principals of my quest and permission to speak to them; to Alexis Jarosz for the School No. 5 image; to Michael Di Micele for the School No. 6 image; to Jules Le Boff for school facts; to Anthony Cataline and Linda Spano for an image of School No. 10; to Bernice Bedrick for the history and images of the schools; to Robert Antonowicz, for school history; to Emil and Helen Pancurak for images including School No. 4 , the ground breaking for School No. 4 Annex, and Peach Orchard Towers; to Pauline Stetz for information on Lida M. Ebbert; to Walter and Stella Tylicki for old school postcards; to Allen Schnirman, Richard Koziol, Rebecca Tatolli, and Alvin and Marilyn Coplan for locations of images; to Jay Colucci for images of the family grocery store, the Villani Bus Company, and the cover image of the

Victory Parade; to Mike Kraynick for the only undefeated football team; to Sylvia Weisbrot for images of her dad, William, author of the *History of Linden* manuscript; to Perry Leib for sharing his knowledge and a historic scrapbook; to Walter Fedor for his interest in Linden history, his support, and a School No. 2 image; to Mary Bodek for her wedding image; to Joseph and Chris Bodek for their support; to Morris Raiffe for numerous possible sources; to Cynthia Hoffman and Morris Leone for use of their respective community studies; to Bruce Howe for speaking to the Linden Coalition; to Vivian and Ray Eriksen for images of Esso and the Linden Presbyterian Church; to Al Palermo for images of the Boy Scouts, the Dutch Reformed Church, and historic information; to Doris Henel for images of early Girl Scouts, the Methodist church, and early Linden; to Mary Kuhtik for images of St. George's Church; to John and Julia Dobosiewicz for early local images including St. Theresa's, John Dobosiewicz Sr., and Volupte Inc.; to Suburban Temple Secretary Ruth Guntherand Gertrude Yellin , for images of the Synagogue; to Harry and Helen Dressig, and Anna Stracensky, for an image of Holy Family Church; to Rev. Hobart C. Utter Jr. for images of St. Paul's Lutheran Church; to Ted Rosenberg, Administrator of the Congregation Anshe Chesed, for images of the synagogue; to Ceil Baldwin for old family images; to Ruth Etta Apalinski for her family photographs of the Winans and McGillvray clans and the loan of the Winans genealogy book; to Raymond Bauer for information on the Winans family; to George Kushner for the early image of Blue Ribbon Pools; to H.G. Clarke for images of the Wood house and the corner of Elizabeth and Wood Avenues; to Donald Clarke for inviting me to speak to the Linden Rotary Club; to Vera Di Leo for an image of Di Leos' Candy Store; to Brian and Doreen Fritchze for family photographs and the 12th Street Candy Store; to Beatrice Bernzott for historic facts of the Tremley area, locations, and encouragement; to Grace Wilson for her image of School No. 1 and her notes; to Mimi Derrig for images including the Roll-Derrig family, Penn Sweet Shop, and the Railroad Station; to Fred Cassel for old postcards of Linden and his gift of Walt's 42nd Street; to Betty and Pat Banasiak for an image of Gordons Gin; to White Castle Inc., O.H., for their photograph of the Linden restaurant; to Allie Motors for an image of Eds' Gas; to Tom Stefanik for Grasselli Park history; to Wanda Knapp for a Village Bakery photograph; to Linda Whitney for her family photograph of Connie's Pizza; to Jean Spinelli, for having me speak at Murowski Towers; to Molly Lenz for an early Linden postcard; to General Motors for their images of the "Wildcats"; to Wayne Szuba for the use of his Eastern Aircraft Division book; to Mike Carlovich of Tosco Inc. for help and information finding a view of the dog track; to the Exxon Corporation for use of the dog track and refinery images; to Mahlon Scott for images of Morey La Rue; to Chris Wade, of Wade Contractors, and Marilyn Donald for images of their families' construction firms; to Bernie Plungis for his images of Edgar Road Garage, Route #25, and the dog track steeples; to Helen Christolis for photographs of her family, neighborhood, and farm; to Edward Truncale for images of his home, an aerial view of the airport, and the Plungis plane on Edgar Road; to Howard Silverman for images of his family, the Silverman Agency, and the Civil Air Patrol; to Sam De Palma and the Worrall Community Newspapers for the author's image; to Luther Carson for images of the oldest house in Linden; to Dan and Jane Stankus for the rescued *Daily Journal* images (now donated to the Linden and Union County Historical Societies); to Charles Shallcross Jr., Robert Fridlington, Charles Aqualina, and Richard T. Koles of the Union County Historical Society, for information; and to Jean Rae Turner, for inspiration and submitting my name to Arcadia Publishers.

A special thank you to my support team: my mom, Irene Pancurak, for family images, memories, and for child care; my in-laws, Richard and Audrey Yeats, for their support and use of the facilities at Quality Graphics Center, Inc.; Raquel Cardet for child care during the sorting of the 450 images submitted; my children, Stephen, Kevin, and Chelsea; and my husband, Darren, for his constant love, knowledge, and support.

Introduction

The earliest residents of the area where the city of Linden is located were the Lenni Lenapi, or "original people" of the Algonquin Indians. On September 6, 1609, Henrik Hudson's ship, the *Half-Moon*, was exploring around the contiguous waters of Staten Island. Five men came ashore to what is now Linden to investigate and saw green land and forests of sweet-smelling trees. They soon came under attack by Native Americans, however, and one man, John Coleman, was slain by an arrow. He is buried at Colemans Point in Sandy Hook, which documents this incident. Dutch settlers soon followed Hudson and established "New Amsterdam."

King Charles II of England presented the land of New Amsterdam to his brother James, the Duke of York and Albany, to conquer. The Duke deployed an army led by Colonel Richard Nicholls, and the Dutch were subsequently subdued. New Amsterdam became New York and Albania (the land across the river), both in honor of James. Governor Nicholls attracted settlers to improve the area. Six Long Islanders petitioned to settle here: John Bayley, Luke Watson, Thomas Benydick, John Forster, and Nathaniel and Daniel Denton.

On September 30, 1664, Nicholls gave them approval to deal with the Lenni Lenapi for land from the Raritan River to Bound Brook. The Long Islanders hired Captain John Baker as an interpreter. Conescoman and Mattano Manamowouc of Staten Island represented the tribe. The deed was signed on October 28, 1664, and goods estimated at £154 were paid to the Native Americans. Nicholls confirmed the purchase on December 2, 1664.

The Associates soon grew from six to eighty men with the following owning land in the Linden area: Luke Watson; Nicholas Carter; William Johnson; Samuel Marsh; Robert Morse and his son Peter; William Oliver; Humphrey Spinage; Thomas Thompson; Charles Tucker; John Winans; Peter Noe; Barnabas Wines; Jonas Wood; Captain John Baker; Caleb Carwithy; William Cramer; Stephen Crane; Joseph Ffrazey; John Hinds and his son James; Abraham Shotwell; Samuel Marsh; Michael Simpkin; John Roll and his son Abraham; John Trembley; Peter Trembly; John Styles, and Nathaniel Tuttle. Upper Rahway, Wheatsheaf, and Trembly were formed by each man receiving a house lot in a village and some outlying territory.

On June 23, 1664, the Duke made Lord Berkley and Sir George Carteret the Proprietors of the land from the Hudson to the Delaware Rivers and south to Cape May and named it New Jersey, in honor of Carteret's defense of the English Isle of Jersey. They appointed Philip Carteret as their governor. Carteret was not told that the area had any residents, and he sold much of the land to new settlers. He and the first group arrived here in July 1665 and named the area Elizabethtown, in honor of the wife of Sir George. New land titles were required by the Associates to prove prior ownership. It was a major issue of the Revolutionary War.

Elizabethtown was very active during the war as the capitol of the colony of New Jersey. Abraham Clark of Elizabethtown was one of fifty-six men to sign the Declaration of Independence. On November 30, 1776, the British took over Elizabethtown, but after battles by the Rahway River, they retreated to Staten Island. The war ended on September 3, 1783, with Elizabethtowns' Elias Boudinot IV serving as president of the Continental Congress and automatically the new nation. In 1789, our first elected President, George Washington, rode on Old Post Road (St. Georges Avenue) to his inauguration in New York City.

One

The First Families of Linden Township

The mid-1800s was a time of changing boundaries, and in 1857 Union County separated from Essex County. The Township of Rahway was formed in 1858. On March 4, 1861, the Township of Linden was created by an act of the state legislature. It was created mostly from Rahway, but included part of Elizabeth and a small piece of Union. In addition to present-day Linden, the area included what is now Roselle, Winfield Park, a small portion of Cranford.

The name of the township was fought over because of the many village names the area encompassed. Wheatsheaf was originally a strong favorite with most of the residents. The name Linden came to the front because of a Mrs. Teeney, who lived on Dark Lane (Park Avenue) and objected to the street name. She made and hung a sign at the corner near Old Post Road (St. Georges Avenue) in a blacksmith shop which read "Linden Road," after the tree of the same name. Abram Aaron Ward saw the sign and thought that Linden would make a fine name for the township. It was not unanimous at first. After the township was named, the two railroad stations in town were still called Wheatsheaf and Tremley respectively until years later.

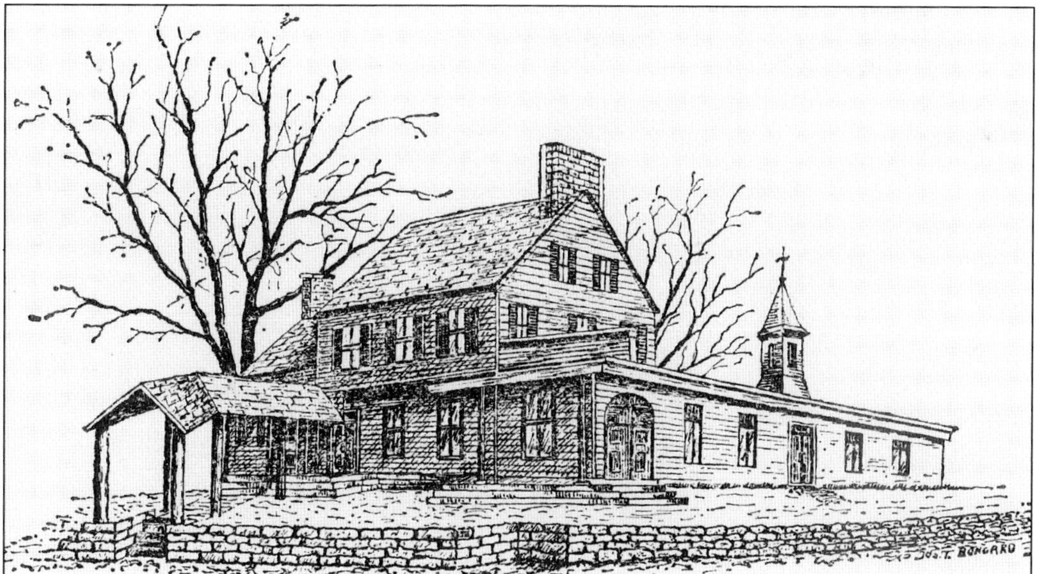

The Wheatsheaf Tavern in 1745.

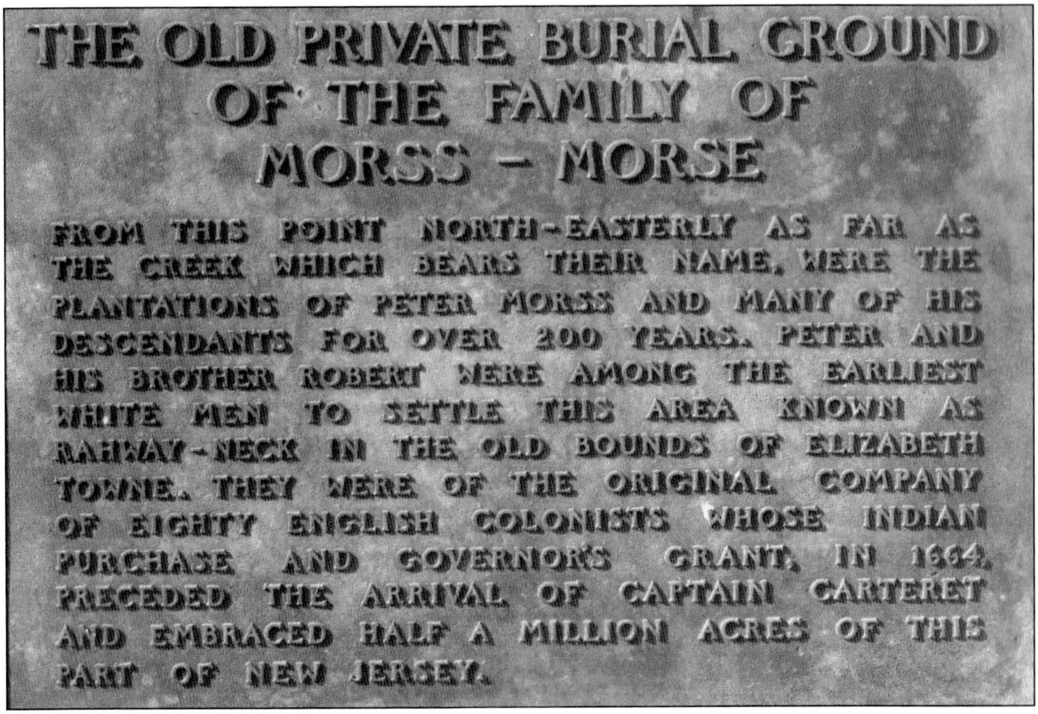

A memorial stone dedicated to the three graves below it. The stone, erected by the Humble Oil Bayway Refinery, is located on the 40-acre property at Lower Road now owned by the Tosco Corporation. This photograph was taken in 1952.

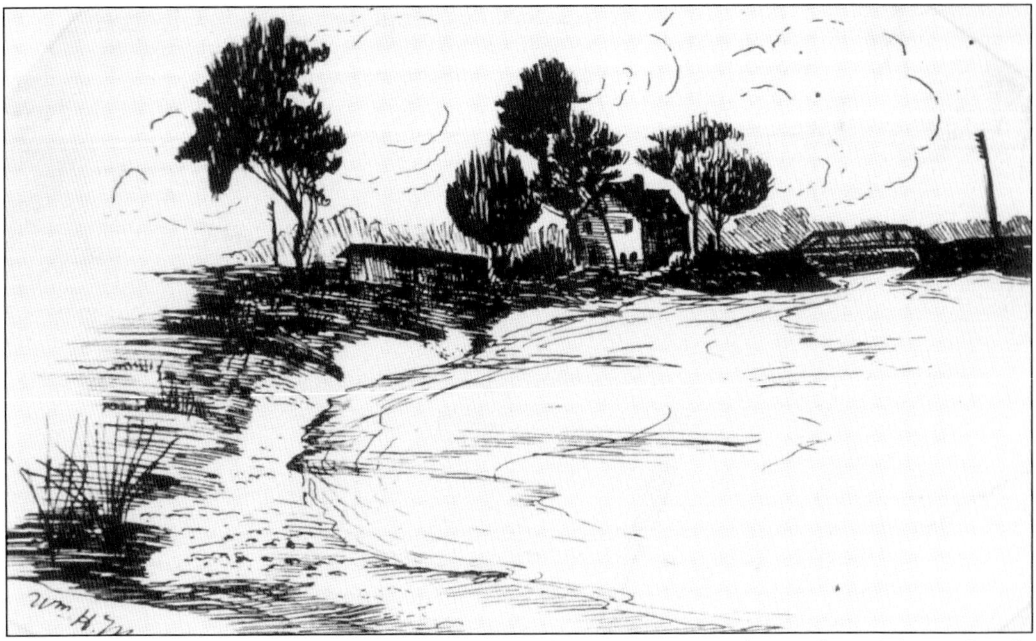

William H. Marbach's sketch of the John Jacob Morse House located on Morse Creek, done in 1936.

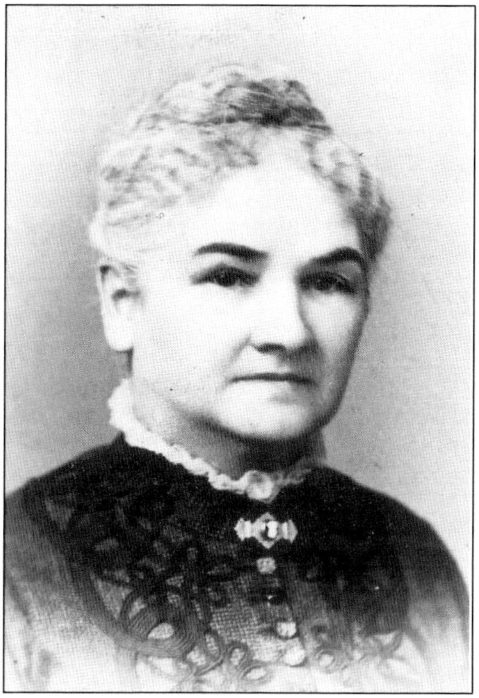

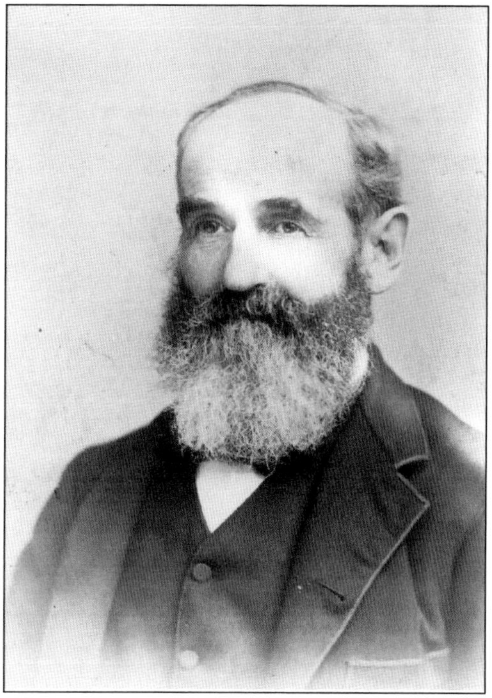

LEFT: Sarah Elizabeth Hatfield Winans (1828–1911) was married to Moses Oliver Winans in 1850 and was the mother of four children: Maline, Clarence, Sarah, and Louise. She left the Presbyterian Church in 1851 to join the Methodist Church. RIGHT: Moses Oliver Winans (1826–1900) was a mason and a farmer. He made many land transactions in the area and was one of the original trustees for the Linden Methodist Church. Moses and Sarah are buried in the Evergreen Cemetery in Hillside.

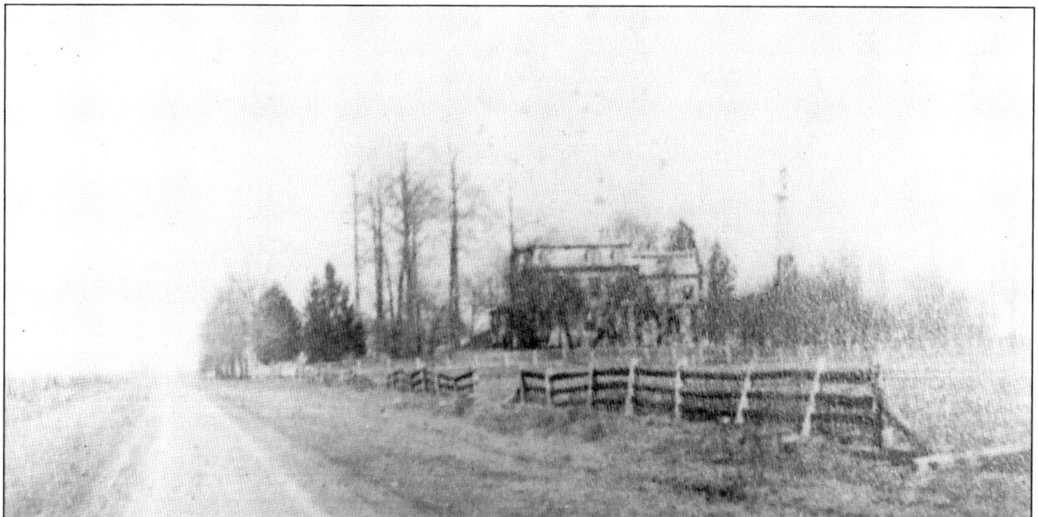

The Winans homestead seen from Linden Avenue. In 1902, Maline sold his part of the property to Clarence. William Smith then purchased it and sold it the same day to the Rosedale Cemetery Association. The Winans homestead was used as a guest house in the cemetery until it was razed during the 1960s.

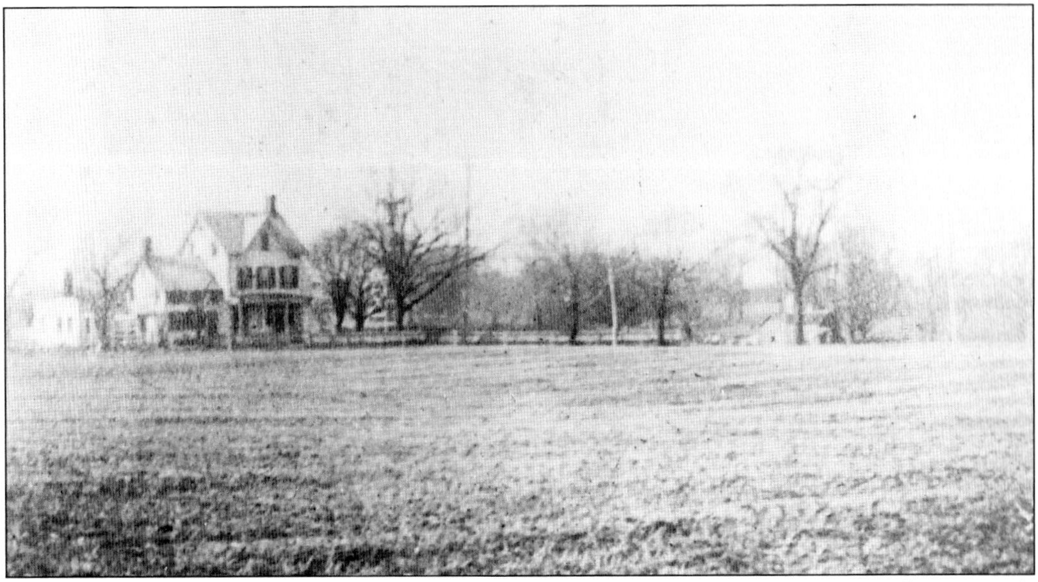

The Winans homestead as seen from inside the property lines. In 1902, William Smith purchased the homestead property from Clarence Winans and sold it to the Rosedale Cemetery Association. The Winans homestead was used as a guest house in the cemetery until it was razed during the 1960s.

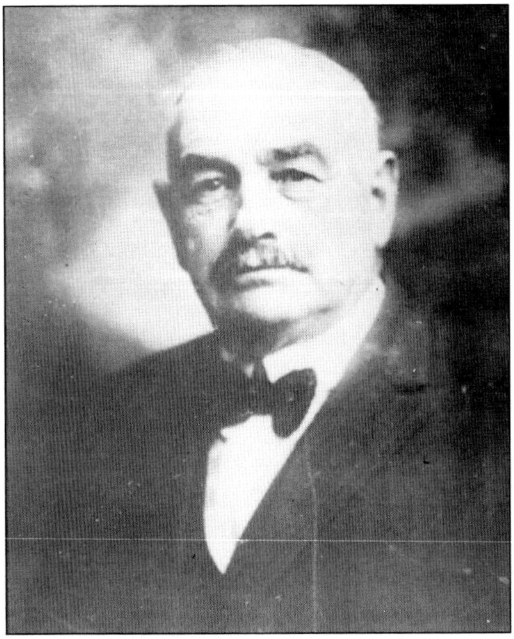

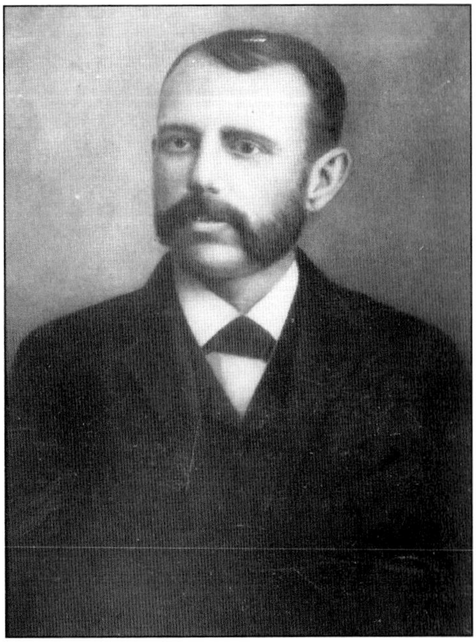

LEFT: Clarence Hatfield Winans (1854–1942). Clarence and his wife, Phoebe A. Wood (1856–1897), raised two children: Ada and Raymond. Clarence was a founder of the Linden Trust Company. He made many land transactions, but is also remembered for starting The C.H. Winans Co. in 1909. In 1910, Clarence Winans, George W. Bauer, Raymond W. Winans, and Walter S. Deniston formed a new corporation under the same name in Roselle. RIGHT: John P. Winans was the son of Jacob Winans, the eighth child of John and Susannah Winans. He bought and sold a lot of land with his distant cousin Clarence.

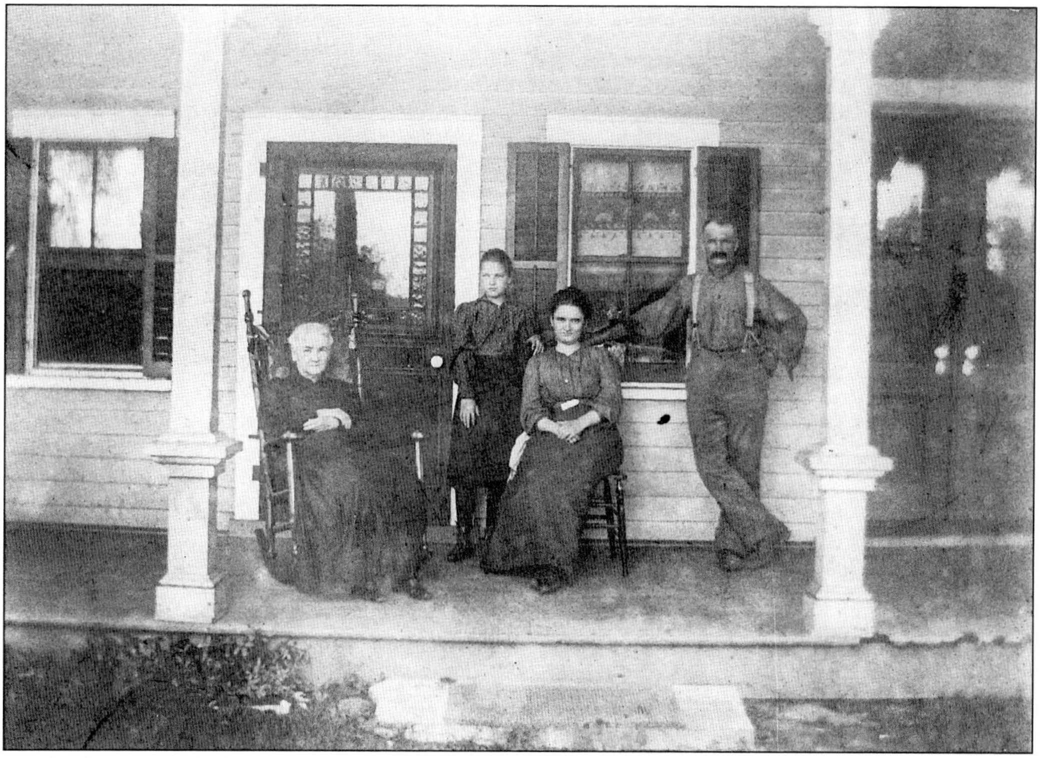

At the homestead where all of the children were born. Shown here are Sarah Elizabeth Hatfield Winans, her son Maline, and granddaughters Etta and Cora Winans.

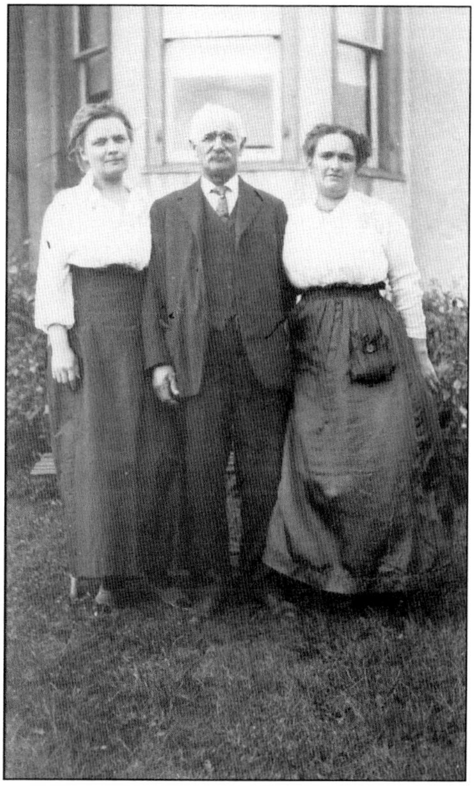

Maline Winans with daughters Cora and Etta Mae (later McGillvray).

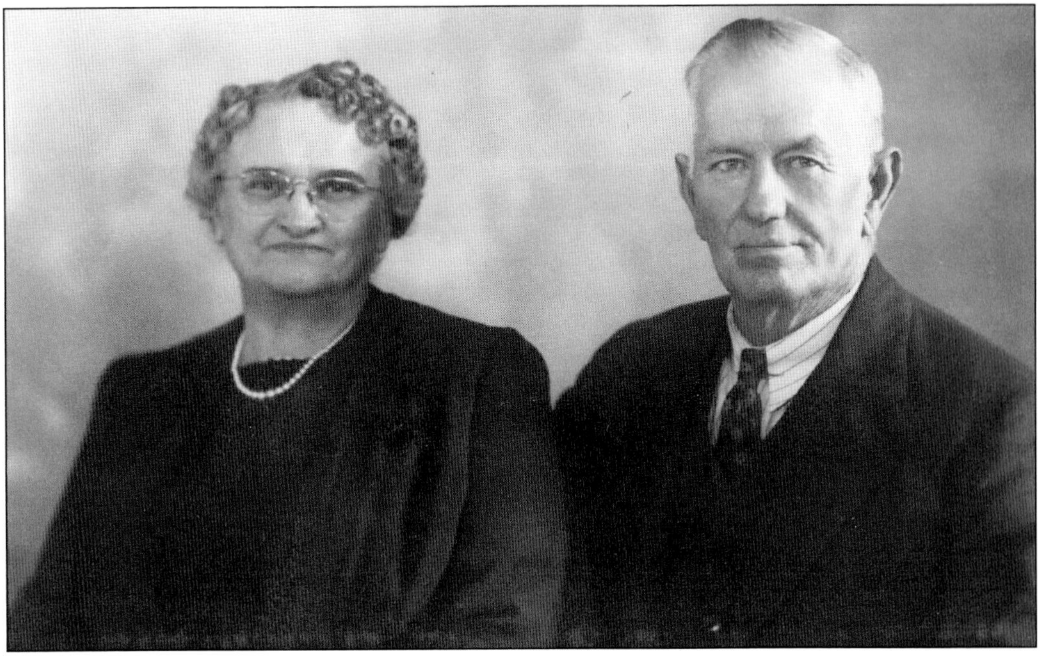

Fred McGillvray (1879–1967) and Etta Augusta Winans (1842–1965), married December 7, 1904. Their children were Fred, Sarah Mahar, Margaret Zimmer, and Ruth Fullerton; the couple had twelve grandchildren. Fred Sr. was a former Linden road commissioner and member of the board of education. He was one of four children along with William, Grace, and George. The family owned a dairy farm on St. George Avenue. This photograph was taken on the occasion of the couple's 50th wedding anniversary.

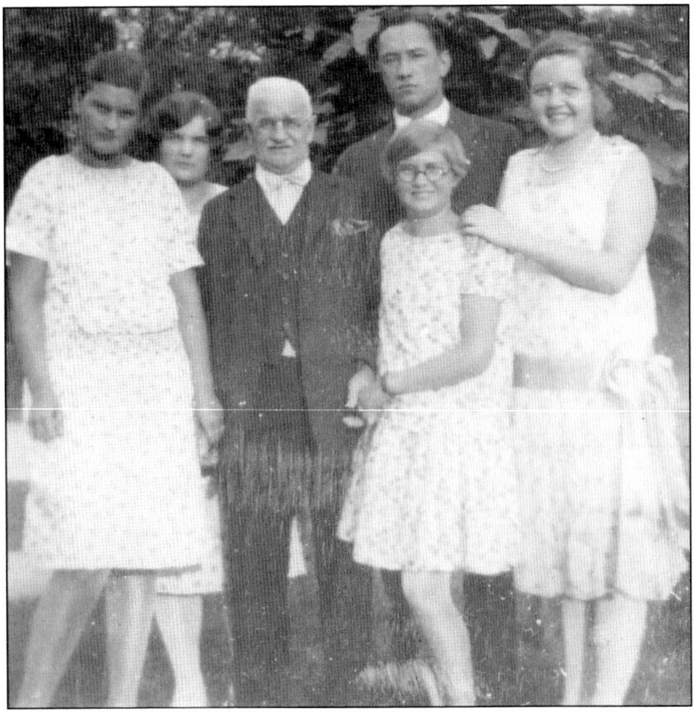

Maline Winans and grandchildren: Frederick, Sara, Margaret, Ruth McGillvray, and Mary Young.

George McGillvray was one of four children along with William, Grace, and Fred McGillvray. He was a very active member of the township committee and also became the first mayor of the city of Linden (1925–26). Albert Weber followed during the 1927–28 term, but McGillvray was reelected for the years 1929–30. In 1931, Jules Verner became acting mayor due to the death of James B. Furber, mayor elect. Verner was elected to fill the unexpired term in 1932. The following mayors have governed the city of Linden since: Myles J. McManus (1933–43), H. Roy Wheeler (1944–52), William Hurst (1953–64), Alexander Wrigley (1965–66), John T. Gregorio (1967–83), George Hudak (1983–86), and Paul Werkmeister (1987–1990). The current mayor is John T. Gregorio (1991–present).

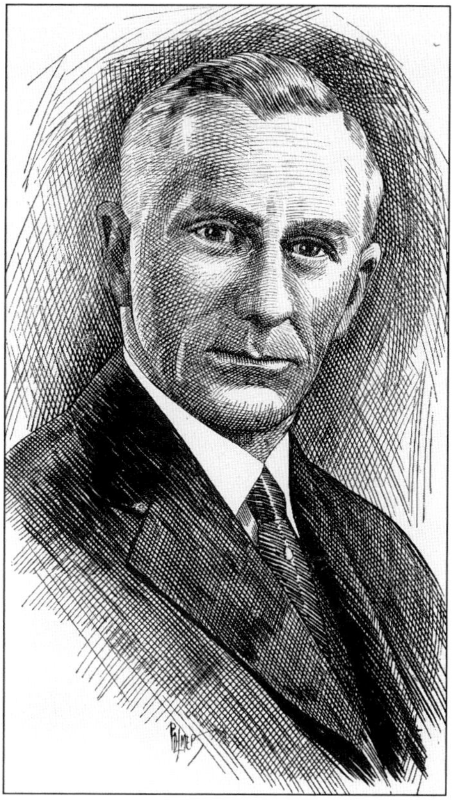

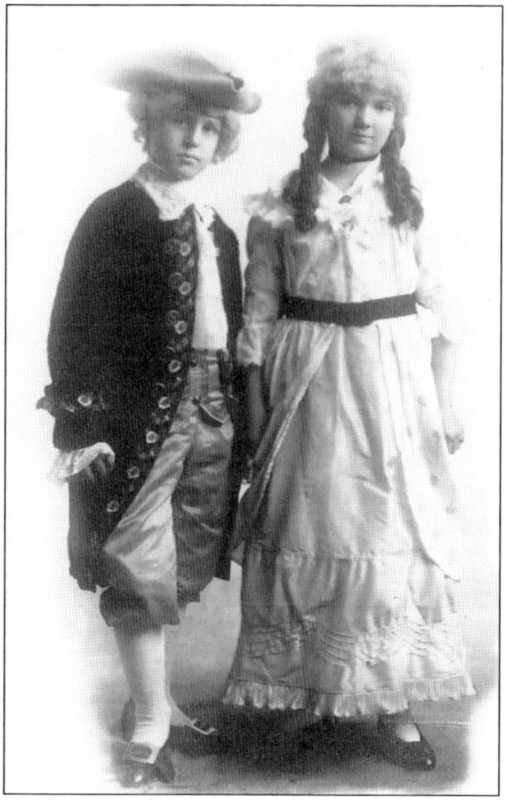

Fred and Sara McGillvray were two of the children of Fred and Etta Augusta McGillvray.

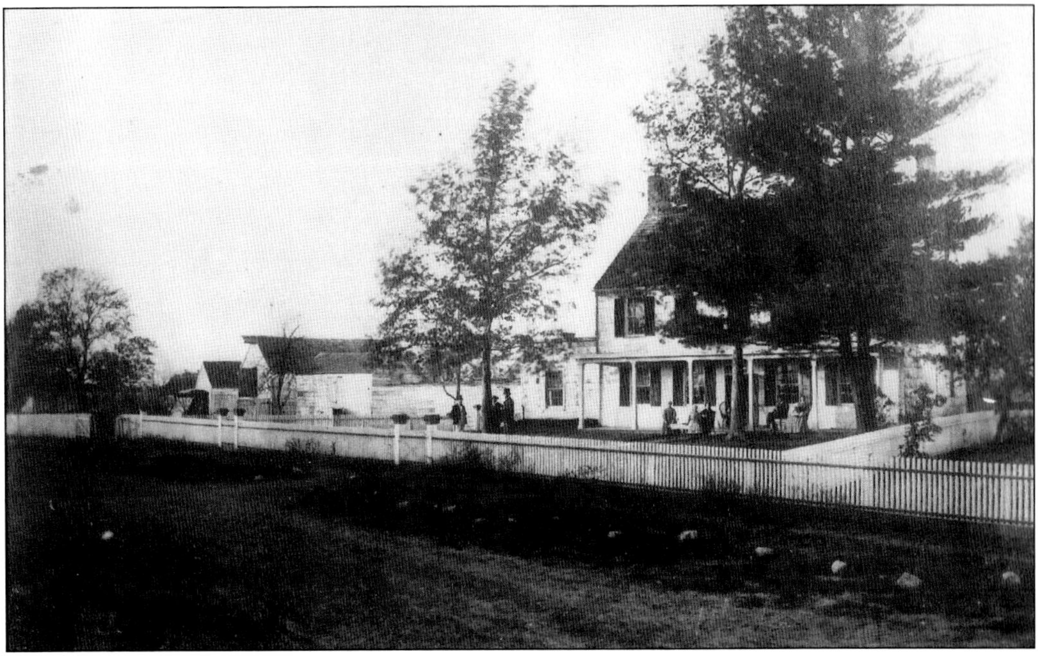

The Wood homestead on North Wood Avenue. There are daisies in the field that would later become Wood Avenue. Phoebe Augusta Wood Winans was the daughter of Meeker Wood and Susan Winans (1856–1897). Their graves are located at Evergreen Cemetery in Hillside.

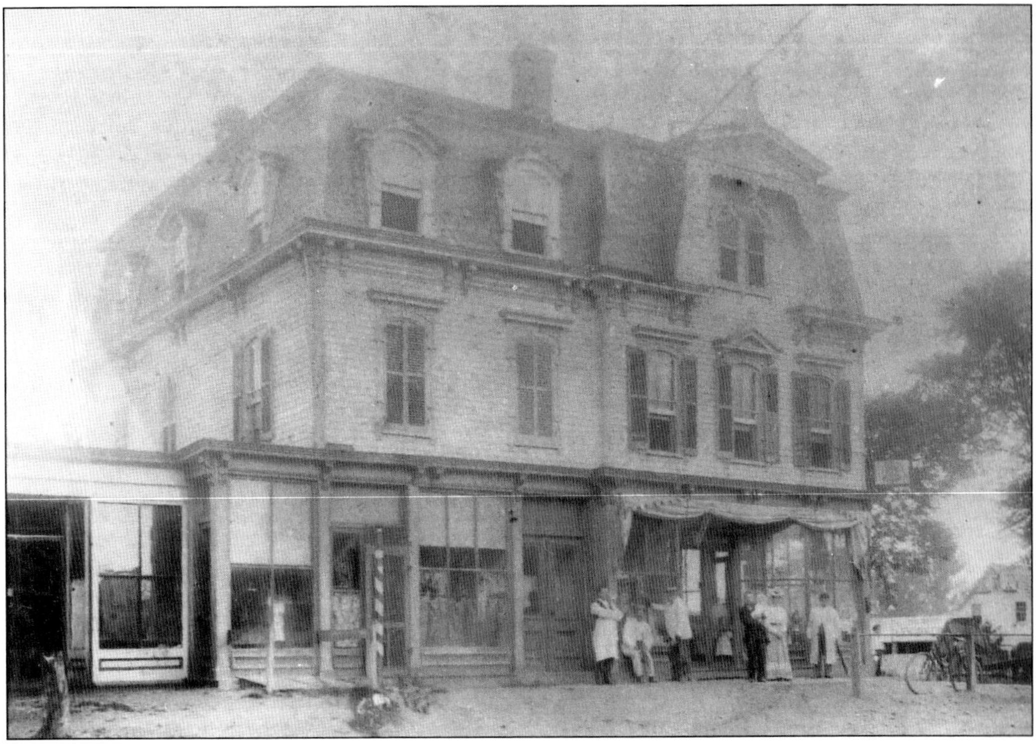

The stores and house that were across from the Wood homestead, where Clarke Engineering and the El-Wood Plaza are now.

Mrs. Christina Dorthea Flaacke (nee Fishler), wife of Henry Flaacke, shown here in 1861. The couple lived in the estate below from 1854 to 1864. Henry was a member of the township committee from 1862 to 1864, and is named in the 1882 *History of Union County* on p. 398.

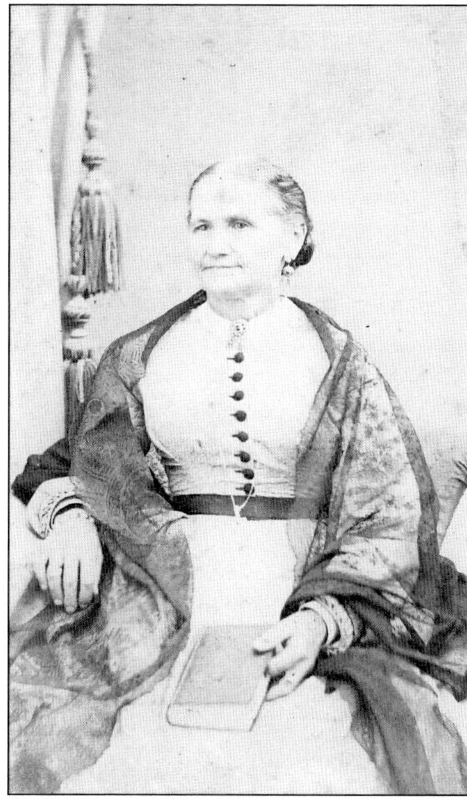

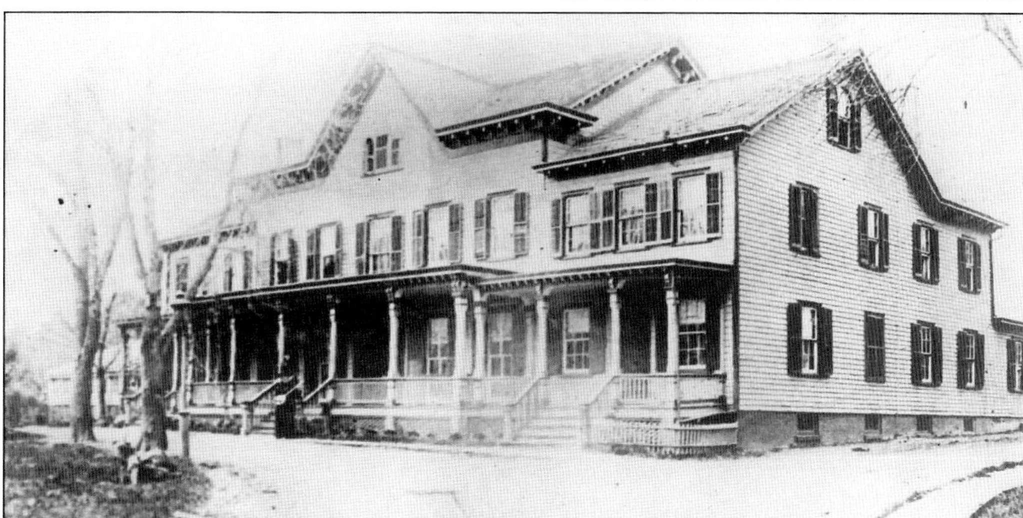

The Henry Flaacke (later Blancke) residence. It would have been located on West Blancke Street. The brook ran through the property. The linden tree-lined driveway would now be Brook Street. Ferdinand Blancke, the son of Frederick Blancke and Anna Snider, bought the property in 1864. He bought a large tract of Linden, sectioned off streets, and built houses. Prior to this he owned Blancke's Lunchroom at 97 Cedar Street in New York City. His wife was Caroline Brah, and their children were Ferdinand Jr., Herman, Emma, and Henry Louis. Ferdinand Sr. died in 1901.

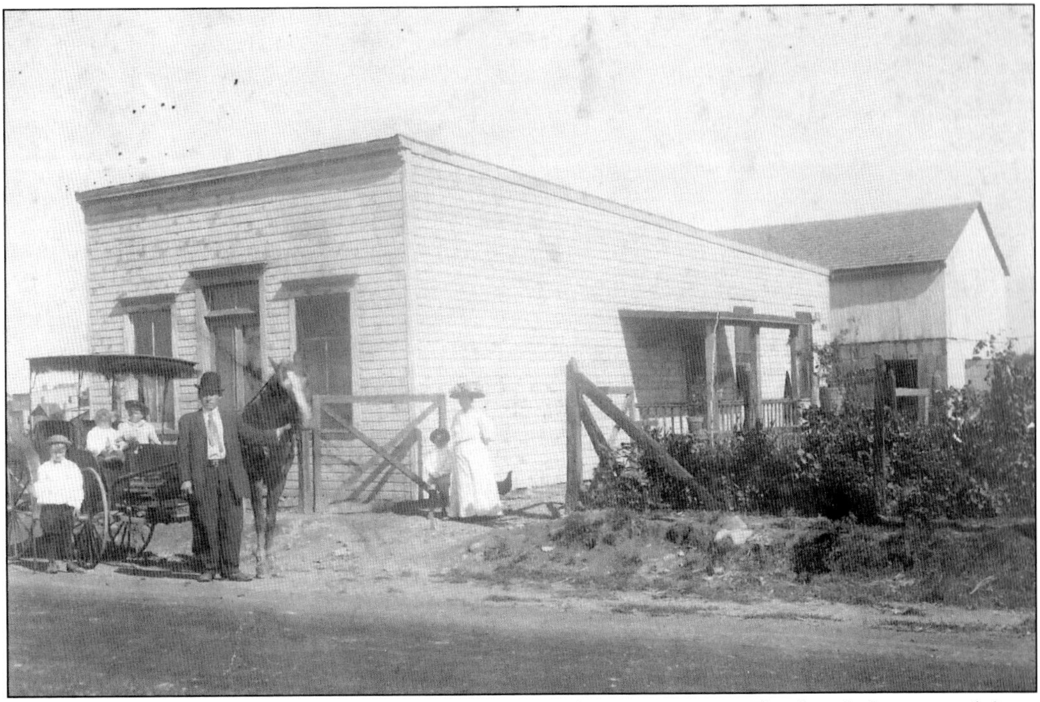

Dora, Charles, Brownie, George, John, and Henry Plungis in 1910. The family home and farm were on East Edgar Road in what is now the eighth ward.

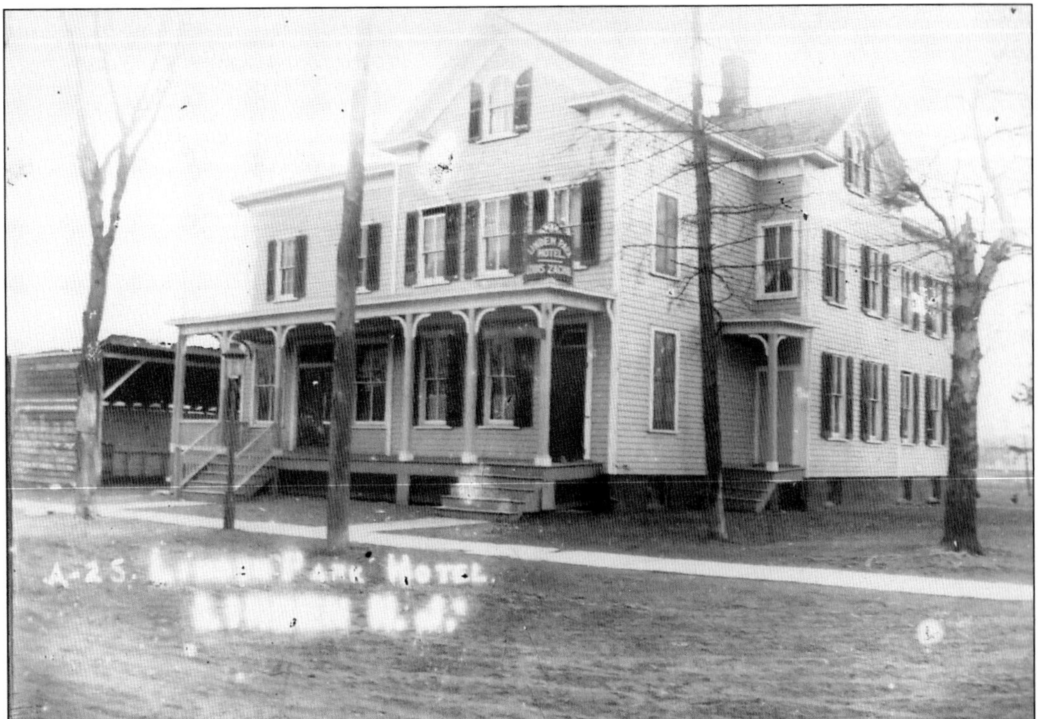

The Linden Park Hotel, located on South Wood Avenue. Its proprietor was Louis Zacher.

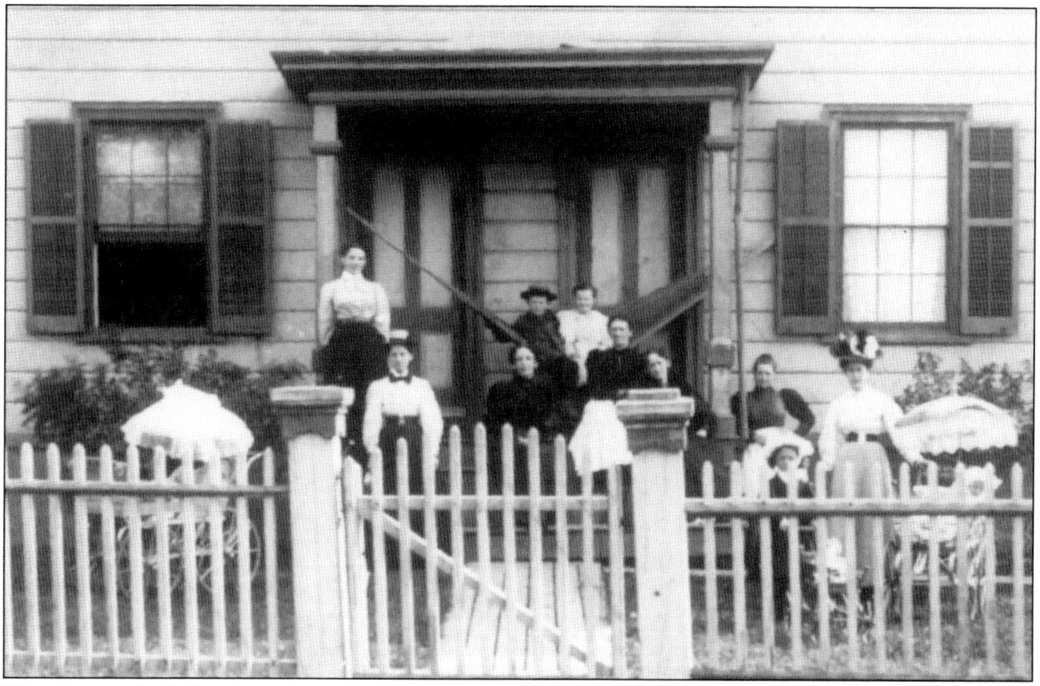

The Derrig-Roll families. From left to right are Louise Roll Derrig, John Derrig, Louise Derrig Farragher, Cassie Roll, Mary Rothery, and Grandma Struber. The little children are Mrs. Pickle (age two) and Martin Derrig (in the carriage).

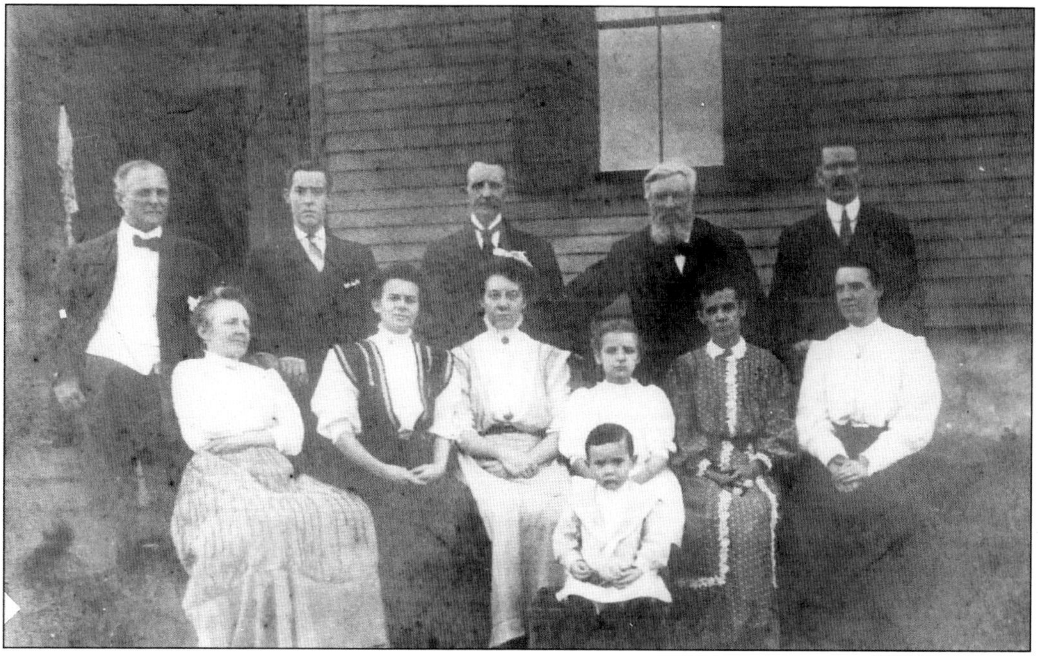

Four generations of the Roll family. Standing from left to right are an unidentified friend of the family, Lloyd S. Roll, Smith M. Roll, Isaac Clausen Roll, Martha Adelia Roll-Depew, Lillie Evelyn Girtauner, Arrena H. Roll, Marion Girtauner (daughter of Lillie), Mrs. Smith M. (Arrena H.) Roll, and Mable Mae Loitch. Seated in front is Jules Girtauner, the son of Lillie.

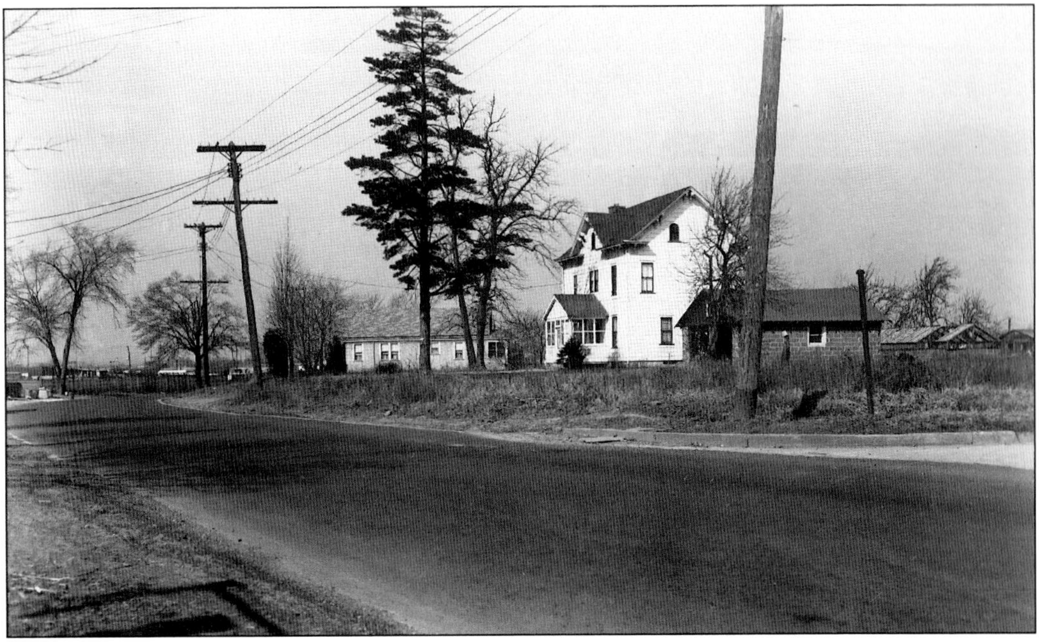

The Truncale family has been residing in this house for many years. At first the family rented it from Harry Mopsick. Mr. Edward Truncale says that there was much more to the original building. The back half of the home was removed in 1923. He should know because he was born in that half of the house in 1917. The Roll family built the home in 1845 and owned the property including the farm that can be seen to the back of the house. Saraphino and Joseph Truncale bought the property in 1939 from Mr. Mopsick and it has been the family home ever since. This is a *c.* 1948 side view of Truncale homestead on South Stiles Street looking toward Edgar Road.

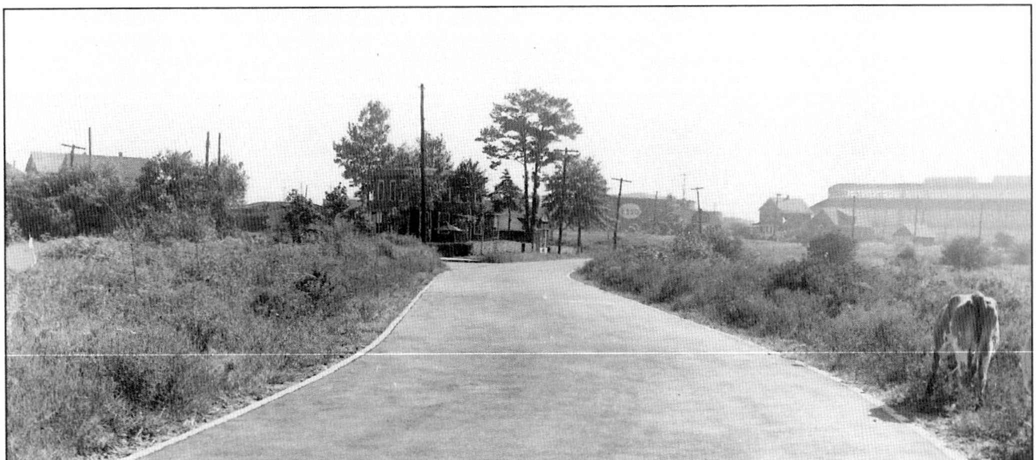

South Stiles Street looking toward 19th Street, *c.* 1950. The engineering department of the city of Linden is responsible for archiving every road in the city through the years. This picture is a big favorite at city hall, but they never knew where the cows came from. These cows belonged to the Rosenbaum family that owned a dairy farm at Clinton and East 15th Street. The cows would be brought over for grazing. To the rear of the image on the right side is the Mather Springs Company.

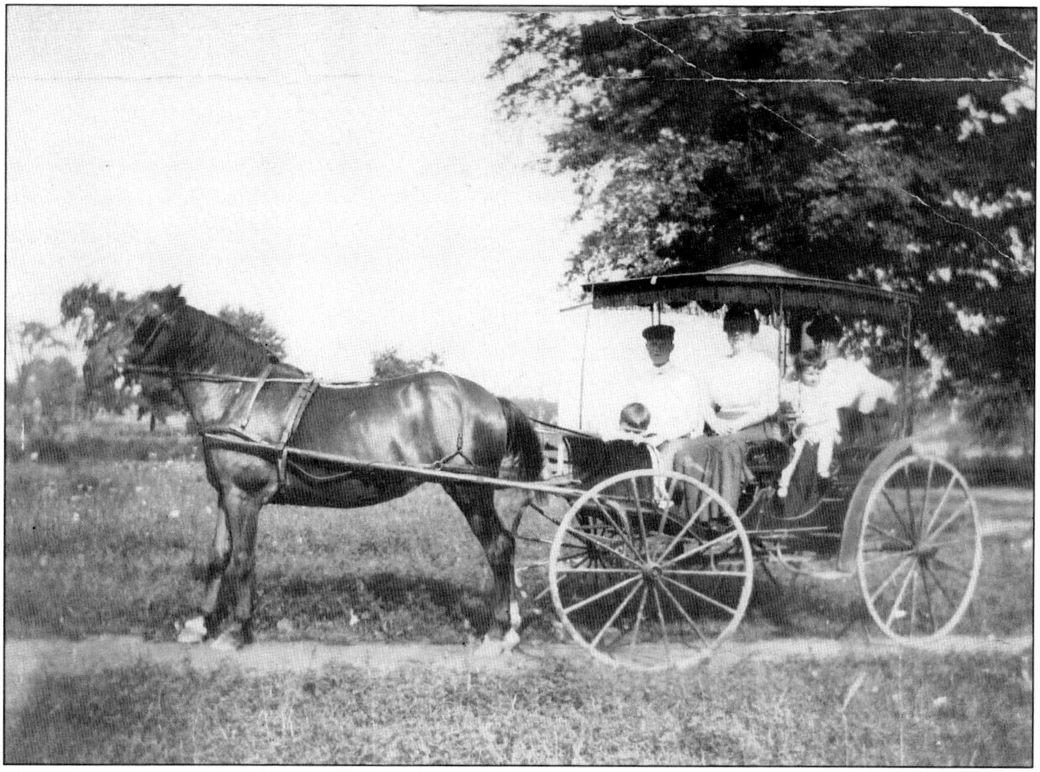

Hussa Street, 1908. Arthur Mellor, Agnes Mellor, Richard Danke, and Arthur Mellor are going for a horse-drawn buggy ride.

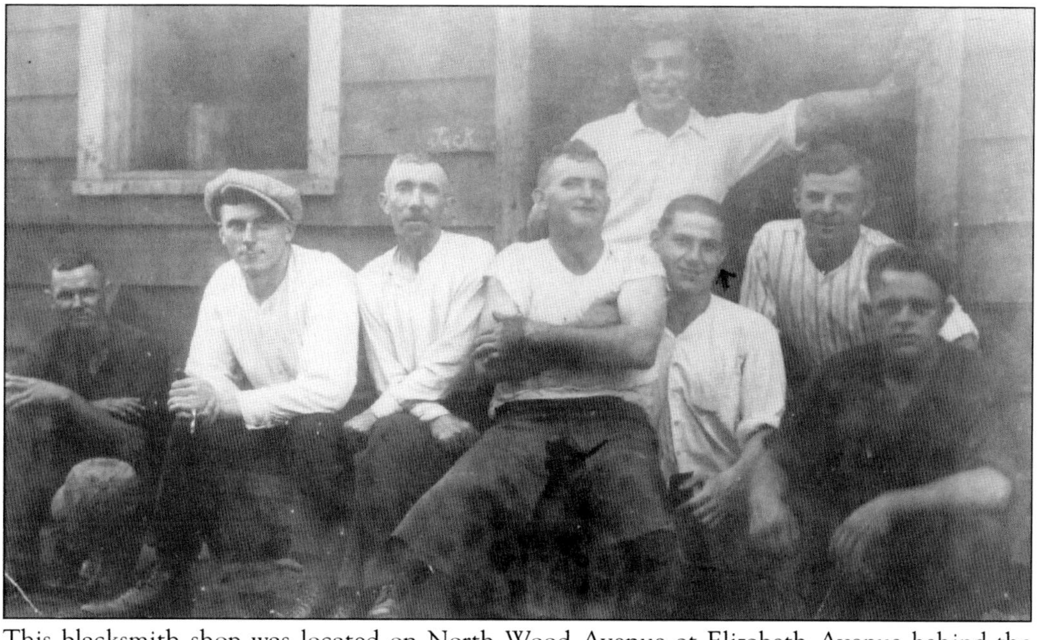

This blacksmith shop was located on North Wood Avenue at Elizabeth Avenue behind the Wood house. Phil Berlinski (second from left) is seen with Jack Sheehy (fourth from left) and Jerry Marhan Sr. (second from right).

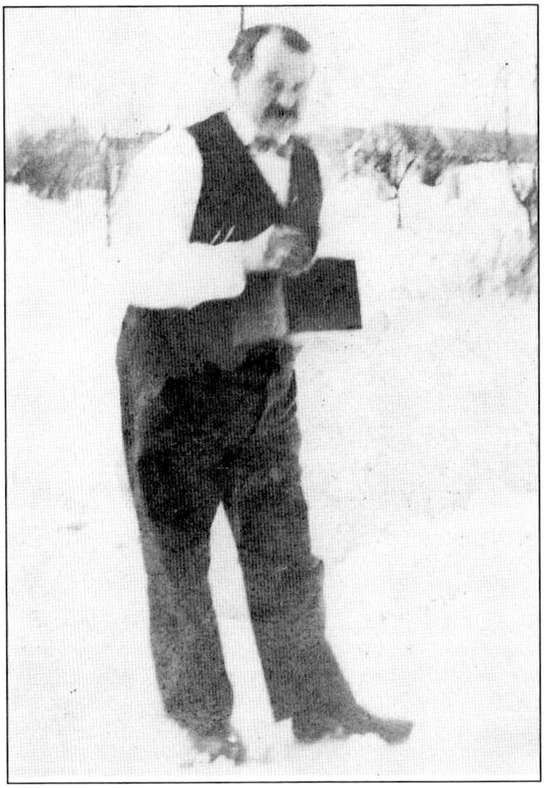

Harry Baldwin, married to Bertha Decker Baldwin. Henry sold real estate in the Linden Park area during the 1920s.

BOTTOM LEFT: Bertha Decker Baldwin, wife of Harry Baldwin. BOTTOM RIGHT: Clifford Baldwin in uniform during World War I. Clifford was the son of Harry and Bertha Baldwin. His name appears on the memorial at School No. 1.

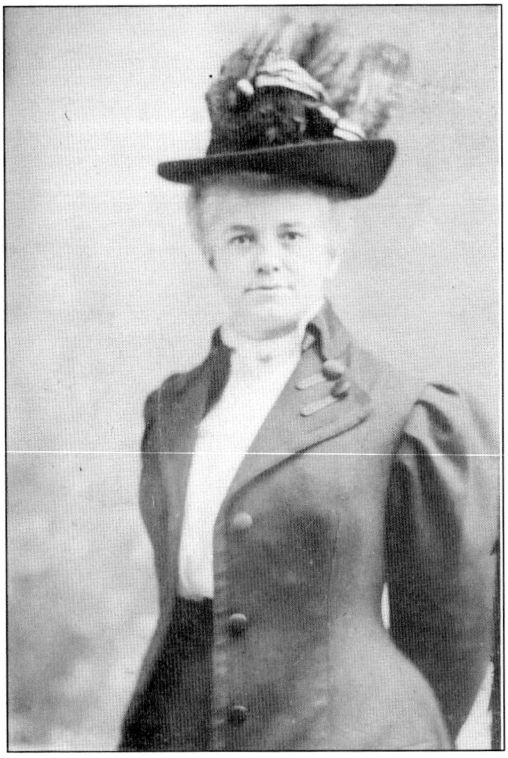

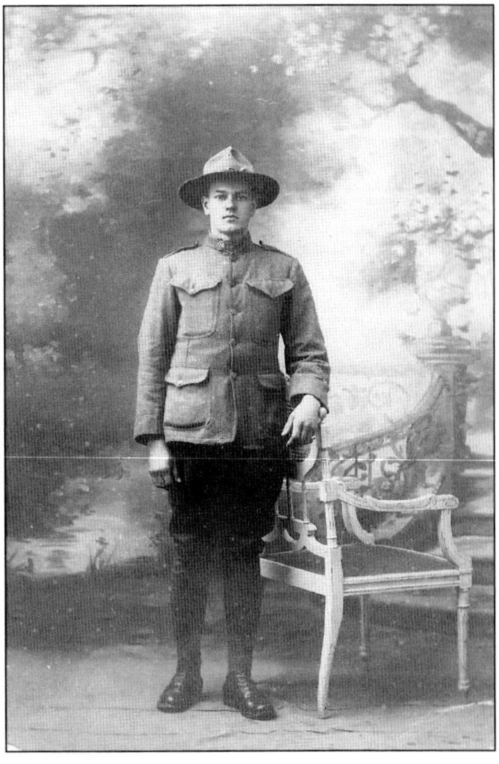

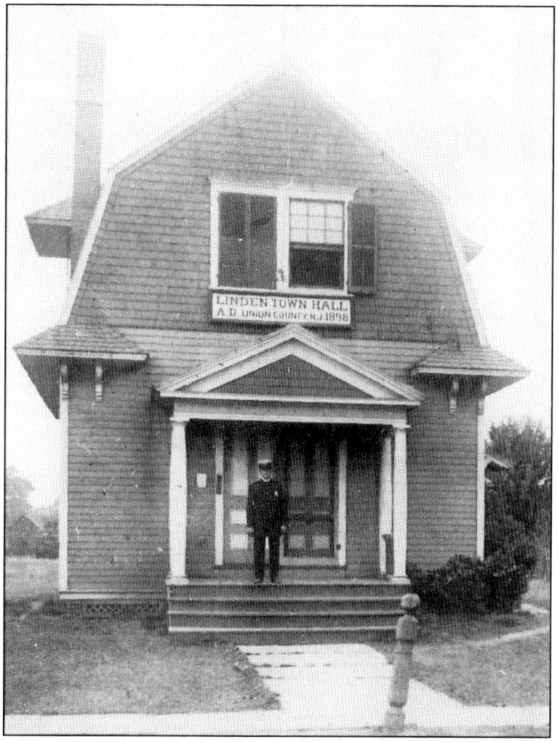

The first Linden Town Hall, 1898. It was located at the southeast corner of Wood and Morris Avenues. It was razed and a new one was built in 1909 (pictured on page 2). The township government was made up of members representing the various districts who in turn elected a chairman. They fixed a tax rate, borrowed money by issuing bonds, and decided on how the money would be spent.

Township officials. From left to right are (front row) Louis Quinn, Alexander Shotwell, John P. Winans, John S. Mesler, Peter Lindsay, John Tucker, and Frank B. Stimpson; (middle row) Frank Schneider, Frank Anderson, Daniel Dippel, and George Cladek; (back row) George S.A. Pickel, William Wright, James Lappin, Arnold Hergenhan, and Fred Covery.

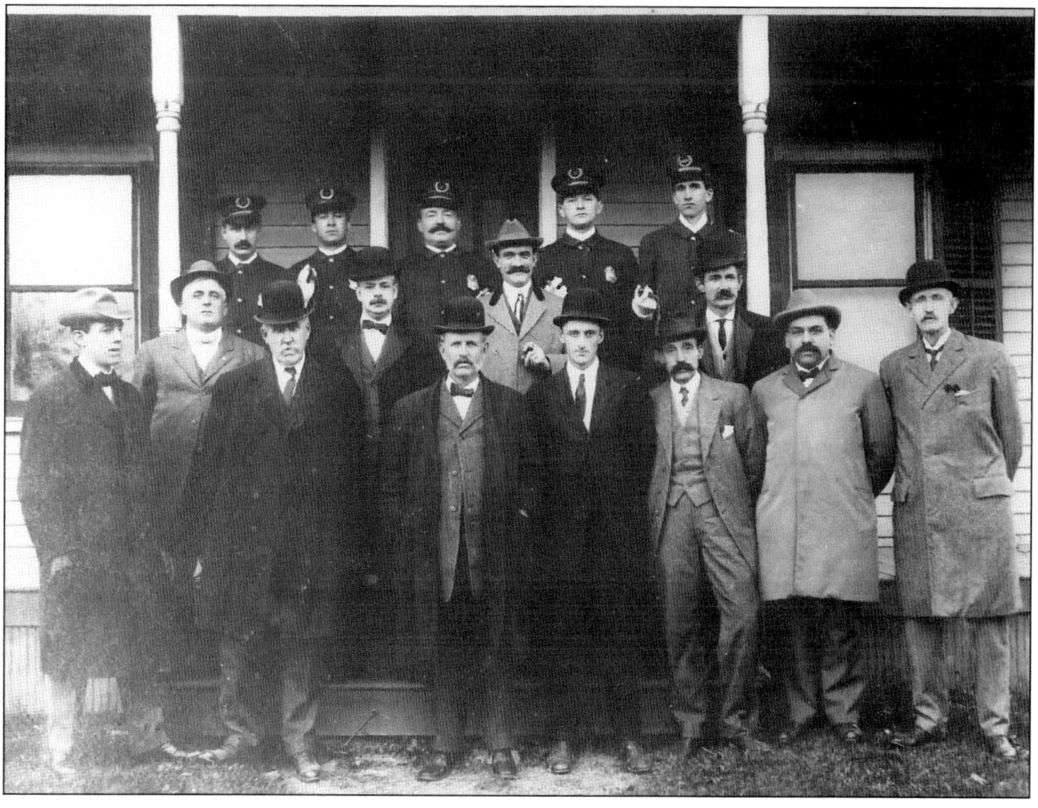

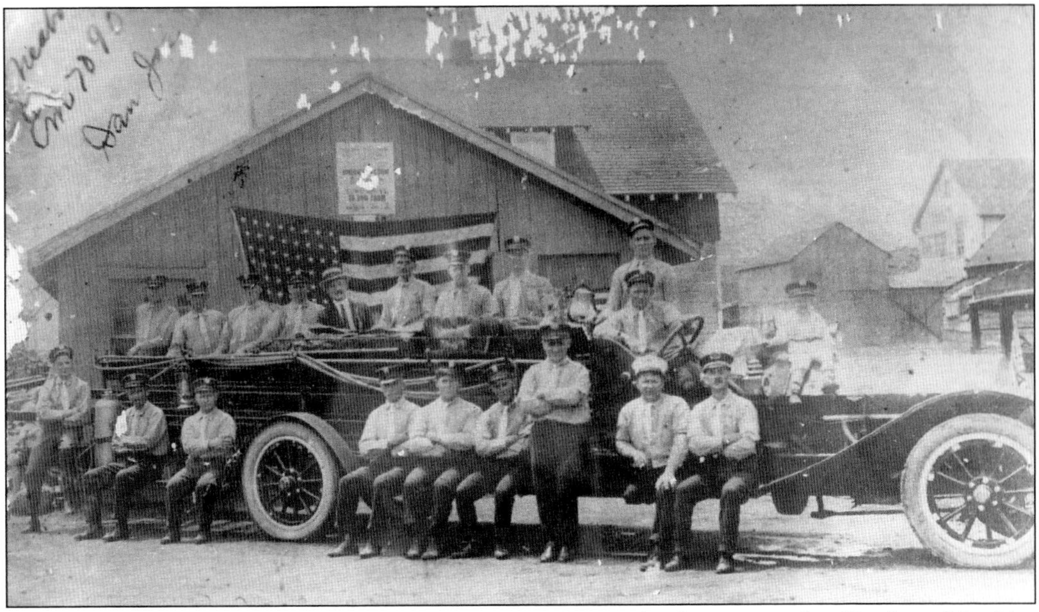

The Linden Township Volunteer Fire Company No. 1, also known as the Hook and Ladder Company. It was first organized in 1908, and was alternately headed by Earl P. Graham, the one-legged man in the center of this c. 1912 photograph, and James T. Bersey, seated to his left. This fire truck replaced a hand-drawn ladder rig. The truck was a Pierce Arrow car that was extended and converted into a ladder truck by members of the company.

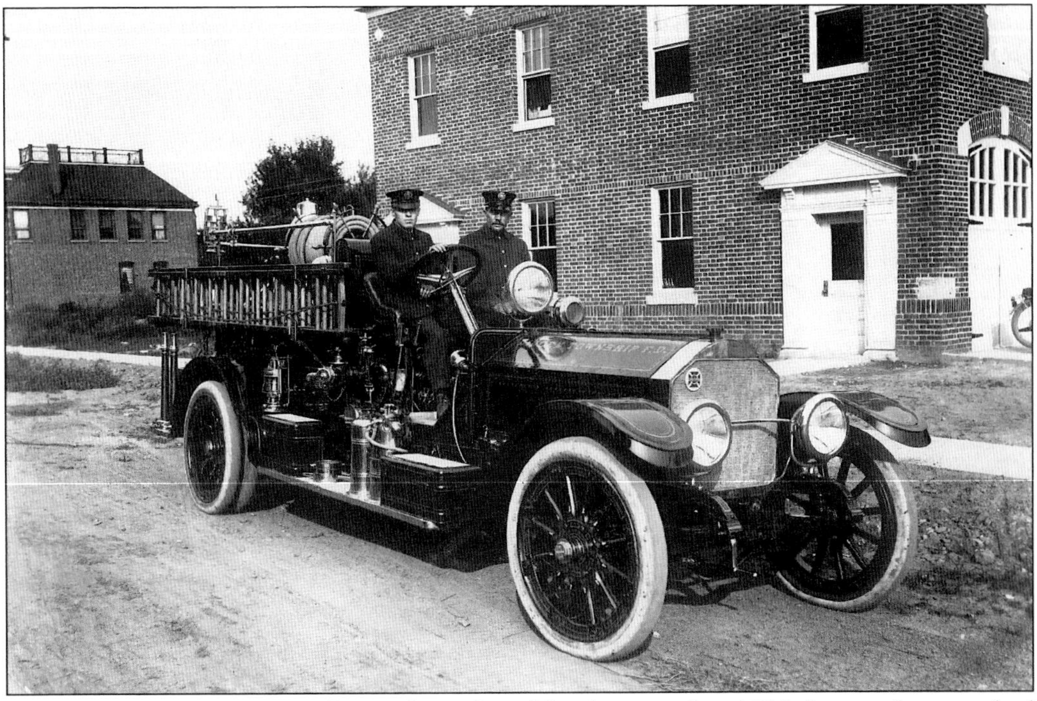

No. 1 Engine "American La France," purchased by the township 1916. It was photographed at the Wood & Morris Avenue fire station. Elmer Glover was the first paid fireman in the combined histories of Linden.

The Tremley Station for the Central Railroad of N.J. (Long Branch line) was built on the site of the Trembly (Traubles) homestead. The building was also used for a post office for the area. The Linden Fire Department posted fire prevention signs on the front of the structure after it had a fire, *c.* 1941.

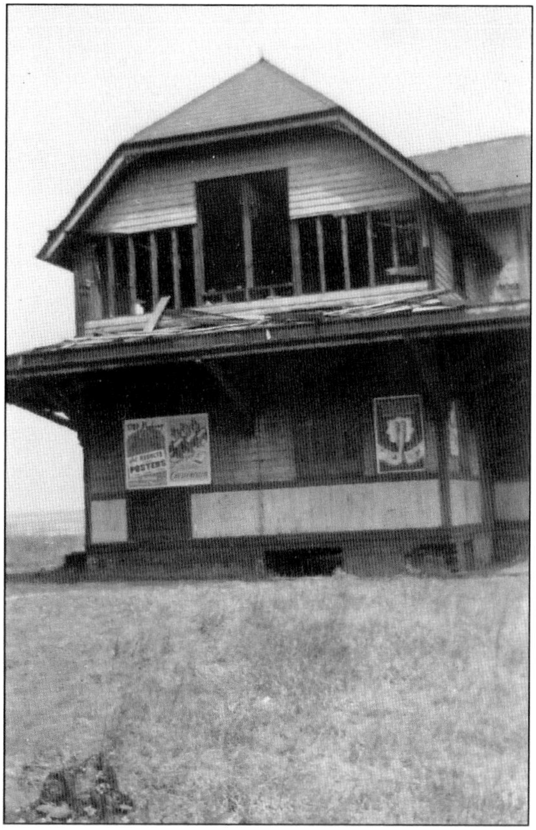

Penn Railroad Station on East Linden Avenue at the entrance to the Rosedale Cemetery. The N.J. Railroad received its charter and began building the railroad through the state in the 1830s. It reached Linden between 1835 and 1836.

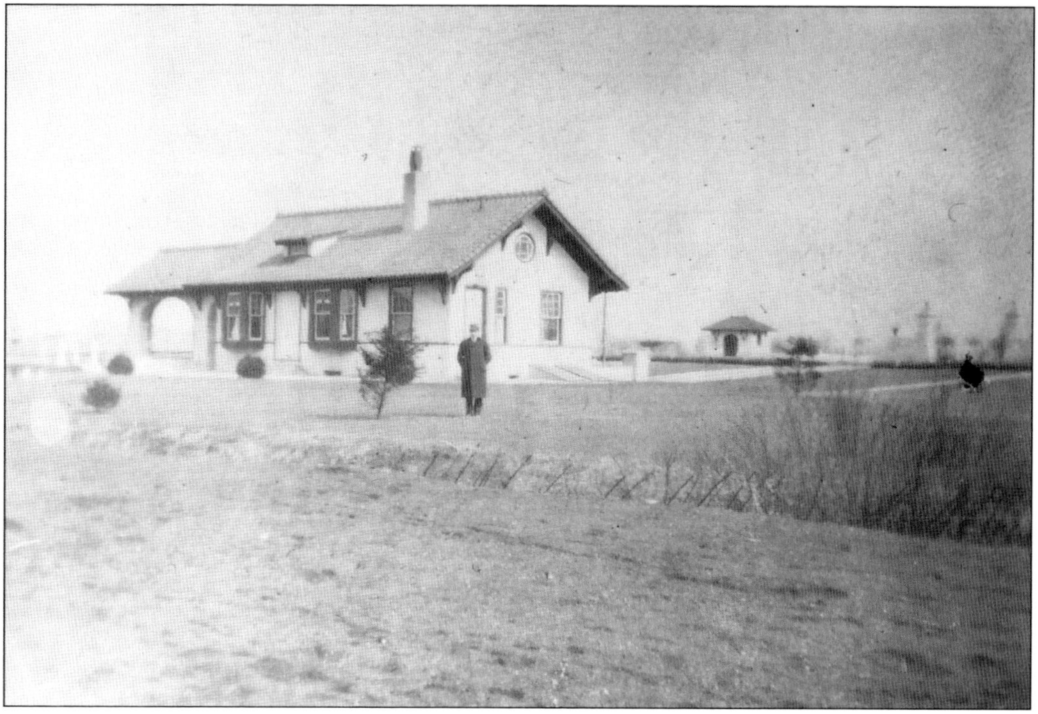

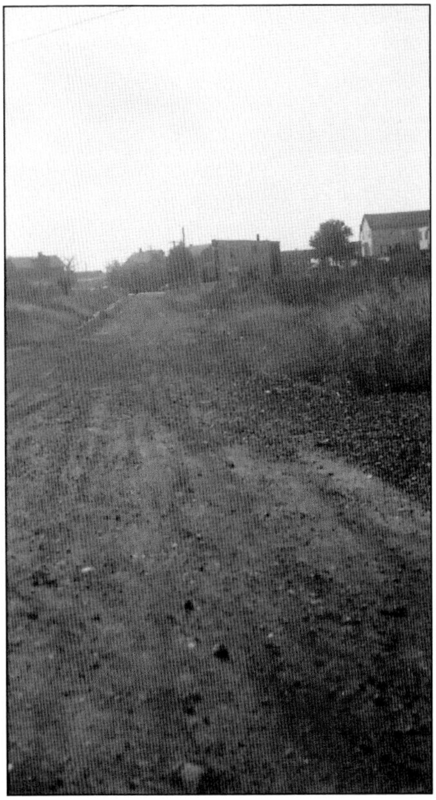

Jean Traubles (John Tremley) married Marie Noe in 1689 in Staten Island and moved to Elizabethtown in 1697, having first been admitted as an Associate in 1695. Both were French Hugonauts. By obtaining 200 acres through a "land pattent" from Governor Carteret and by buying some more land he came to own the whole point that jutted out into the Arthur Kill—thus the name, Trembly Point. The village of Trembly was also named for him. His son Peter operated a ferry crossing to Staten Island for many years. In time, the "B" was dropped from the name. Tremley Point Road was once part of the Minisink Trail. The Central Railroad Station in the Tremley Point section was located on the site of the homestead. Many streets are named in this area for family members of John Fedor, who began developing the area in 1916. Tremley is part of Linden's Seventh Ward. Many industries have made Tremley their home too.

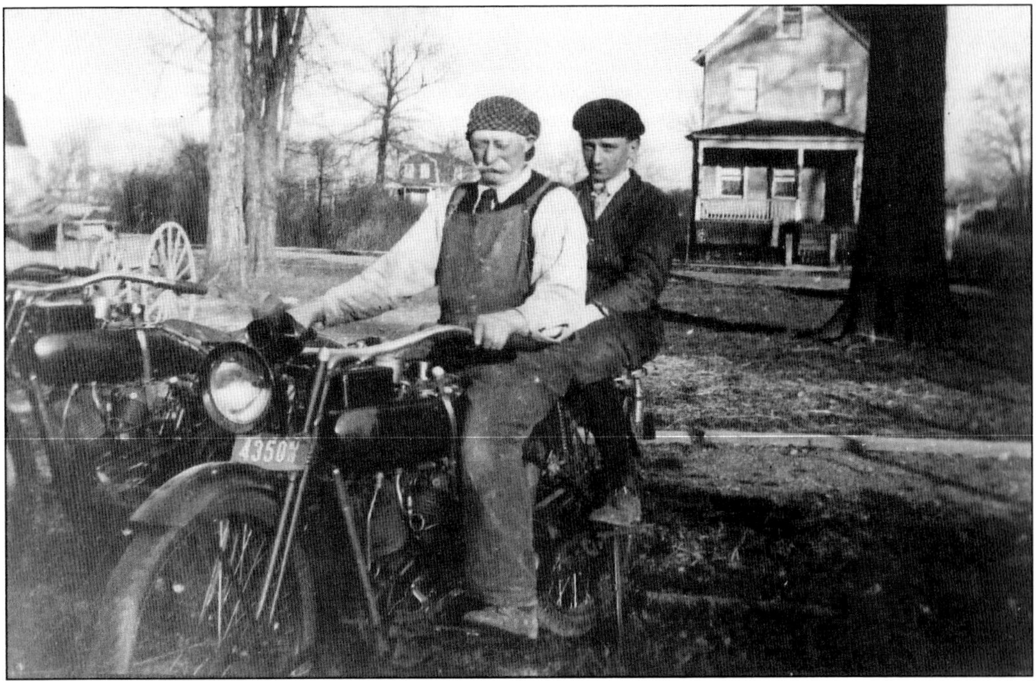

John Mellor and Carl Vanderwall on a motorcycle, Hussa Street, 1908. John would soon become the plumbing inspector for the borough and Carl would become the Linden Postmaster.

Two

Separation to Consolidation

Linden Township was mainly farmland. The area located near the railroad became well-to-do as many of these residents were the owners of businesses in New York. People would use the N.J. Railroad, which was built over the Essex and Middlesex Turnpike, to commute from work to their country homes in Linden. In time, they requested improvements including sidewalks, indoor plumbing, electricity, and sewers. These residents decided to start their own community, since township officials didn't feel there was a need for these modern conveniences.

On March 28, 1882, the borough of Linden separated as an "island Municipality" from the middle of the township. The government of the borough was very similar to the system we know today. There was an election each year for a mayor and councilmen.

During the early 1920s, the Wood Avenue Improvement Association felt that consolidation would be good for the financial future of both municipalities. Petitions from the township were delivered to the borough and approved. The idea was put up for election.

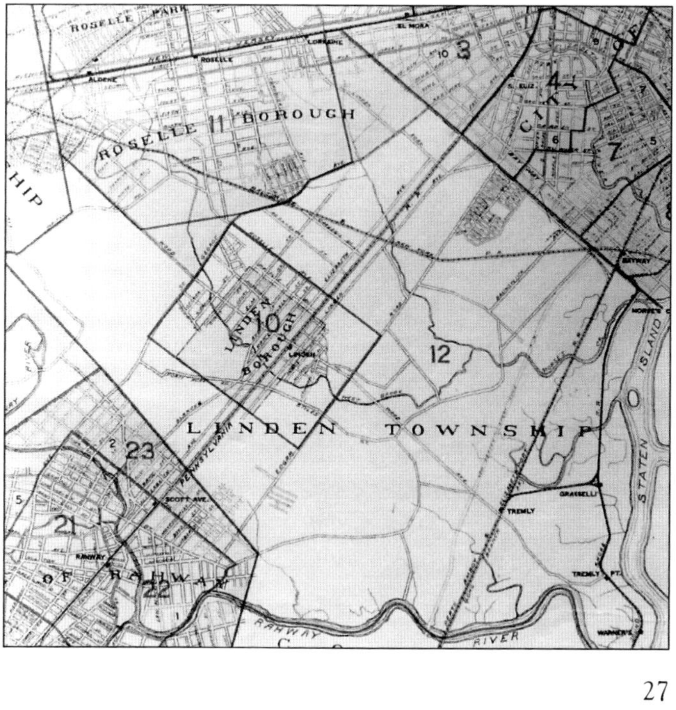

The election results were for consolidation! Legislation was passed for the two municipalities to incorporate as the City of Linden on April 3, 1924. Linden actually started to function as a city on January 1, 1925. This 1902 map depicts Linden Township with the Linden Borough inside. The borough of Roselle was originally part of Linden. It also became a separate community in 1895.

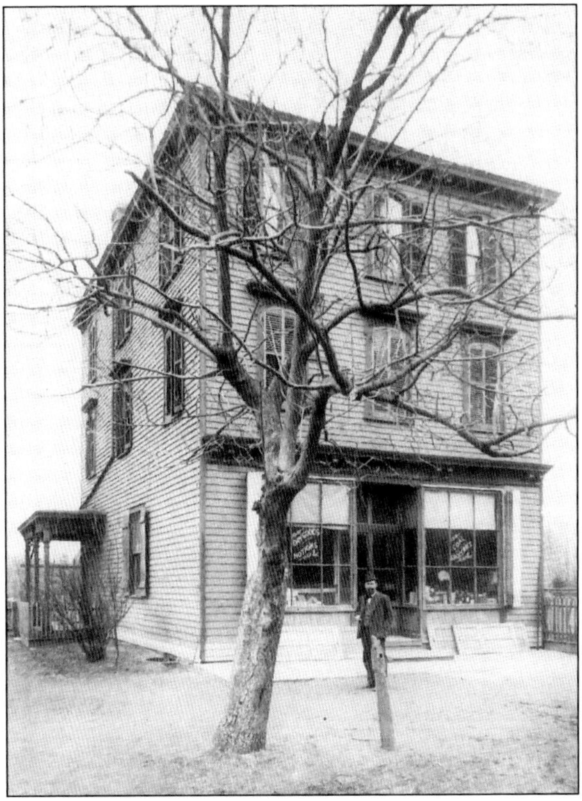

A general store at the corner of Blancke Street and Wood Avenue, where Linden City Hall is now. Mr. Gesner is standing in front. The store was used as a post office and as a site for borough meetings. It was knocked down to build borough hall.

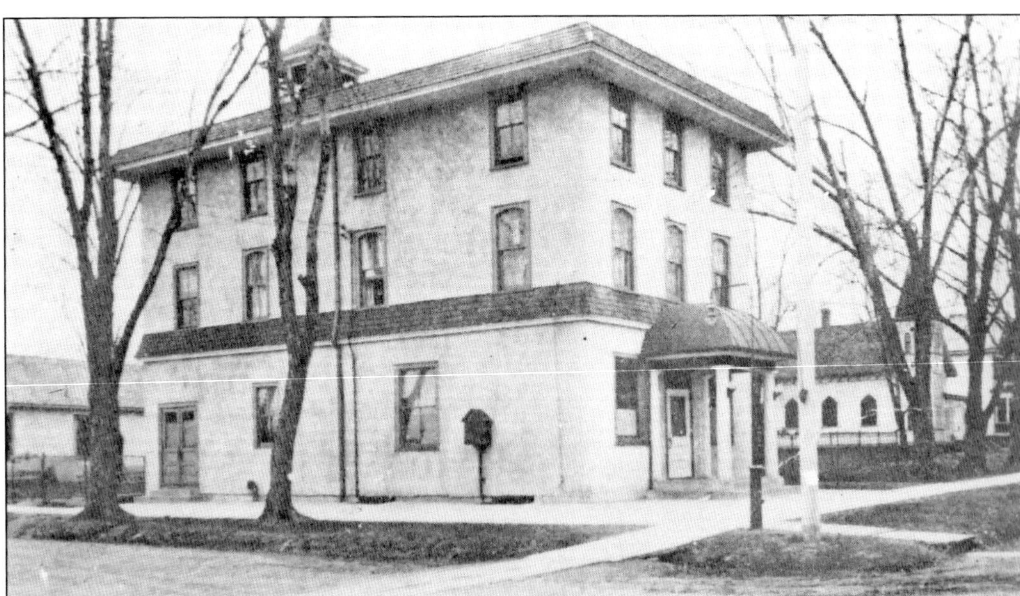

Borough hall, in the present location of city hall at the corner of Blancke Street and Wood Avenue.

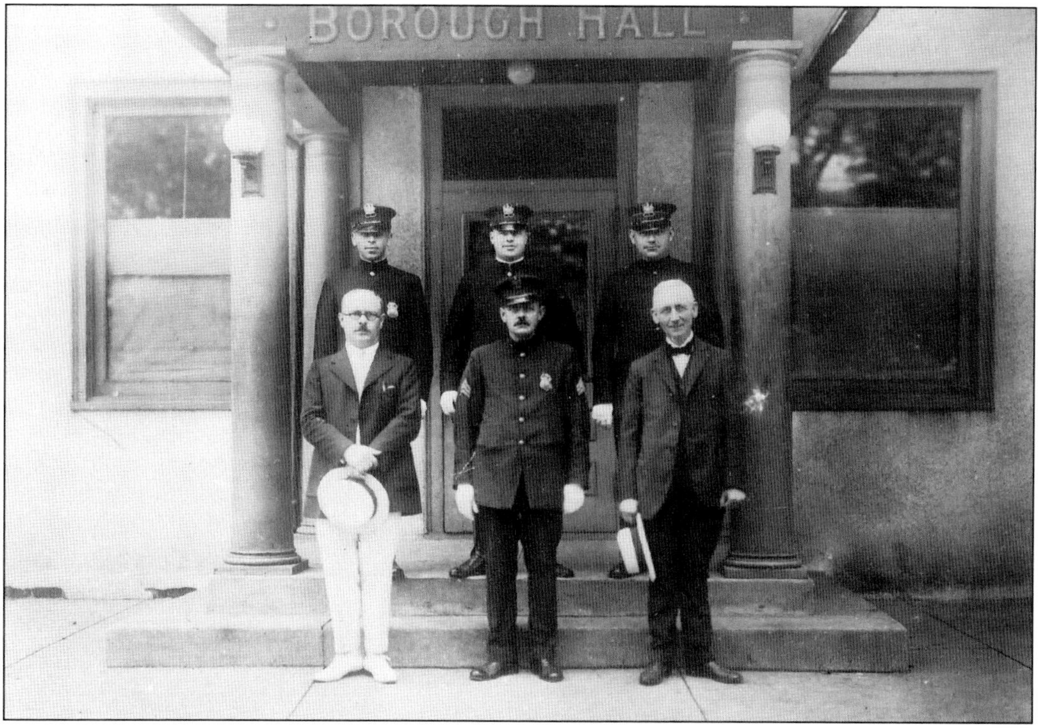

The Linden Borough Police Department. From left to right are (front row) Mayor Verner, Charles Miles, and Mr. Murray; (back row) Harry Wagner, Charles Bedle, and Charles Virager.

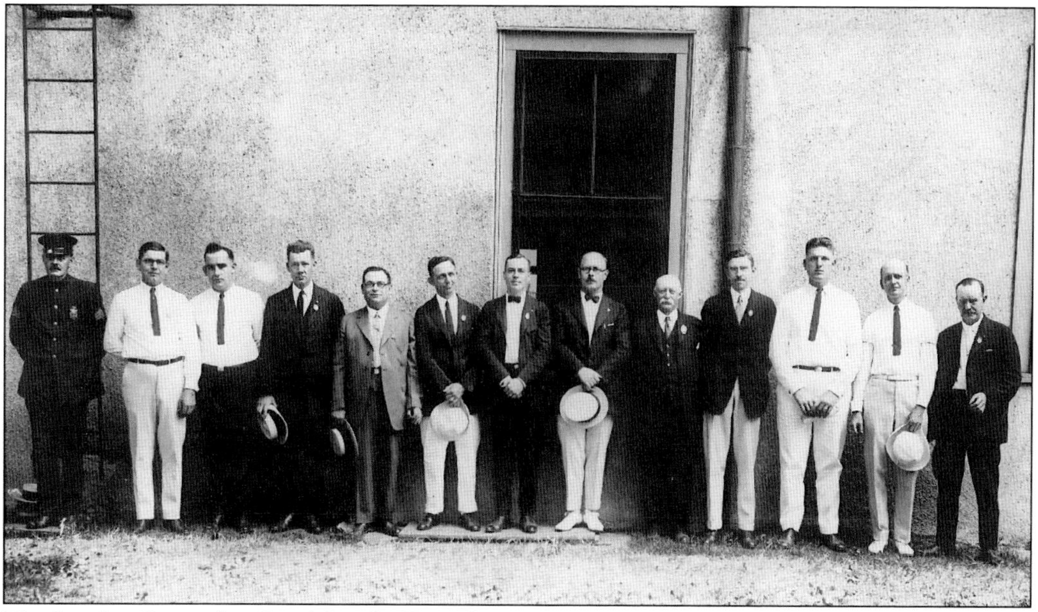

The Linden Borough official family. From left to right are Police Lieutenant Miles, Fire Chief Harry Blancke, Town Clerk Thomas Sullivan, Councilman Hugh Carpenter, Neil O'Donnell, John Demorgije, Councilman Frank De Montmorency, Mayor Jules Verner, John Mellor, Councilman William Doe, Assistant Engineer Dudley Blancke, Treasurer Henry Dabb, and Councilman Charles Walters.

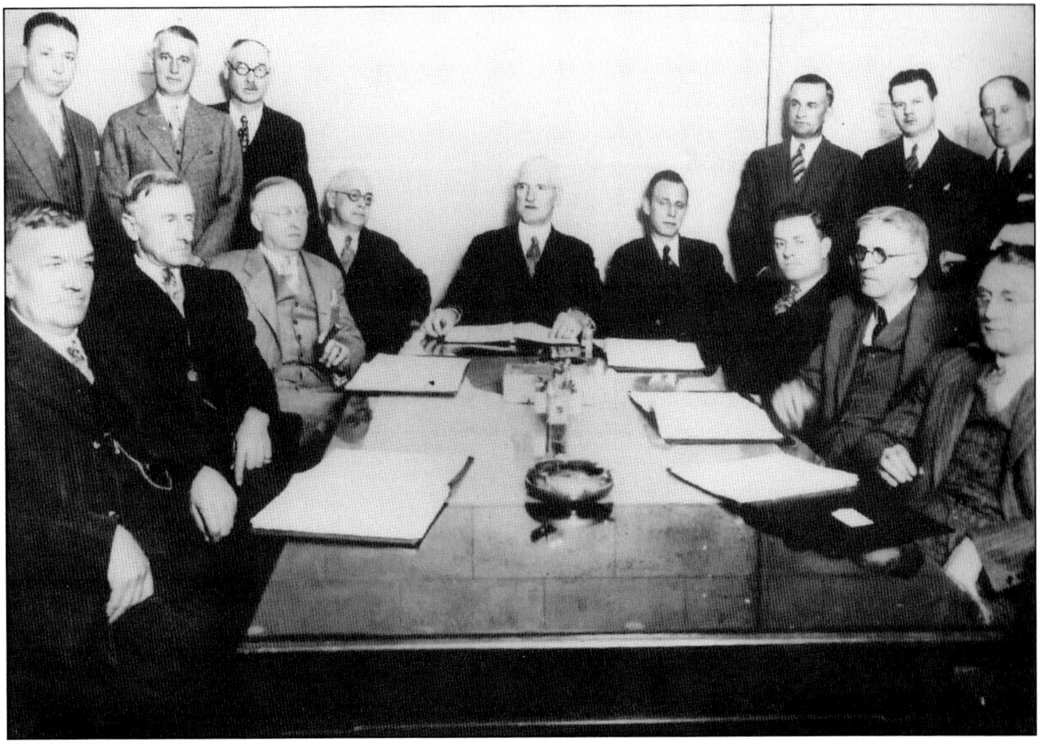

The Linden National Bank and Trust Company. On February 4, 1920, this bank opened with capital of $25,000. By 1928, the capital grew to $200,000. During this year, the bank moved to the corner of Elizabeth and Wood Avenues. Bank records show that the population of Linden had grown from 3,000 to over 20,000 since the community's incorporation as a city. This photograph depicts the formation of the bank. From left to right are (front row) John Molson, George McGillvray, Herbert Banta, Frank Anderson, H.B. Hardenburg, Harold DePew, Thomas Archipley, J. Lappin, and Judge Morris; (back row) Richard Post, J. Van Devinter, Alexander Amon, Mr. Farmer, Frank Newell, and William Feller.

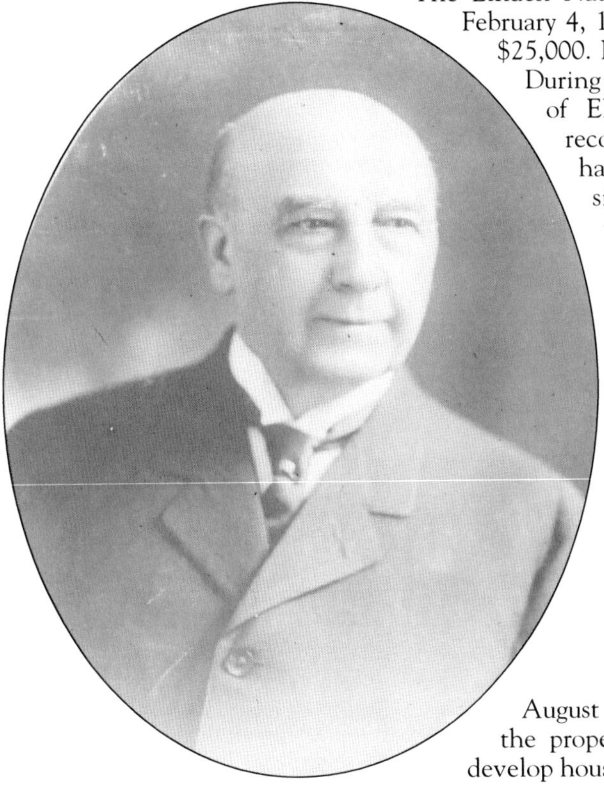

August E. Knoph. August purchased much of the property owned by the Blancke family to develop housing. Knoph Street is named for him.

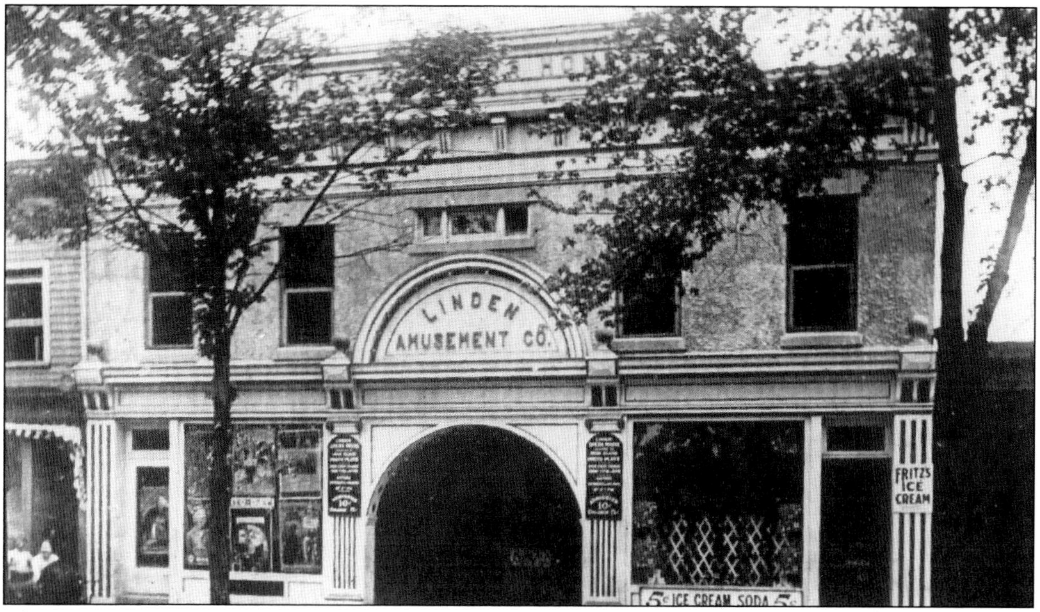

The Opera House, built in 1915. It was located on the 100 block of Wood Avenue, and became the Roxanne Theater in the early 1920s. It was also the original home of Greenbergs' Department Store.

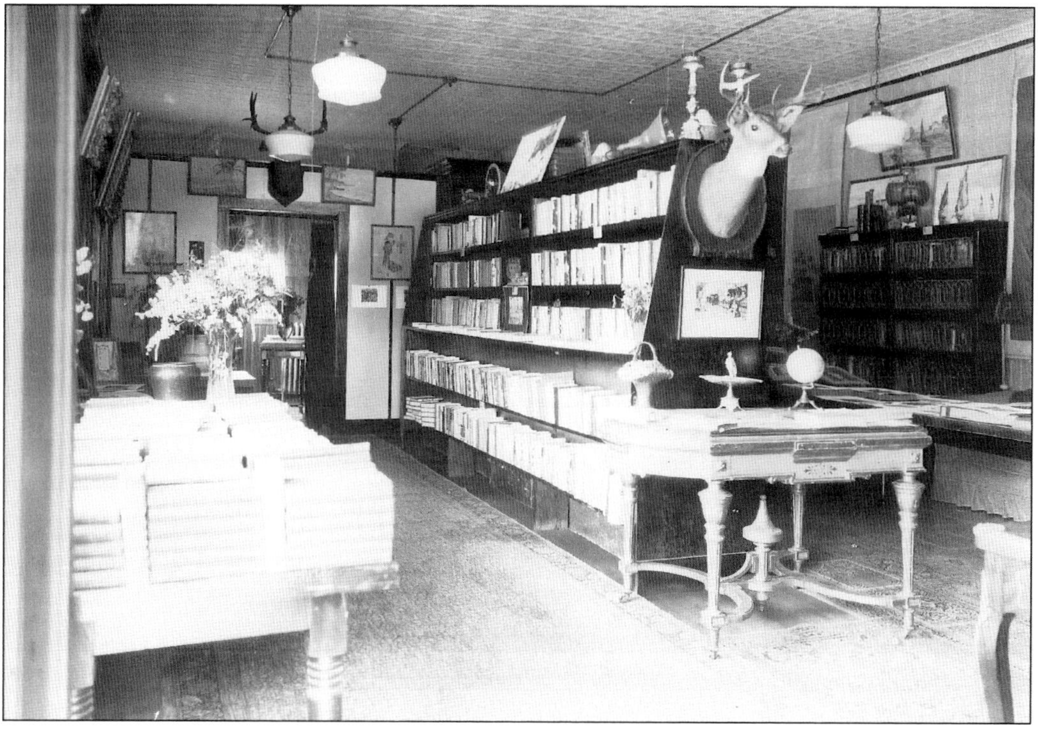

The Linden Bookshop Gallery at 210 North Wood Avenue in 1926. Stanley Sredzinski was a learned man with a love of rare books, which he sold here. He had a real estate office at 124 South Wood Avenue at the corner of Morris Avenue at the same time. This was the time of the real estate boom in the new city of Linden.

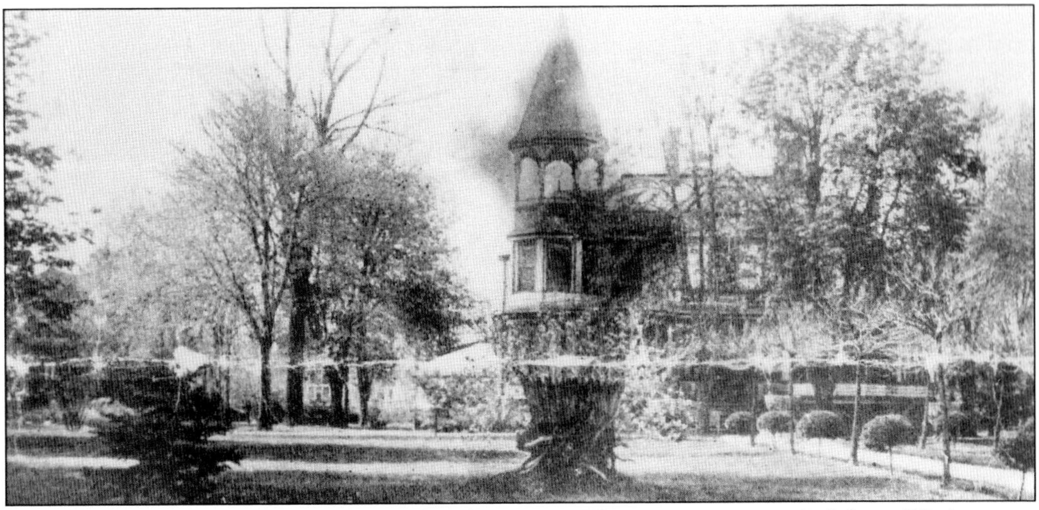

The Luttgen country estate on East Blancke Street. The property extended from Washington Avenue to Elm Street. When Luttgen moved to Connecticut, the house was divided and moved. The front half of the house was moved forward to Blancke Street, and was eventually razed to build the apartments. The back half moved to Luttgen Place when the street was cut through. The property was divided into house lots and this structure became a boarding house. Walter Luttgen, a banker and a true philanthropist, was responsible for paving Wood Avenue to the waterfront. He also built a kindergarten on Henry Street and sent Mrs. Bateman, his wife's friend, to Germany to study kindergarten teaching methods.

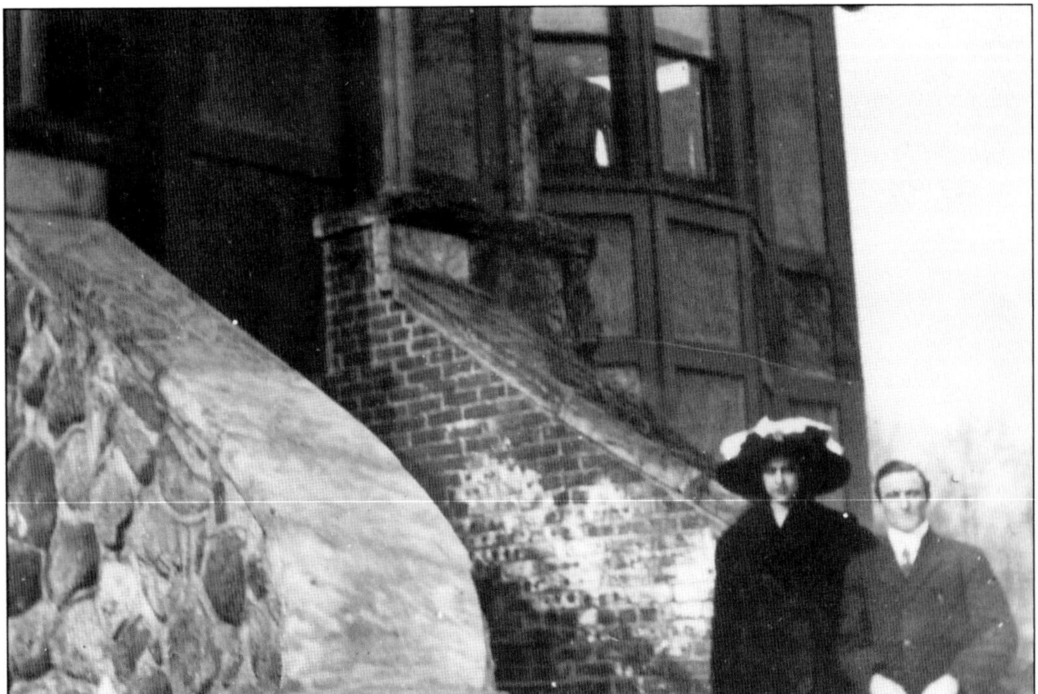

Mr. and Mrs. Philip Capraun (Anne Zutter) bequeathed the property they lived on to St. Elizabeth's Church. (The property was located where the church is now.) The couple is standing in front of the Luttgens' front door. That is Mr. Luttgen in the window above.

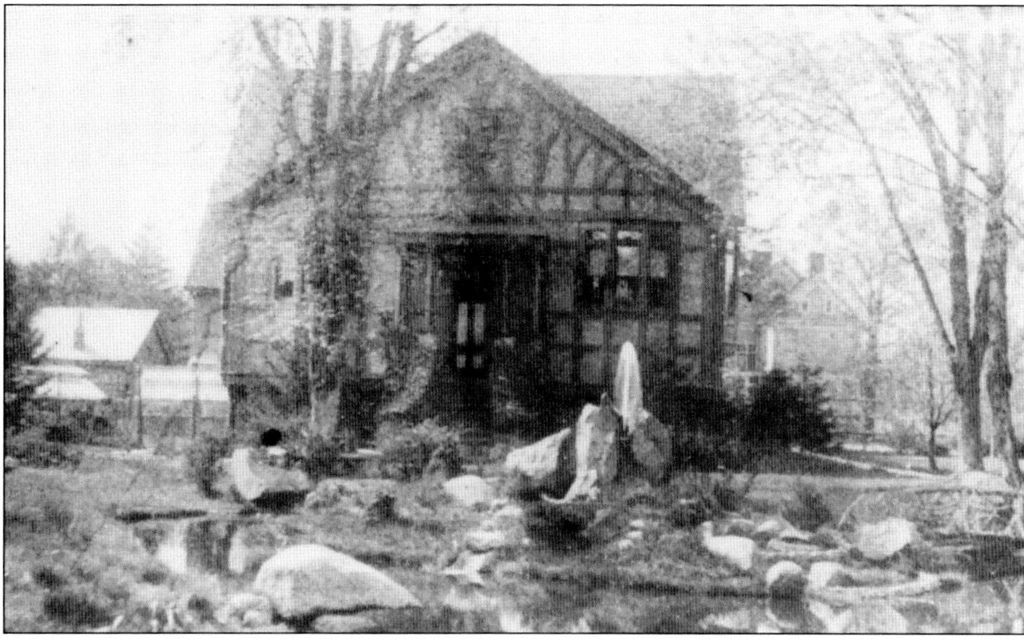

On the grounds of the estate was the building now occupied by the Loyal Order of Moose fraternal organization. It had stables attached to it, and there were living quarters for the help in the building. There was also a small auditorium with a stage and a bowling alley. The building was taken over by the Linden Country Club before the Moose arrived. The Linden Public Library was also housed here in 1927.

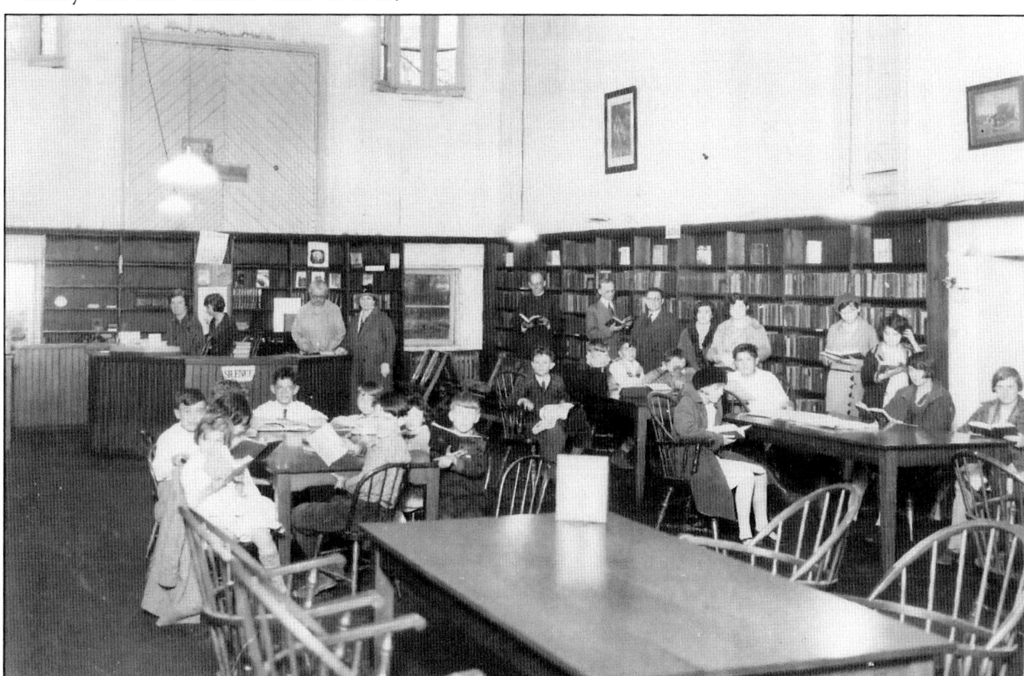

The original Linden Public Library, located in the stable wing of the Linden Country Club in March 1928. The library was sponsored by the Linden Rotary Club.

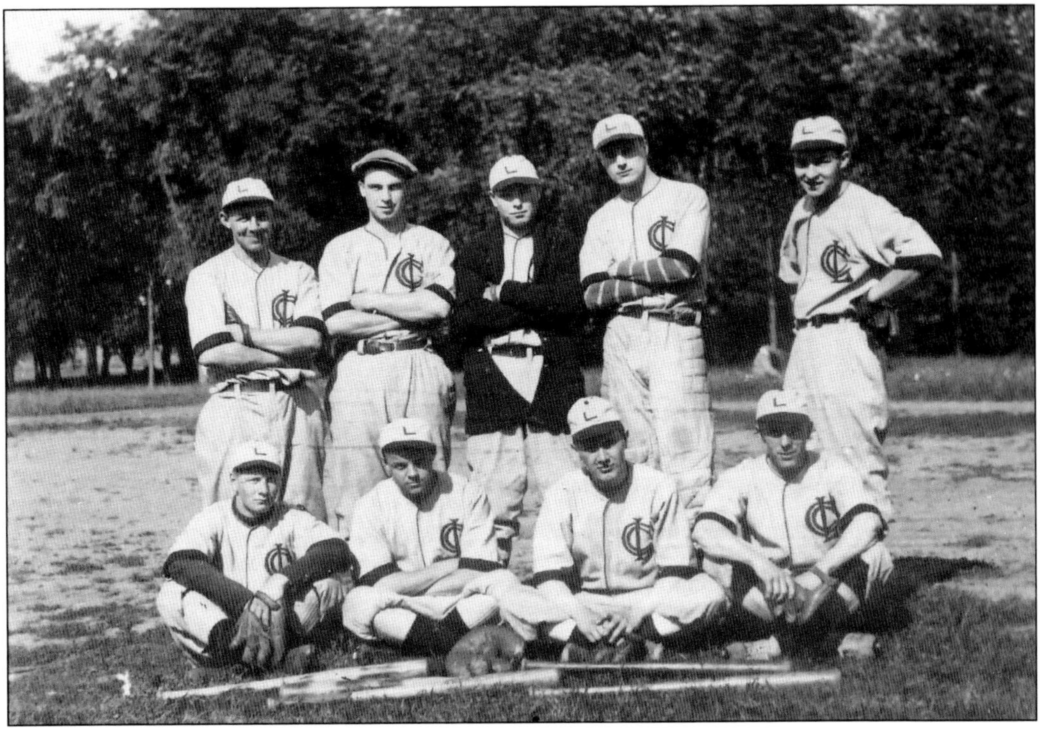

The 1914 Linden Country Club Baseball Team.

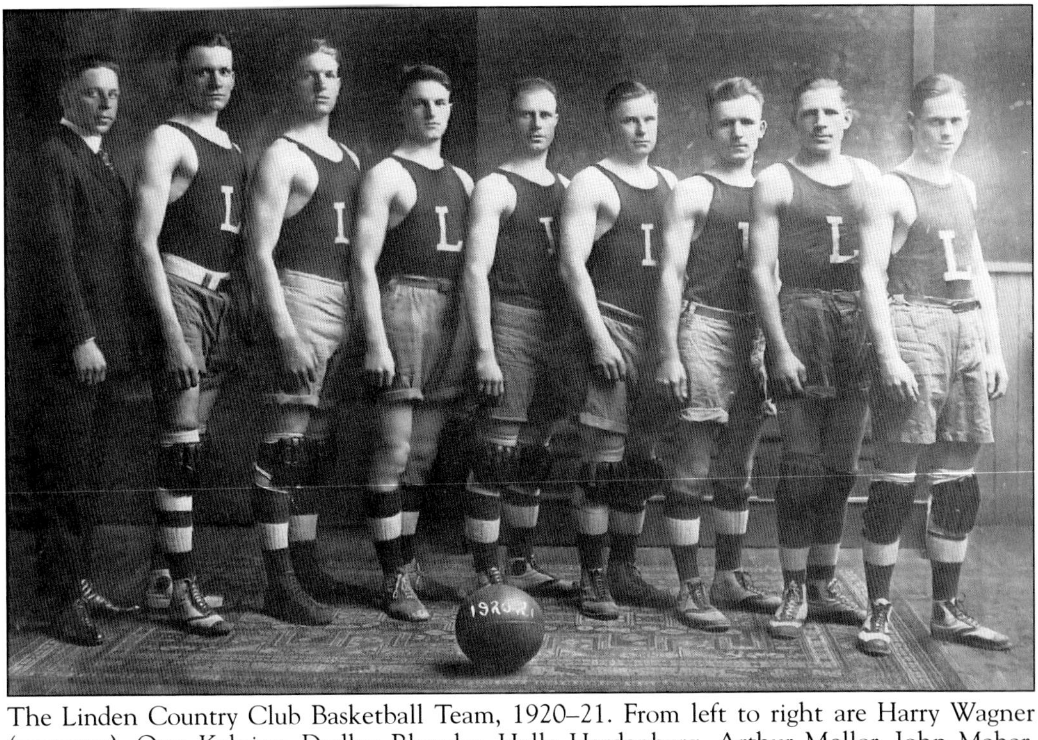

The Linden Country Club Basketball Team, 1920–21. From left to right are Harry Wagner (manager), Otto Kalning, Dudley Blancke, Halle Hardenburg, Arthur Mellor, John Mahar, Hugo Wendel, Andrew More, and Norman Anderson.

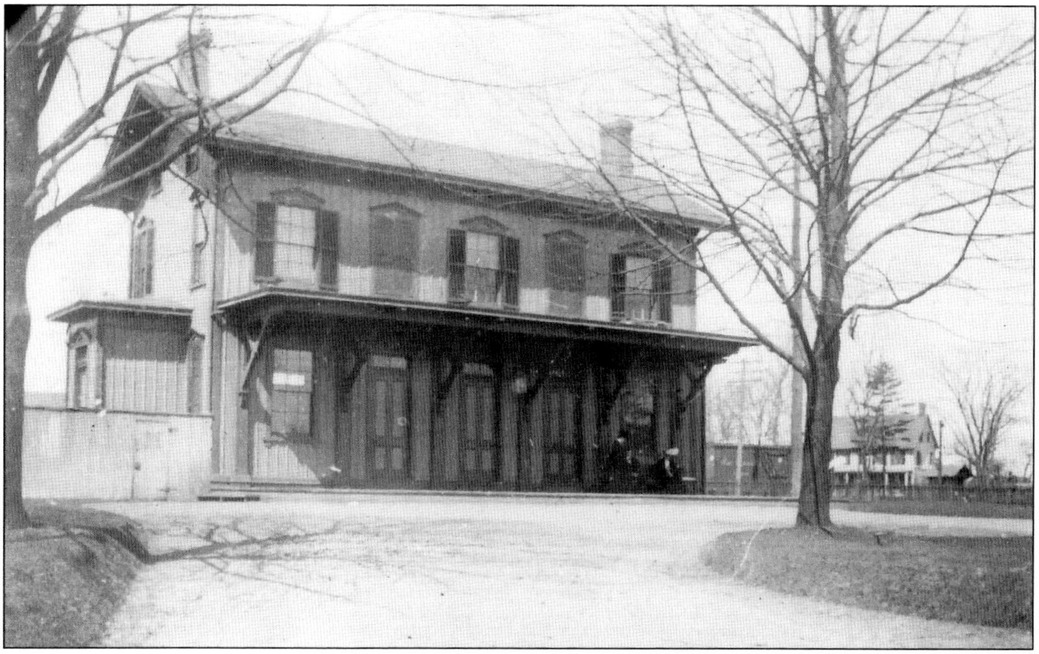

The Wood Avenue station known as Wheatsheaf for the Pennsylvania Railroad in 1910. The Wood homestead is at the rear, across the tracks. This photograph was taken before the depression of Wood Avenue to go underneath the tracks beginning in 1912.

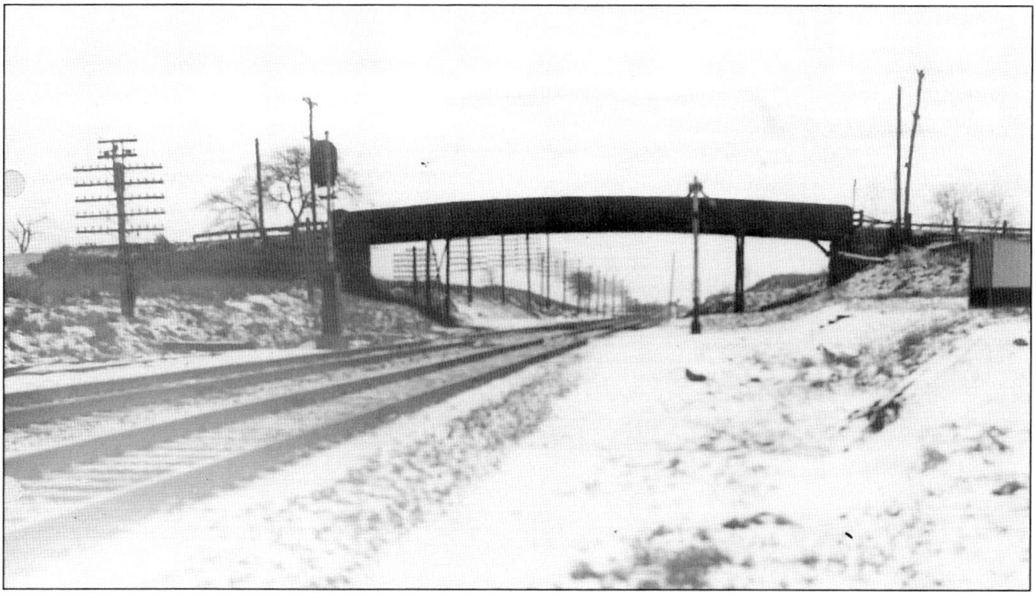

Prior to being a railroad, this was a private road known as the Middlesex and Essex Turnpike. Farmers paid a toll of 3¢ at each end. To avoid the expense, farmers gave up land to create the Edgar Road Shunpike (Edgar Road) that went from Elizabeth, N.J., to Morses Mill Road. It was constructed by the N.J. Railroad, became the Pennsylvania Railroad, and is currently operated by N.J. Transit. This image is the old Park Avenue bridge. Park Avenue was once called Dark Lane. It originally went all the way to Gallopping Hill Road and was renamed due to much of it disappearing when Warinanco Park was constructed.

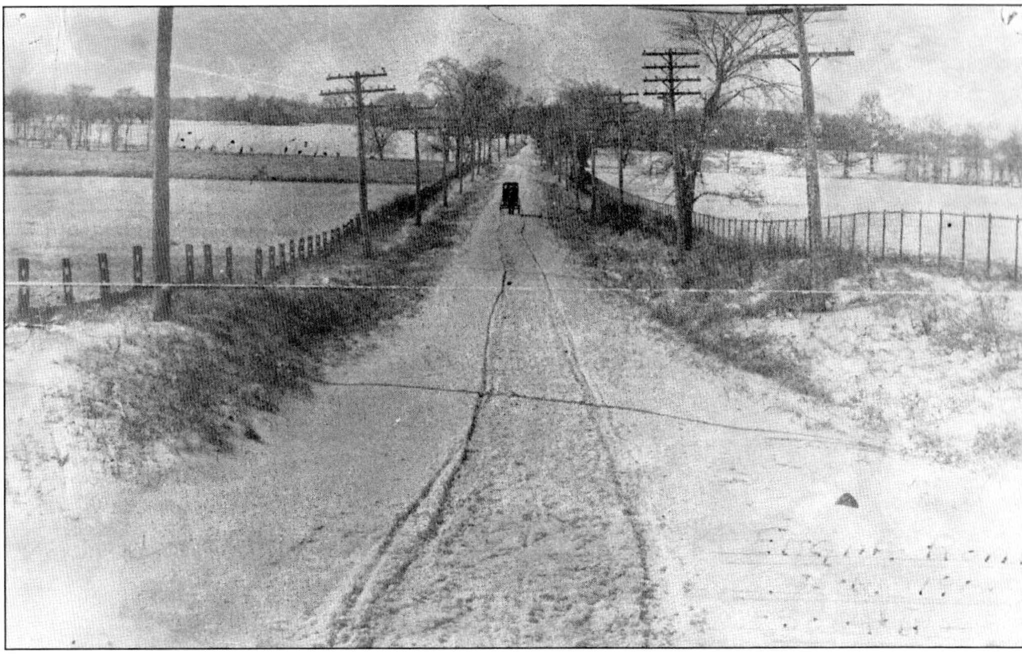

The Edgar Shunpike, now Edgar Road. It was called Route 25 before it became Route 1. As you can see, it was once a dirt road. The view is looking south from atop the railroad overpass, near what is now the Tosco entrance (upper left dark area). Edgar Road, Tremley Point Road, St. George Avenue, and the Lower Road to Rahway were once part of the Minisink Trail.

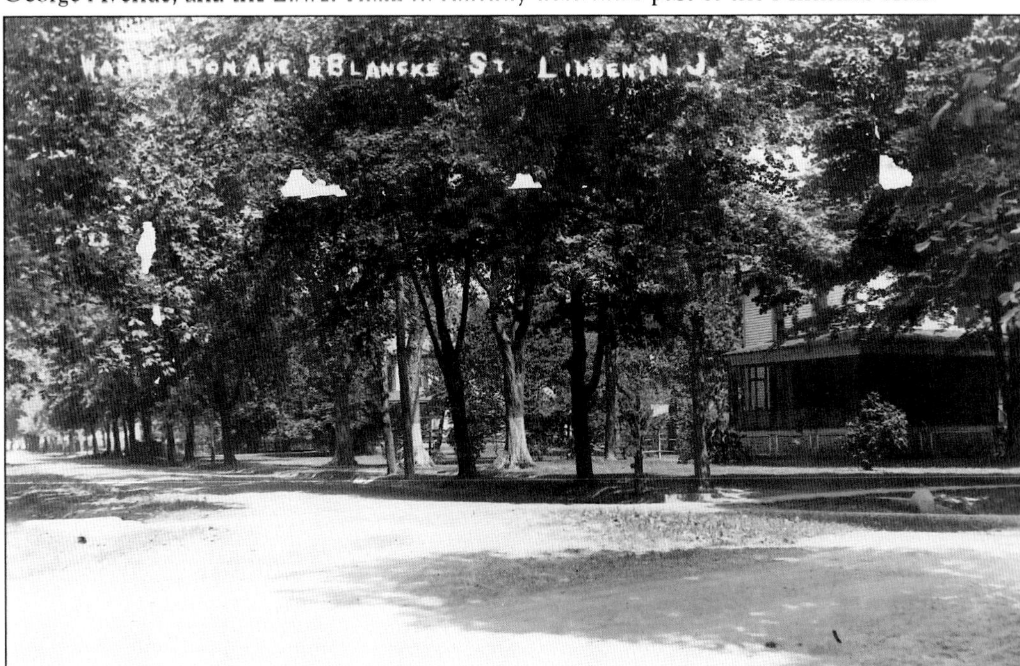

The corner of Washington Avenue and East Blancke Street. The McDonagh home is on the right. By 1925, Joseph McDonagh had been president of the bank, a member of the borough council, and president of the board of education.

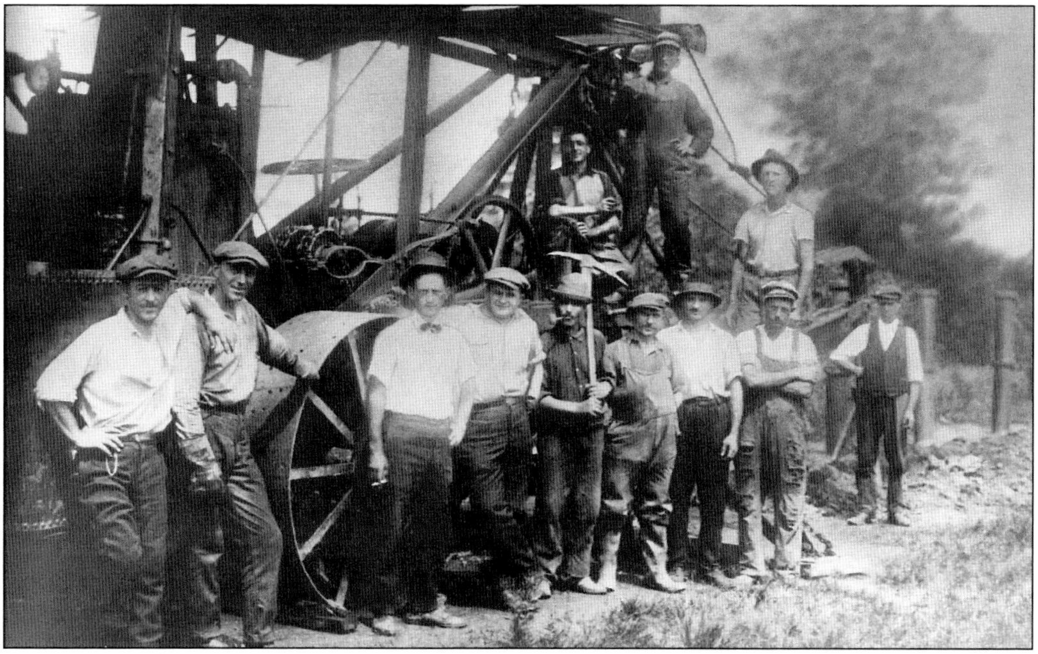

Christian Wade Sr. and the crew from Wade Contractors Inc. of Elizabeth were hired by the borough to construct sewers. This photograph depicts work being done on Washington Avenue in 1922. Christian M. Wade Sr. married Emma Hergert from Linden and had eight children: Christian Jr., Russell, Raymond, Bertha, Evelyn, Dorothy, Elanor, and Marie.

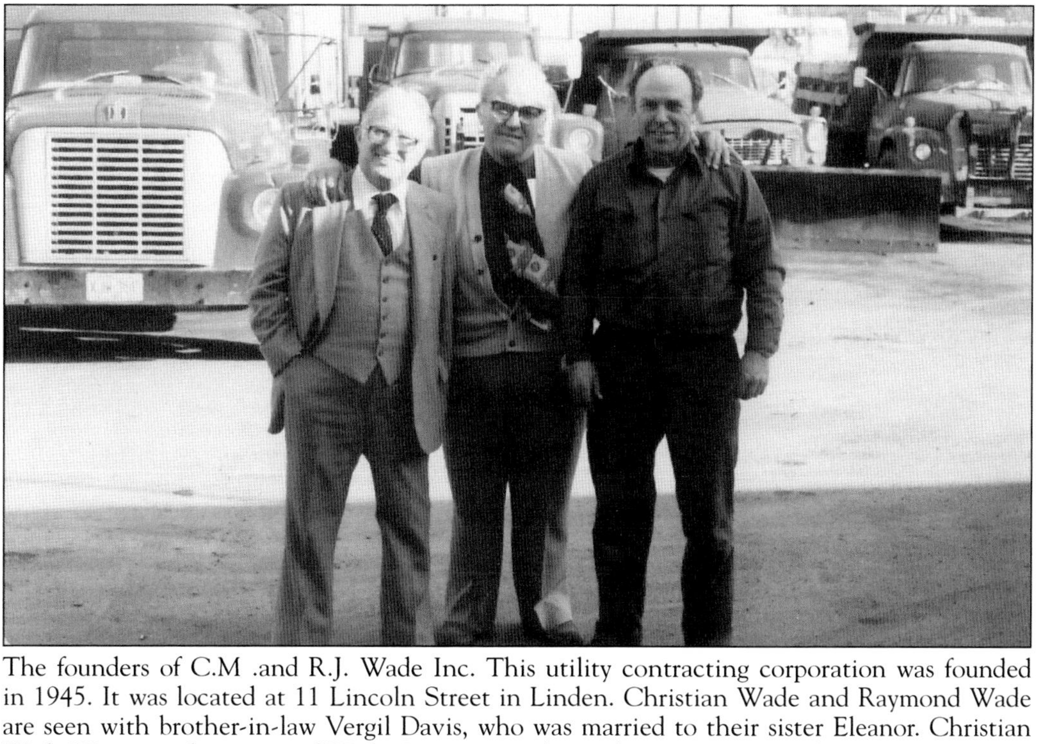

The founders of C.M .and R.J. Wade Inc. This utility contracting corporation was founded in 1945. It was located at 11 Lincoln Street in Linden. Christian Wade and Raymond Wade are seen with brother-in-law Vergil Davis, who was married to their sister Eleanor. Christian Wade III is now the owner of Wade Contracting, located at 1701 East Linden Avenue.

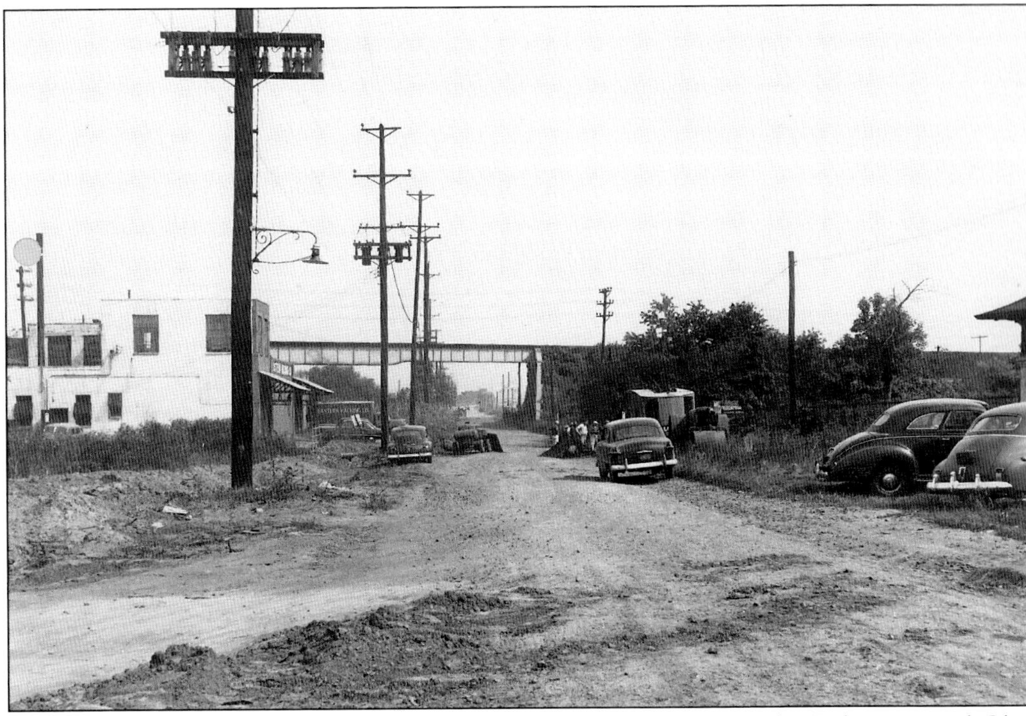

The history of Linden Avenue begins in the seventeenth century. The Baltimore and Ohio Freight (B&O) Railroad traversed the city to Tremley on the overpass above. The Eastern Packing Company is shown here on the left. This photograph was taken in September 1952.

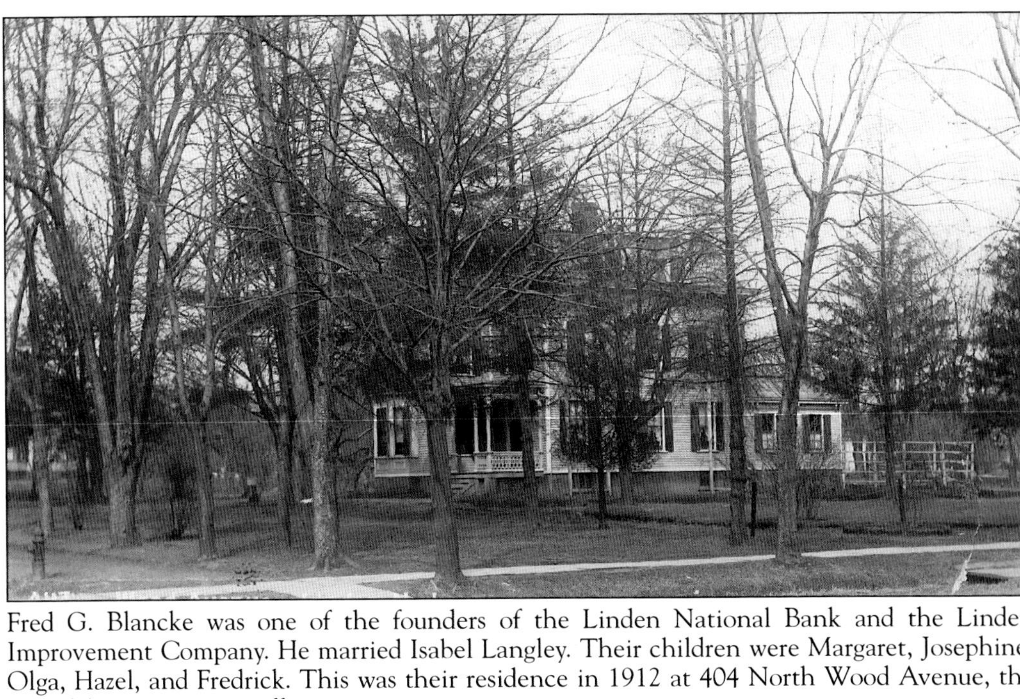

Fred G. Blancke was one of the founders of the Linden National Bank and the Linden Improvement Company. He married Isabel Langley. Their children were Margaret, Josephine, Olga, Hazel, and Fredrick. This was their residence in 1912 at 404 North Wood Avenue, the site of the current post office.

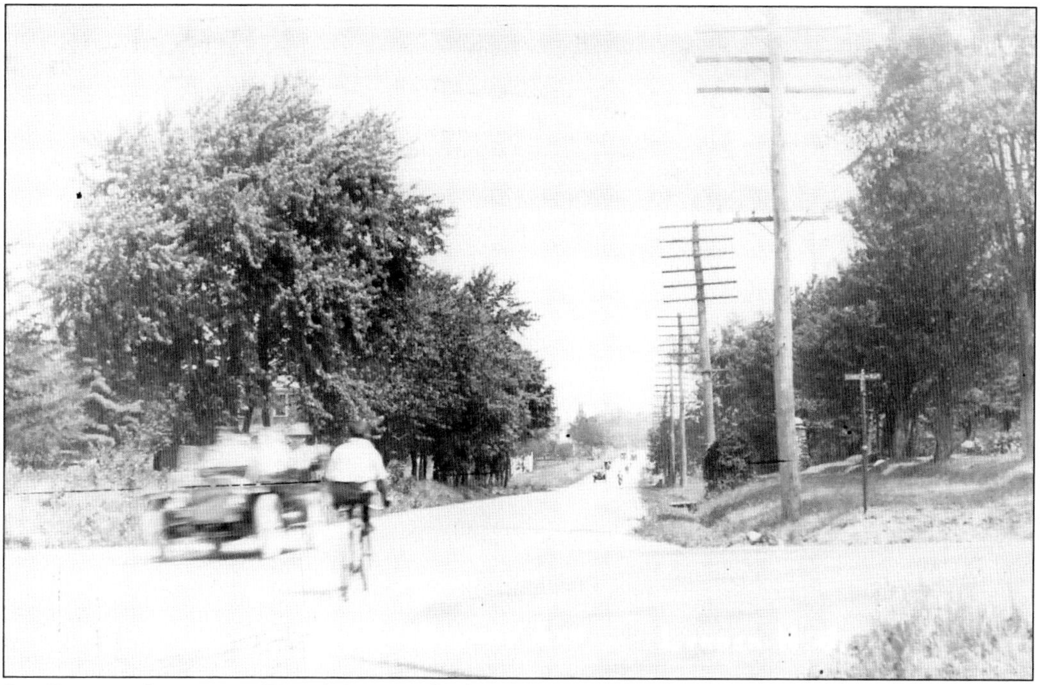

St. Georges Avenue at Wood Avenue looking east, c. 1904. The oldest road in Linden is St. Georges Avenue, part of State Highway 27. It was built and called Queen Anne's Highway during the reign of Queen Anne (1665–1774). It extended from Perth Amboy to Elizabethtown, and then more was added to go to Newark, taking part of Broad Street. It was formerly a unit of the Lincoln Highway, the transcontinental highway of the United States. During King George's reign, it extended all the way to Jersey City and was called King George's Road.

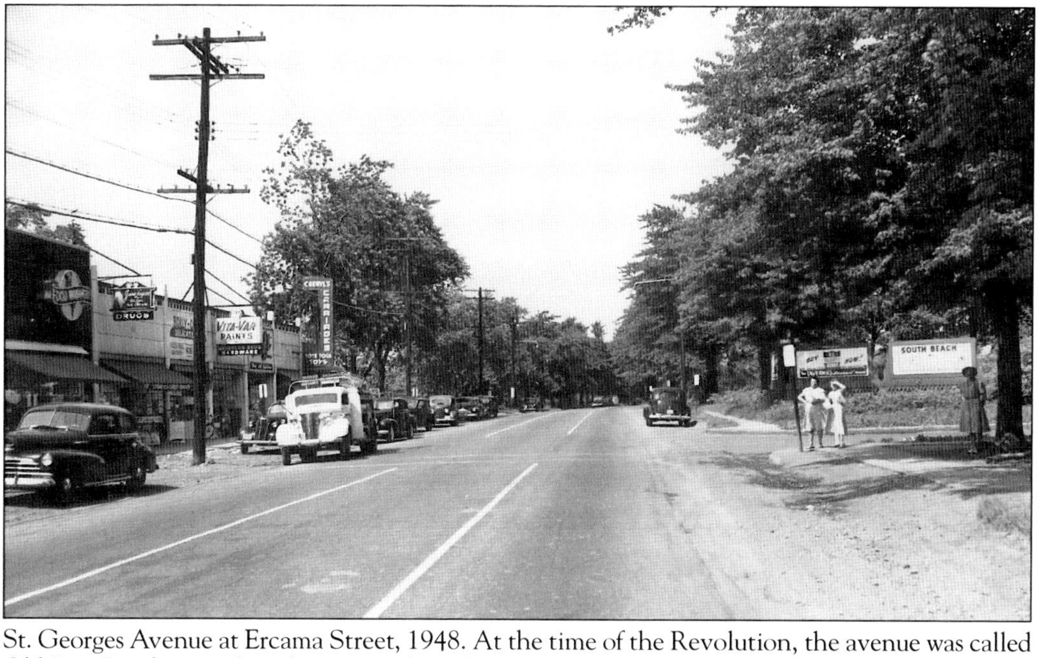

St. Georges Avenue at Ercama Street, 1948. At the time of the Revolution, the avenue was called Old Post Road; it was later known as the Old Country Road when Rahway became a city.

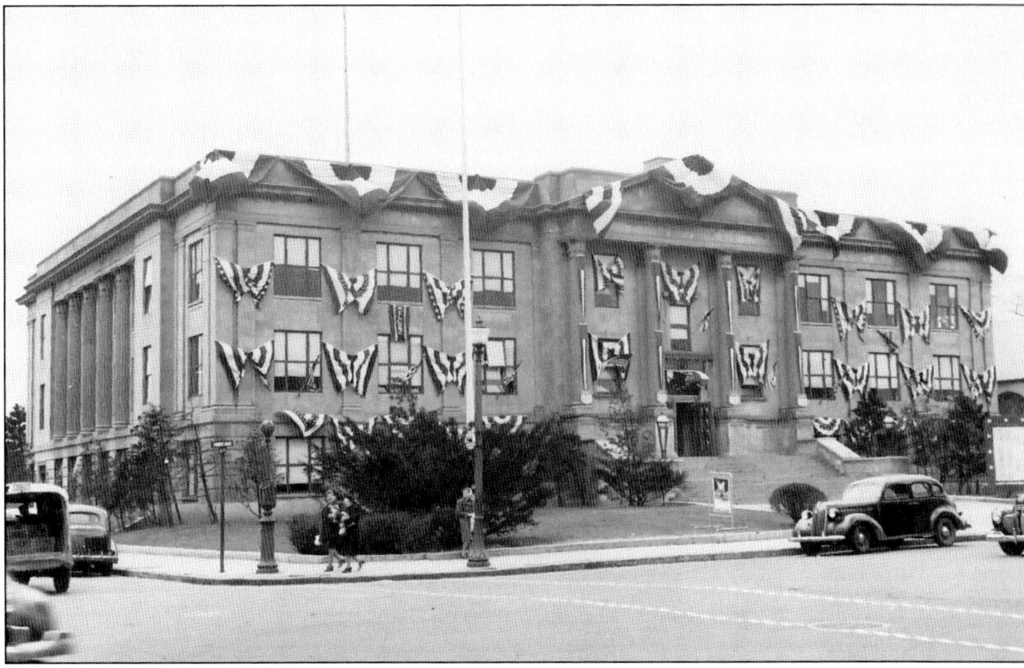

Linden City Hall dressed with banners, celebrating the 1946 Linden Victory Parade. The War Honor Roll is to the right on the front lawn. City hall was built on the site of the borough hall and dedicated in 1930. It housed the fifth district court in 1931.

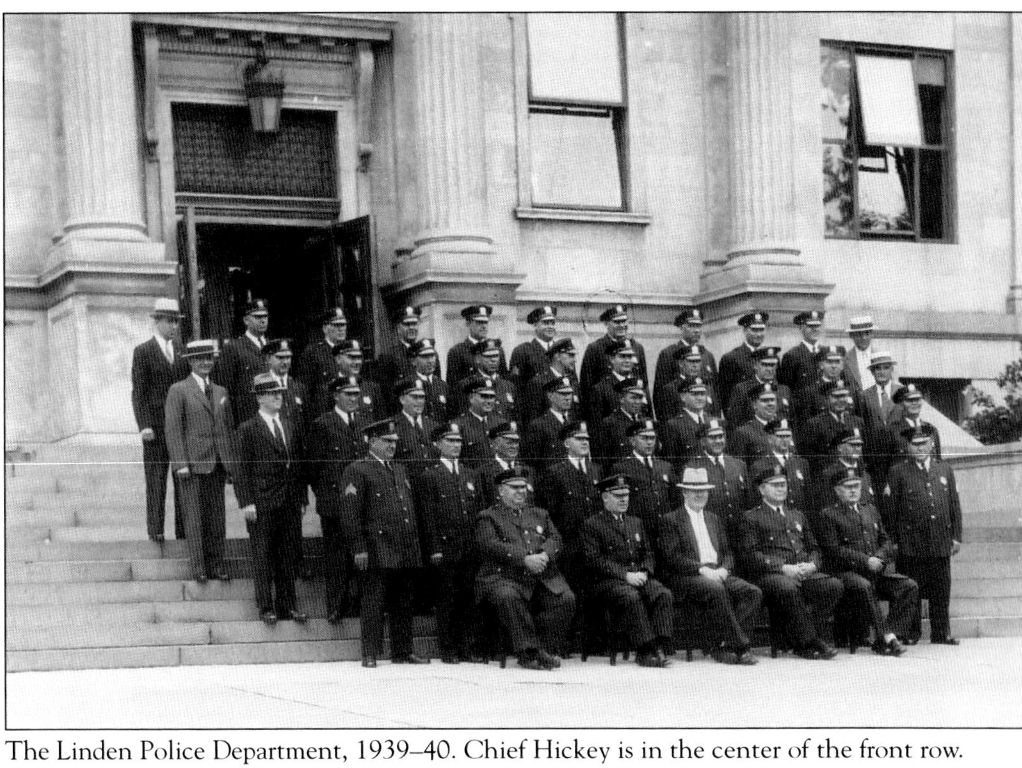

The Linden Police Department, 1939–40. Chief Hickey is in the center of the front row.

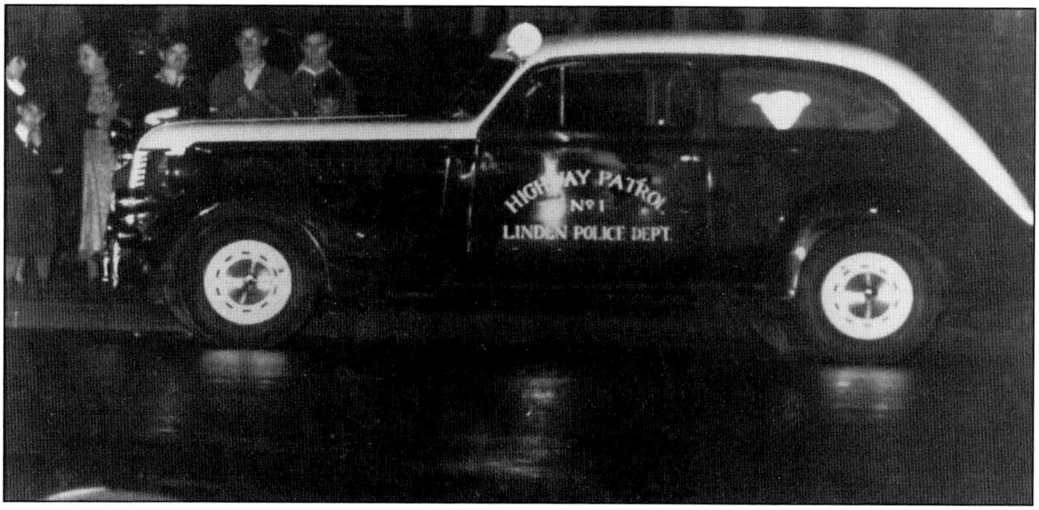

Highway Patrol #1 of the City of Linden Police Department.

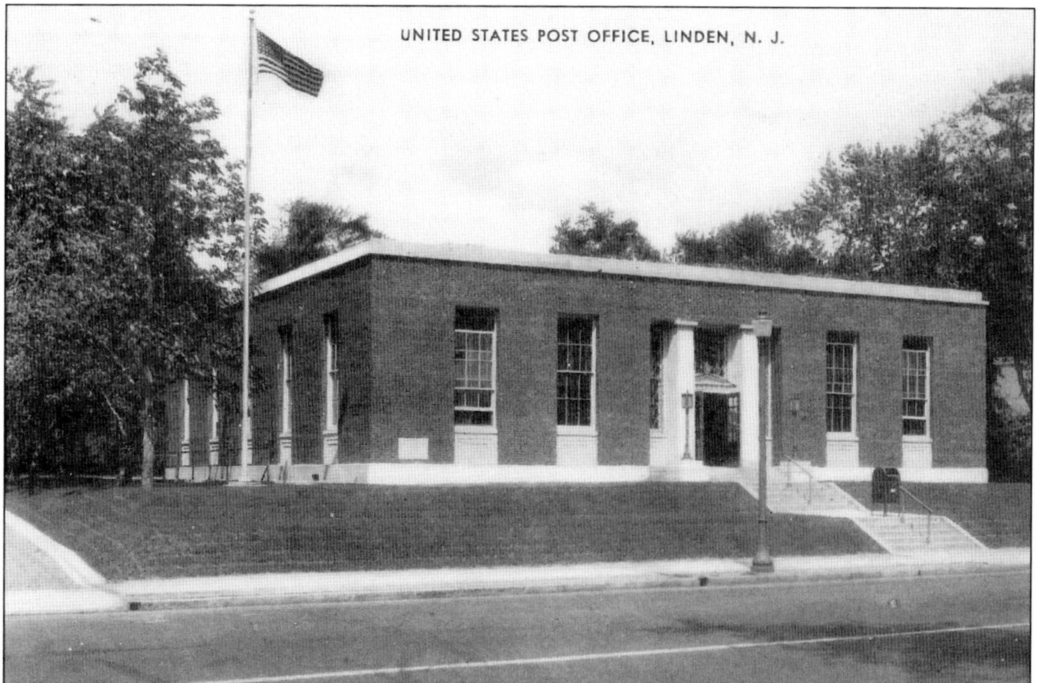

Post office, *c.* 1938, in its present location at 400 North Wood Avenue. This property originally housed the Fred G. Blancke homestead.

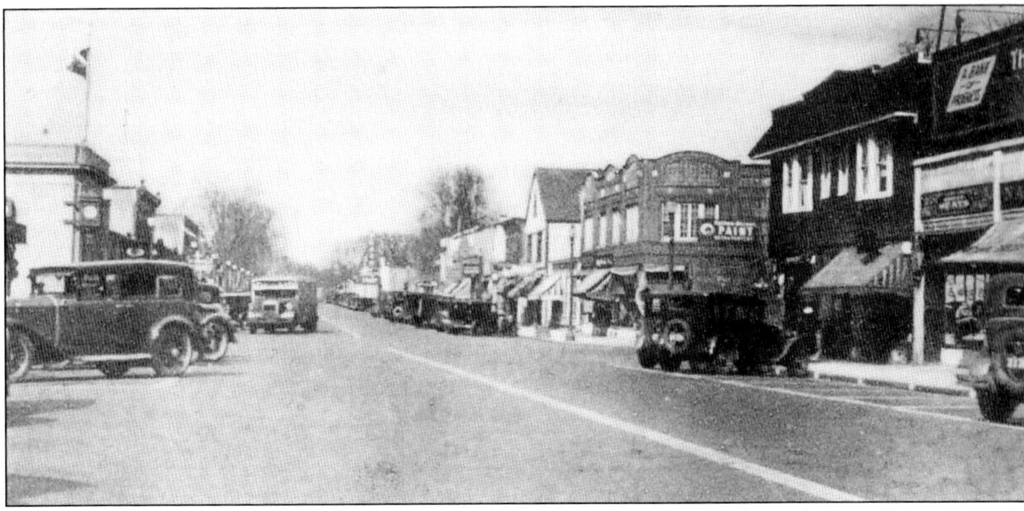

A postcard featuring North Wood Avenue in the 1920s. Cars are parking diagonally against the curb. The image captures Koenig Hardware (on the right), the Linden Trust Company (across the street), and the Plaza Movie House (in the background).

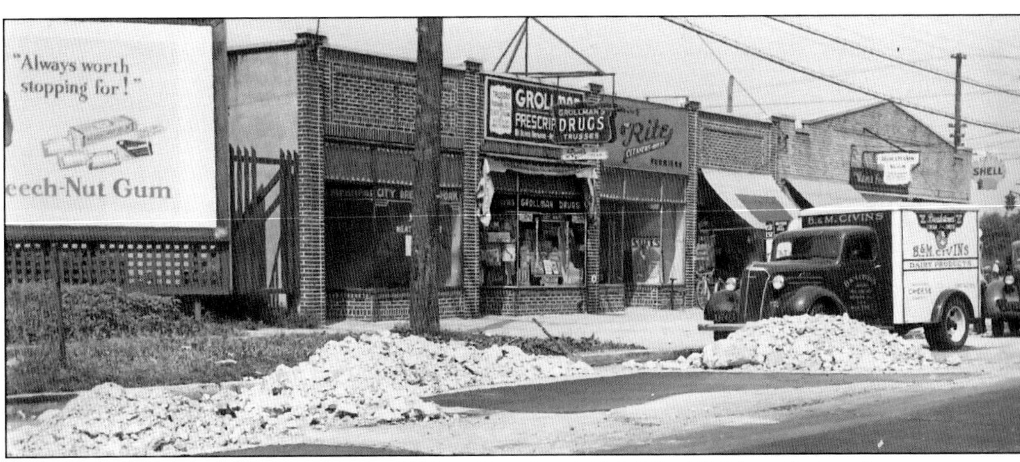

South Wood Avenue looking toward Edgar Road *c.* 1936. The WPA is fixing the pavement of the street.

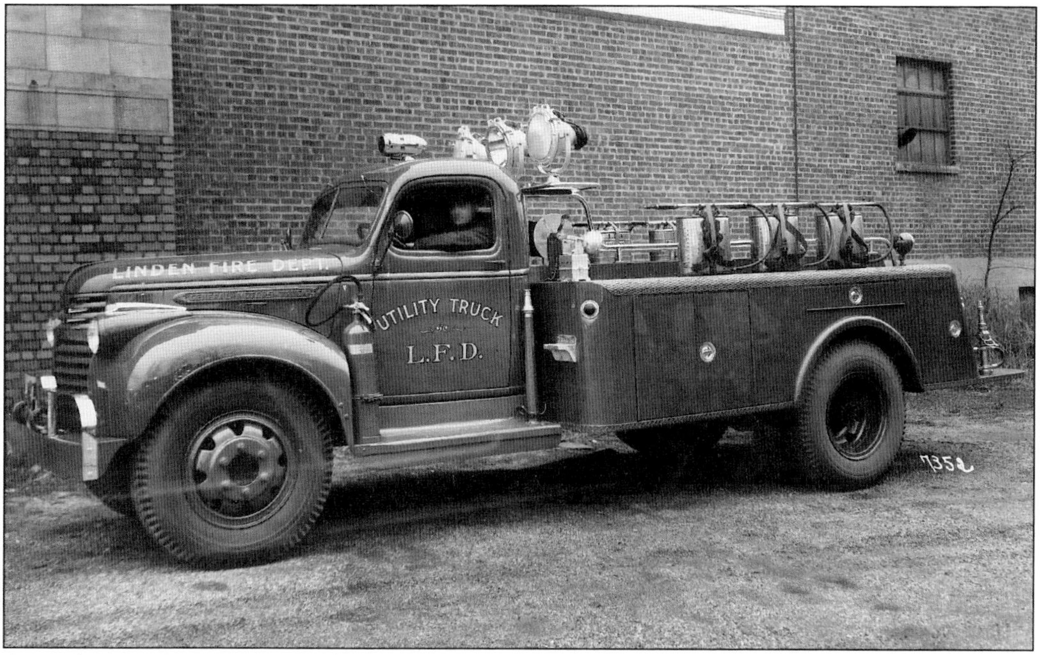

A Linden Fire Department utility truck manufactured in 1952 for the city.

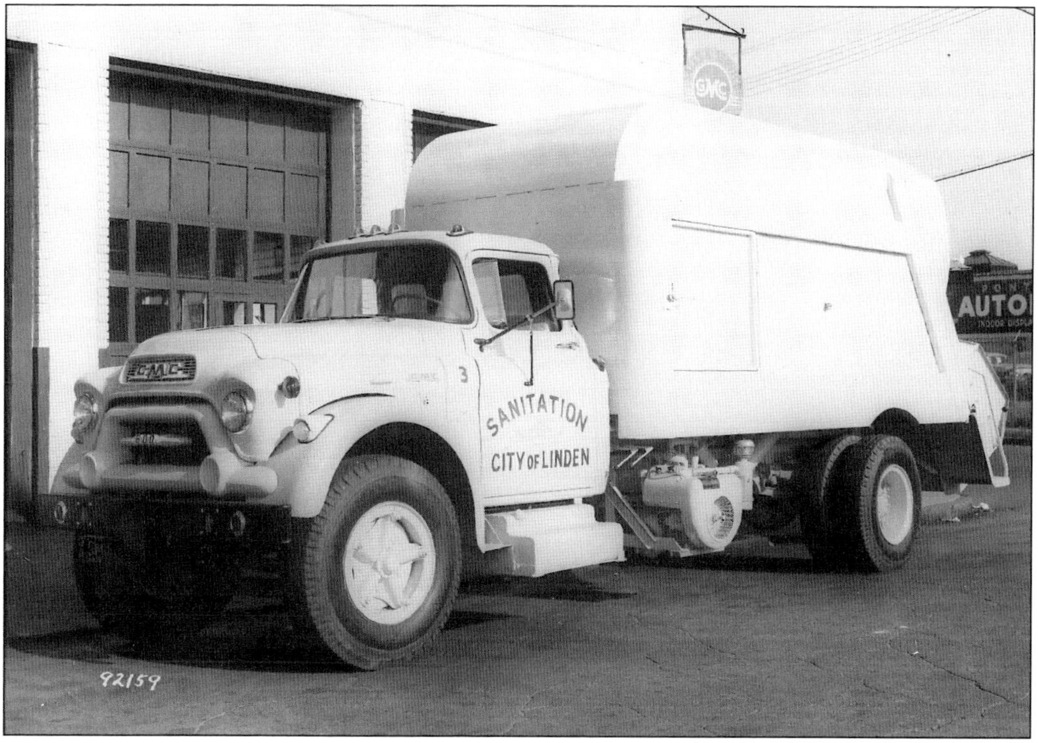

In December 1920, the Linden Township passed an ordinance calling for the collection of garbage by municipal means. It was supervised by the overseer of the poor. The borough of Linden hired a private firm for garbage and ash removal in 1922. This is an image of City of Linden 1959 Sanitation Truck No. 3.

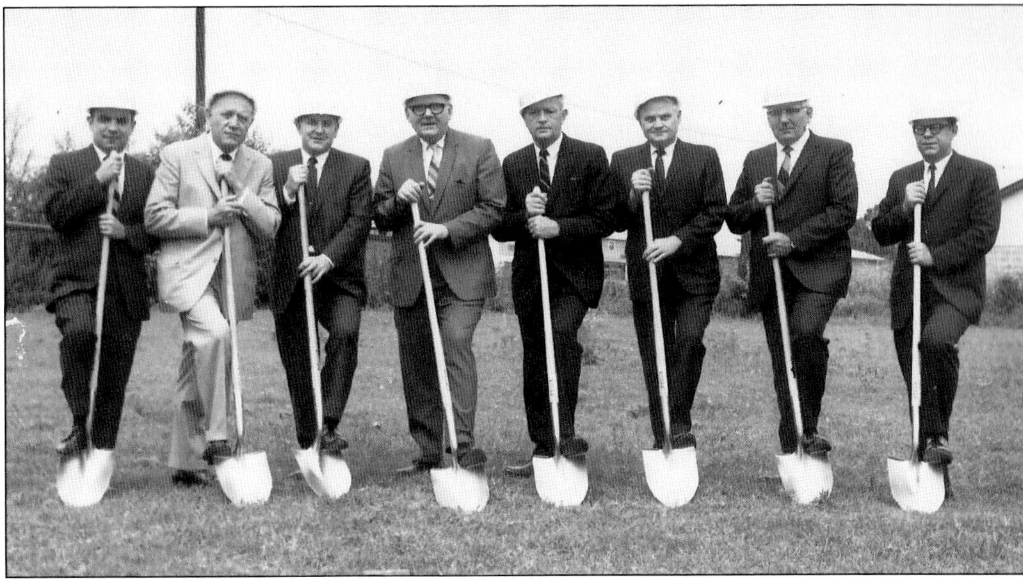

Groundbreaking for the Peach Orchard Towers Senior Complex. This was the first housing authority in the city. Members are, from left to right, Mort Weitzman, Charles Komorski, Bernard Seget, John Tieman, James Scanlon, Stanley Novalany, Steve Morris, and Emil Pancurak.

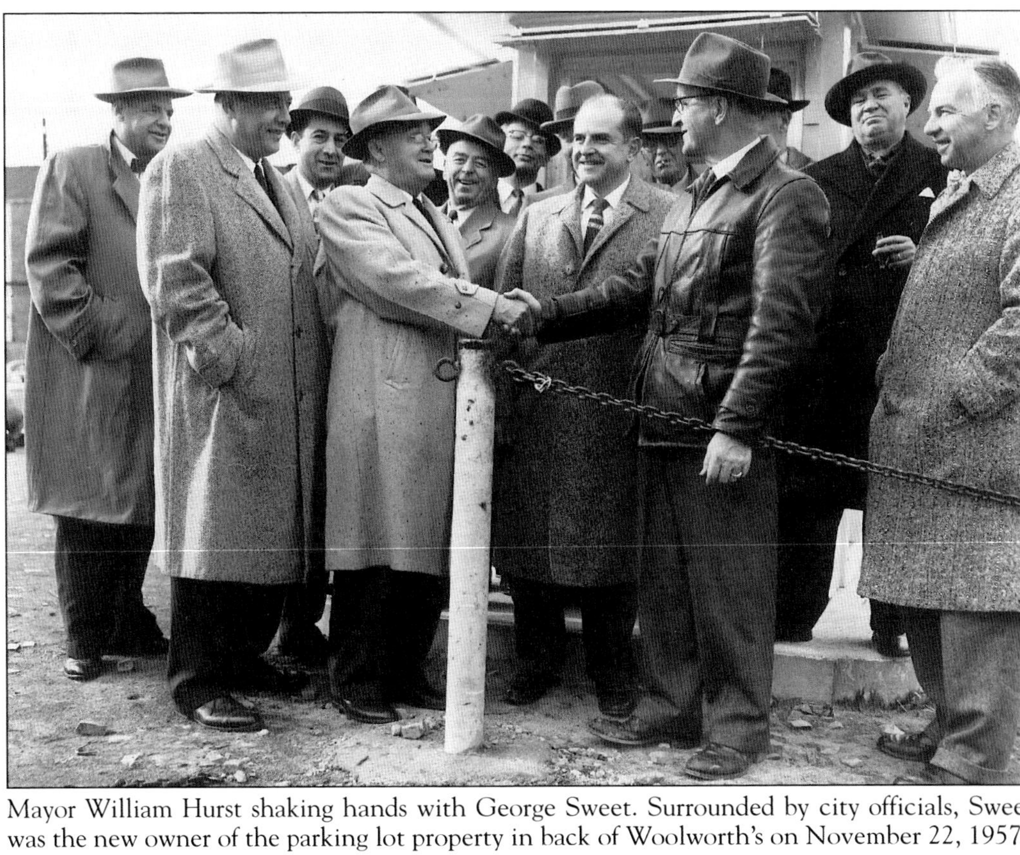

Mayor William Hurst shaking hands with George Sweet. Surrounded by city officials, Sweet was the new owner of the parking lot property in back of Woolworth's on November 22, 1957.

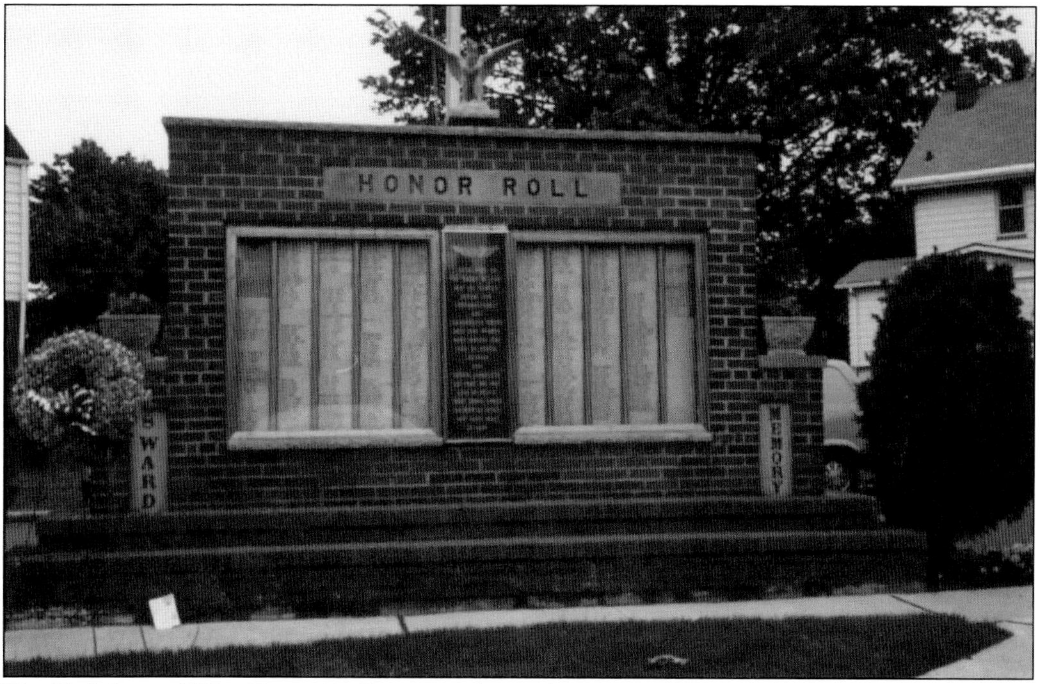

The Eighth ward War Honor Roll memorializing the servicemen and women of World War II.

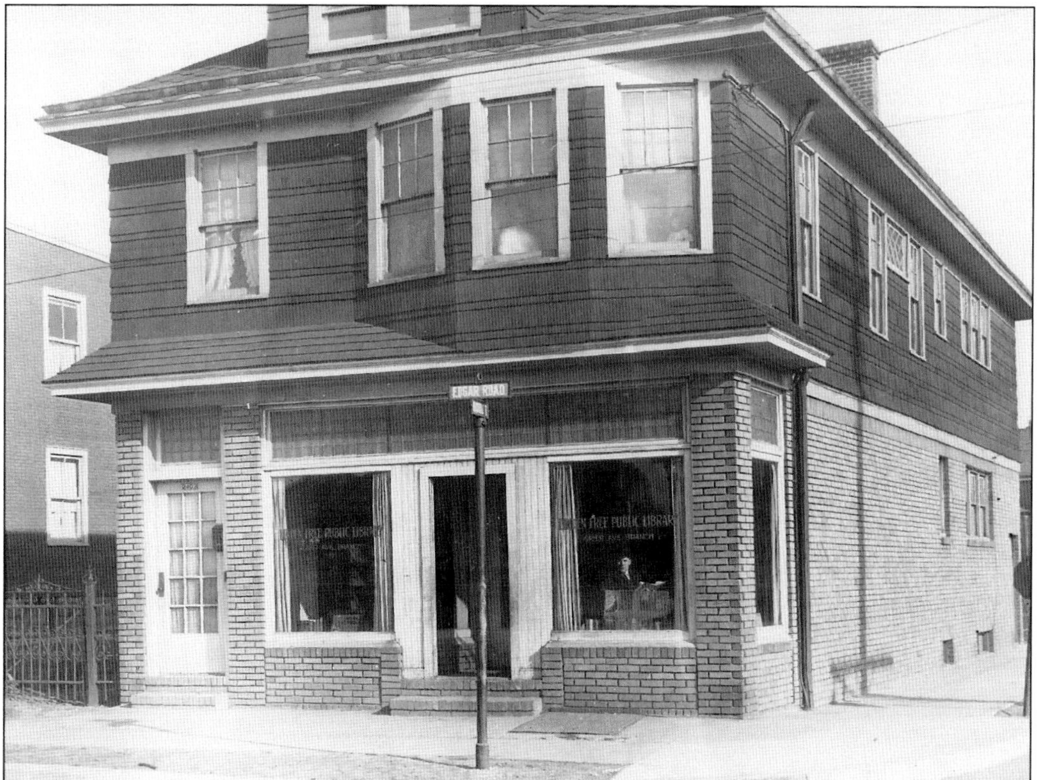

Linden Public Library, Edgar Road and Bachellor Avenue, 1929.

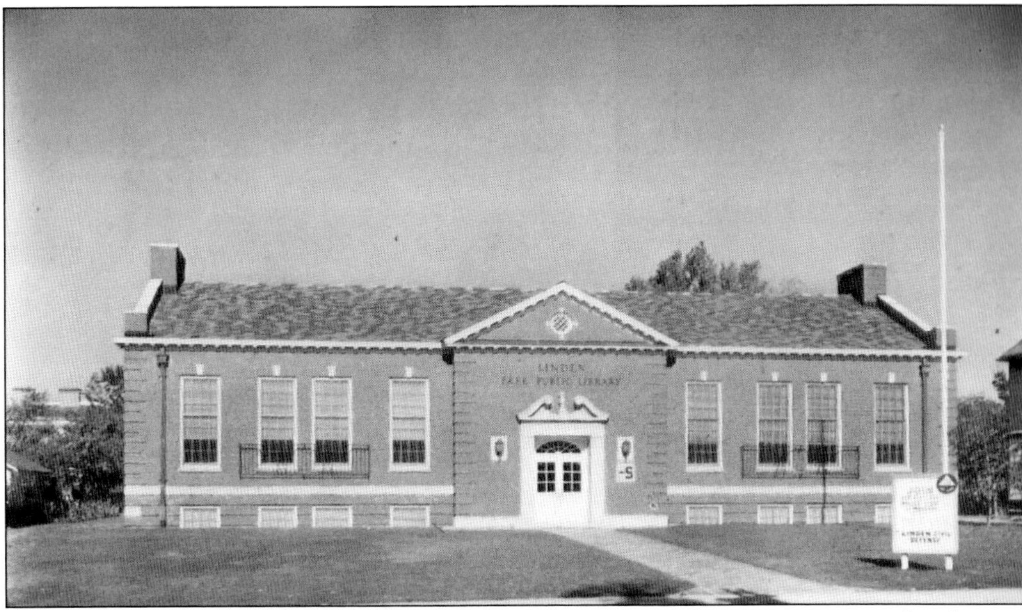

The Linden Public Library (main branch) on East Henry Street. The cornerstone is dated 1939.

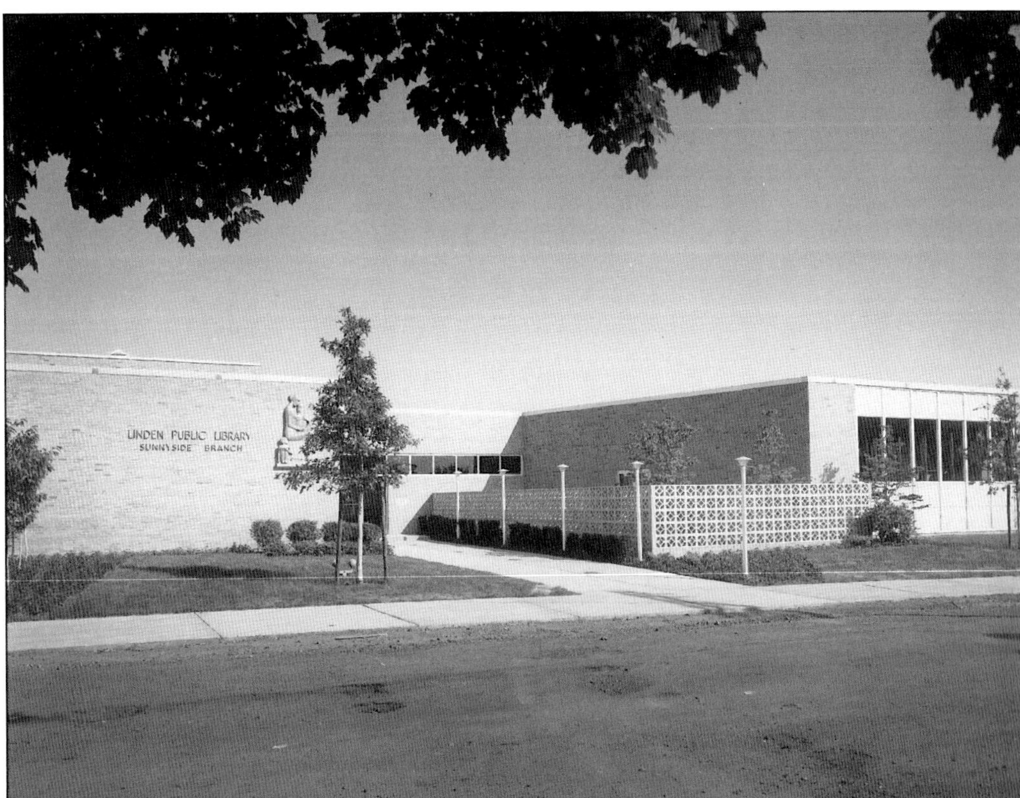

The Sunnyside branch of the Linden Library is located at 100 Edgewood Road. The east branch is located at 1425 Dill Avenue.

Three

Celebrate Wood Avenue

One way to experience beautiful downtown Linden is through our parades. They have always been natural to Wood Avenue. During the early 1900s, the township's Fourth of July parades took place on South Wood Avenue. In later years, the two municipalities welcomed home our war heroes. The city then hosted Memorial Day parades, commemorating the heroes of all the wars: those who came home and those who died for our country.

In 1950, the Linden Halloween Committee was formed. The group is still sponsored by the Linden Recreation Department. Individuals, organizations, and schools create lavish floats for parades occurring each year. Many local and professional marching bands participate. Youngsters are given awards for creativity in costuming and artwork.

Linden has also orchestrated parades for special occasions, too, with thousands of spectators coming from all over to experience them. The direction of the marchers changed sometimes but they always marched on Wood Avenue. Some early images are included along the route depicting the changing facade of our beloved Wood Avenue.

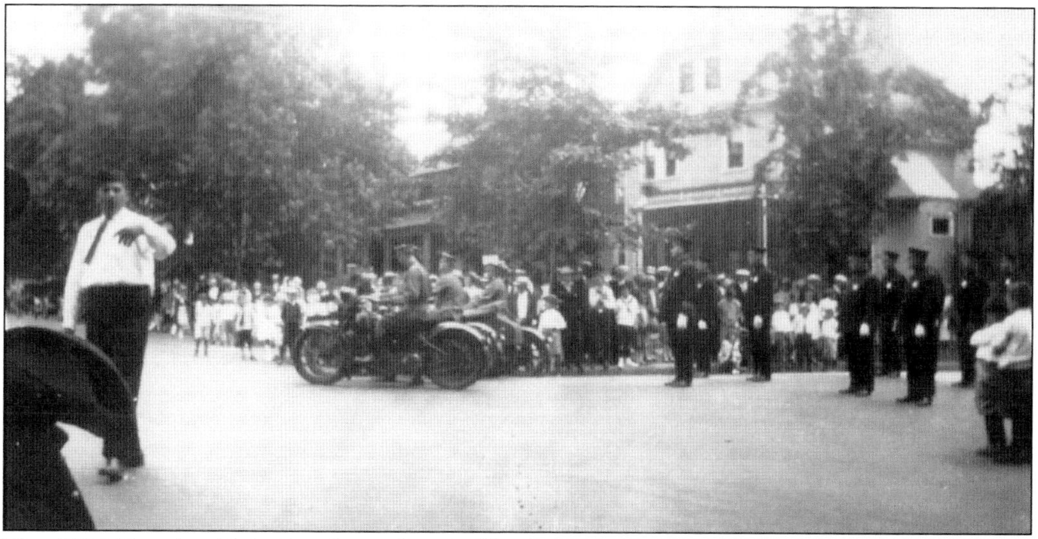

The 1924 Fourth of July Parade on South Wood Avenue and 16th Street. Wood Avenue was paved only up to this street until Mr. Luttgen continued the paving to the waterfront, where his yacht was docked.

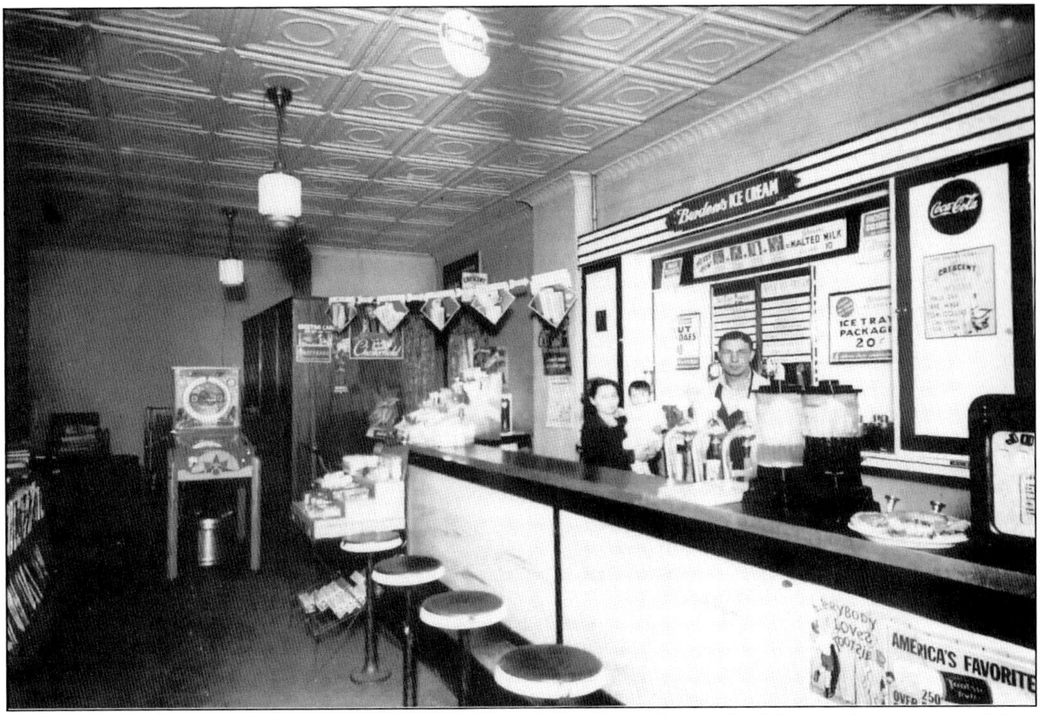

Di Leo's Candy Store, 1707 South Wood Avenue. We see Vera (holding Sebastian) and her husband, Anthony Di Leo, in June 1939.

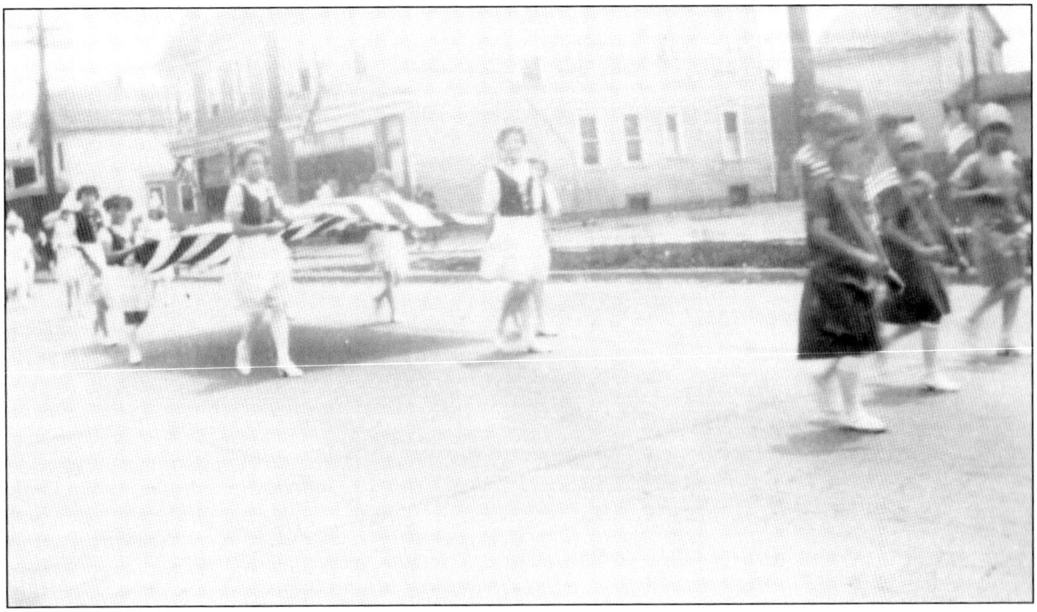

The 1920 July Fourth Parade at South Wood Avenue and Eleventh Street, looking where Big Stashes Restaurant would be today.

John Dobosiewicz with Dotsie, Junie, and Dickie Bullers in front of the Twelfth Street Candy Store c. 1935.

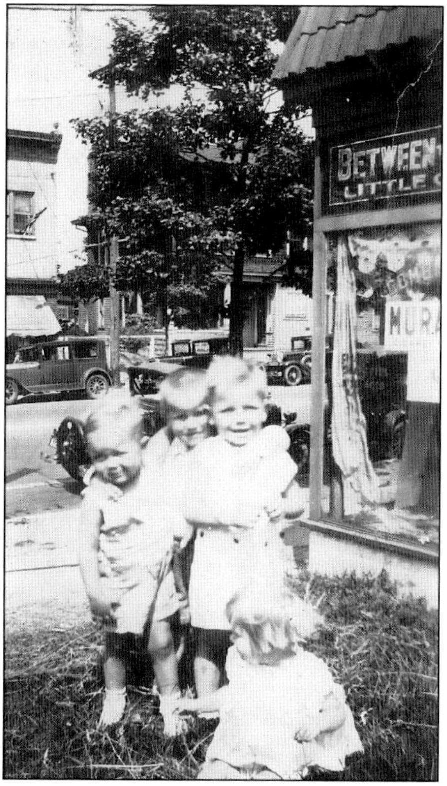

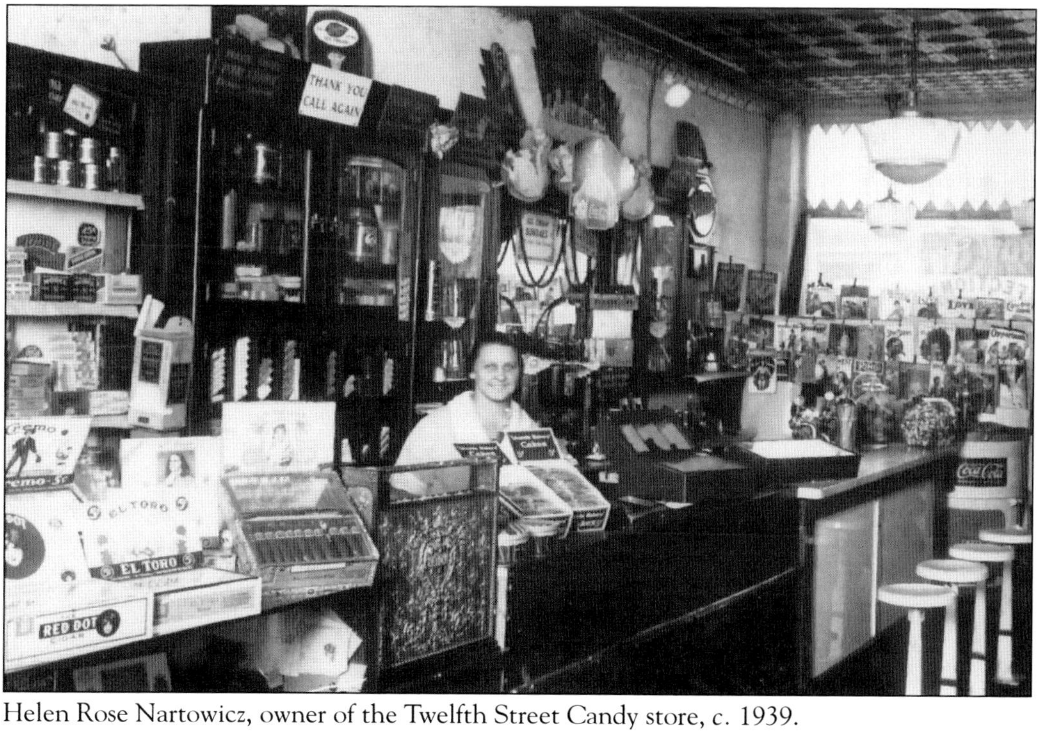

Helen Rose Nartowicz, owner of the Twelfth Street Candy store, c. 1939.

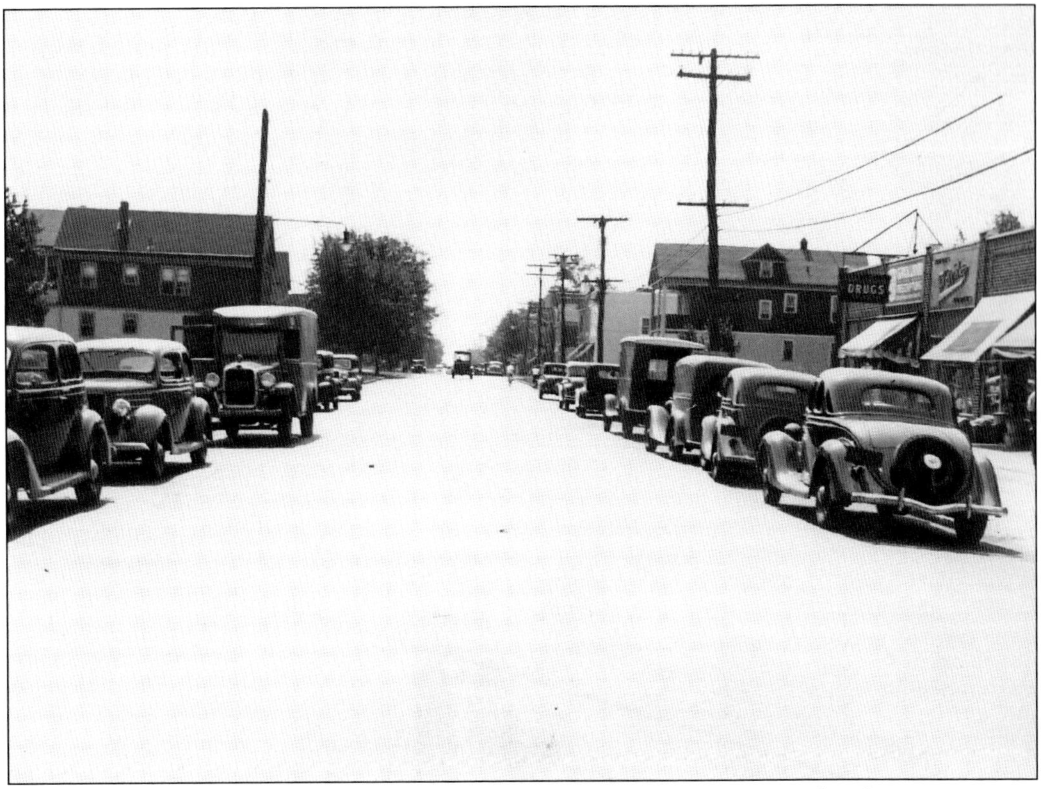

South Wood Avenue looking south after some WPA street work was completed.

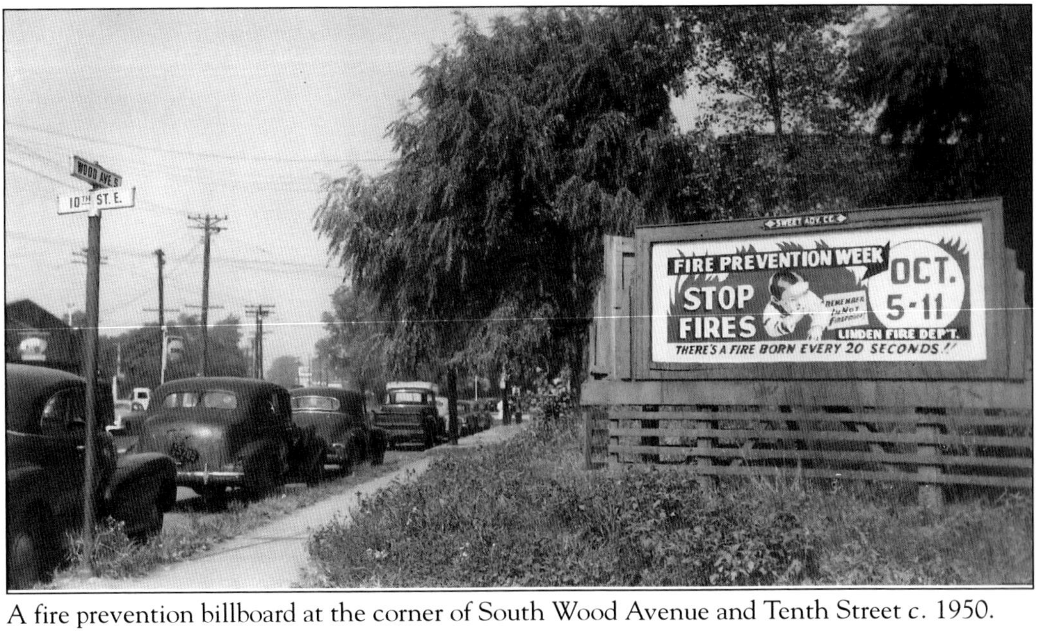

A fire prevention billboard at the corner of South Wood Avenue and Tenth Street *c.* 1950.

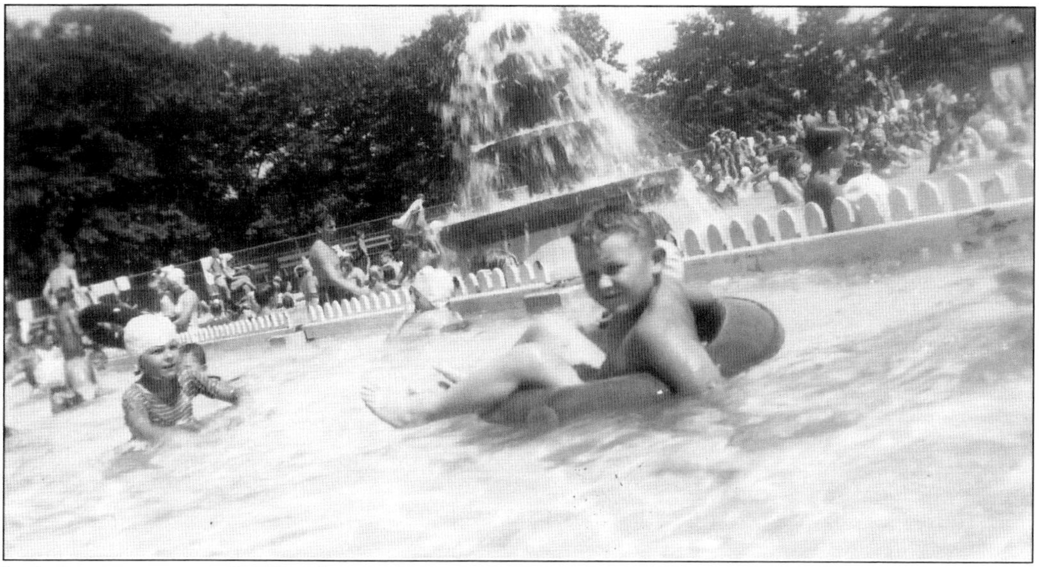

Jack Crane enjoying J. Wheeler Pool on August 23, 1948.

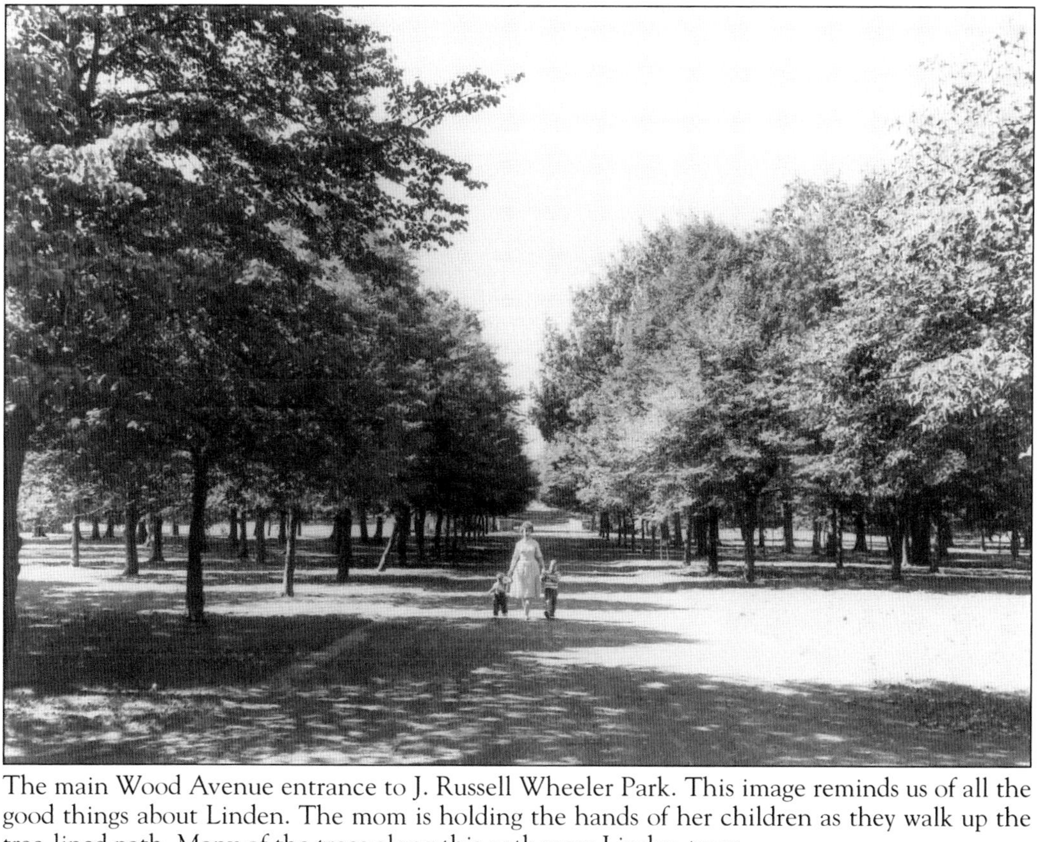

The main Wood Avenue entrance to J. Russell Wheeler Park. This image reminds us of all the good things about Linden. The mom is holding the hands of her children as they walk up the tree-lined path. Many of the trees along this path were Linden trees.

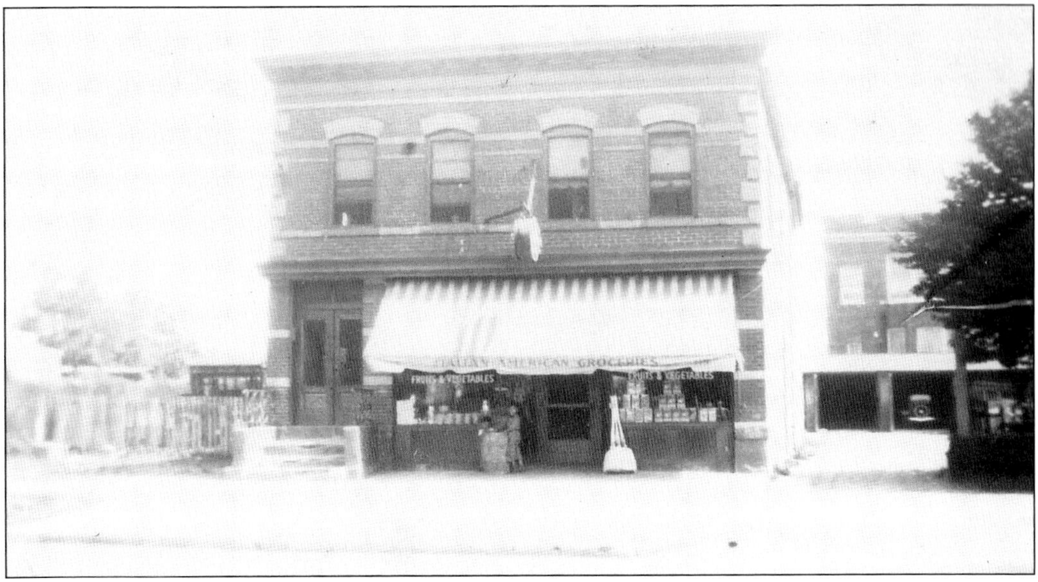

The American-Italian Grocery Store opened in 1931. It was a family-owned business run by Frank and Palma Villani and was located at 115 South Wood Avenue. All of the foods were imported from Italy. During World War II, importing came to a halt and the store closed. This photograph was taken *c.* 1934.

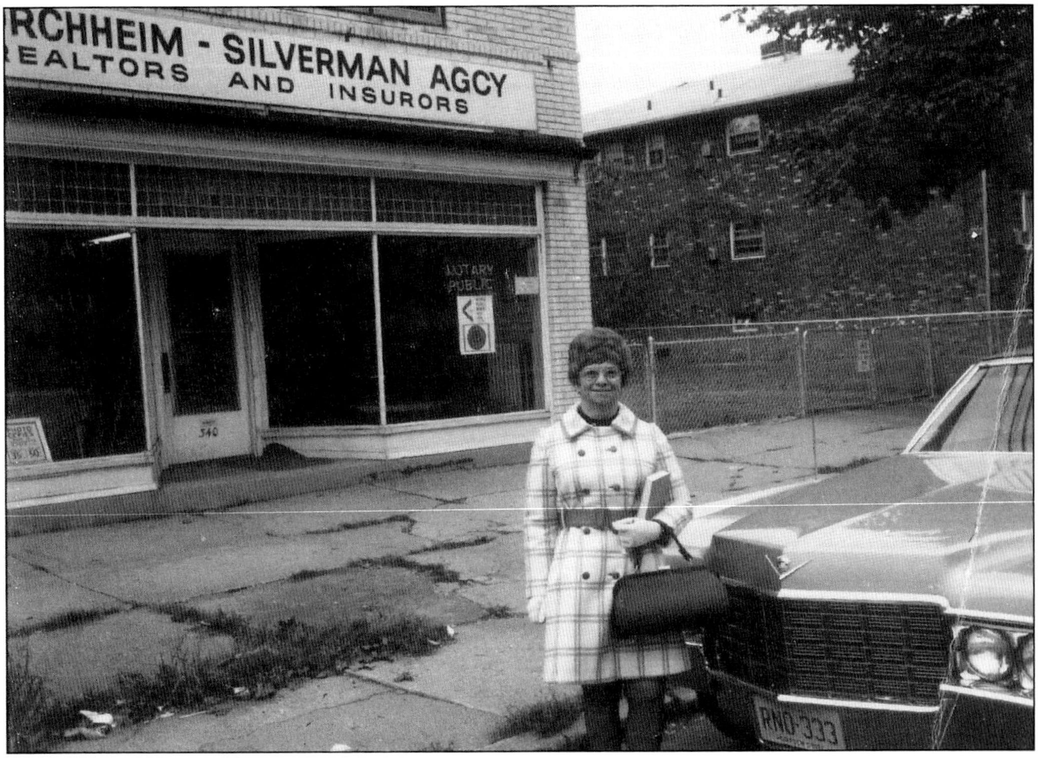

Rae Silverman outside the Storchheim Silverman Agency. It is because of this woman that the word "Realtor" is now capitalized in the dictionary.

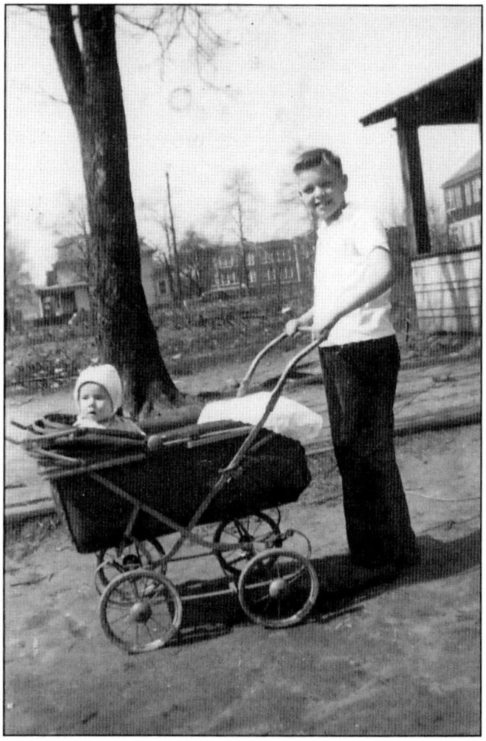

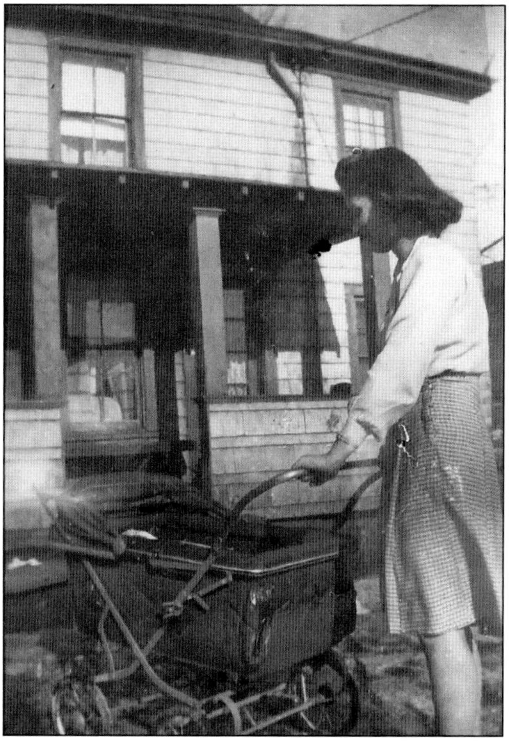

The oldest documented house in Linden is at 417 South Wood Avenue. It was the home of Luther Carsons' family from 1935 to 1955. Alton Carson with nephew David is to the left and Phyllis Carson, also with first-born son David (at nine months of age), is to the right.

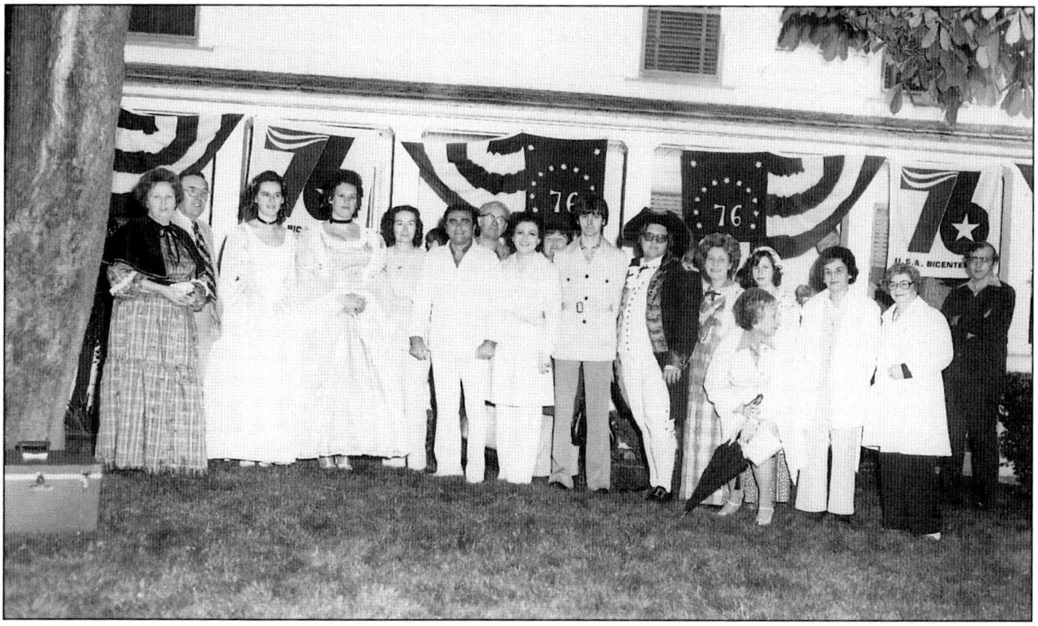

Mayor John T. Gregorio and the Bicentennial Committee at the dedication of the Evia House in 1976. A plaque is on the front lawn as a dedication to the past of the house. It was built in the 1700s and is Linden's oldest house on record.

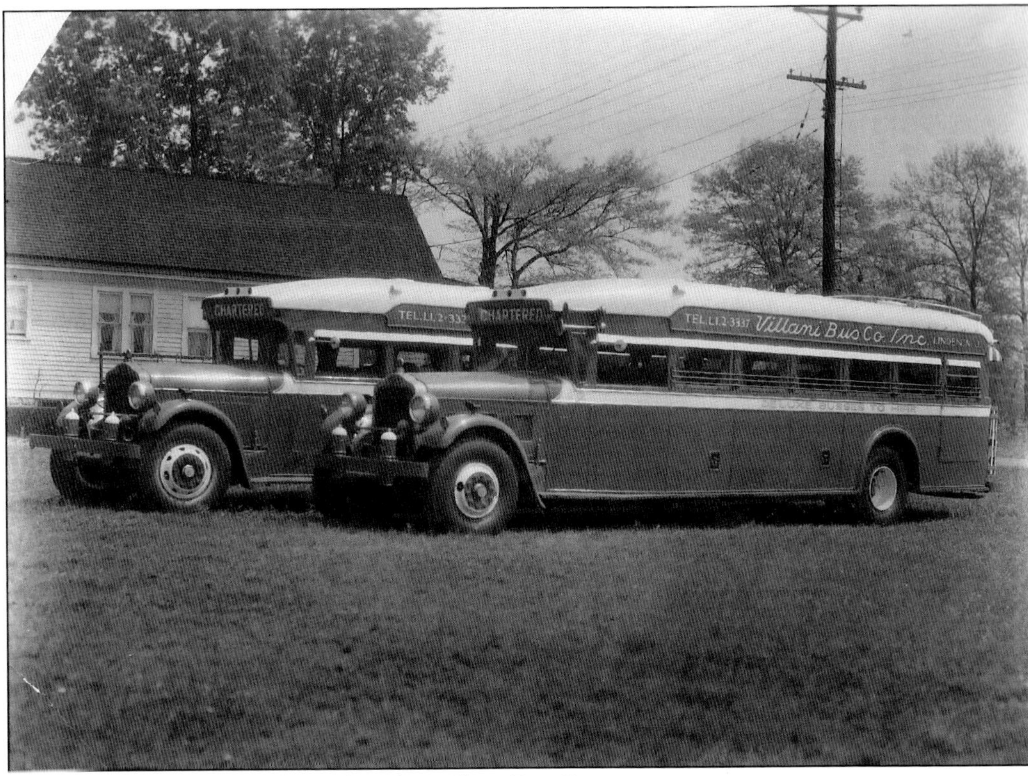

Two 1937 models that belonged to the Villani Bus Company.

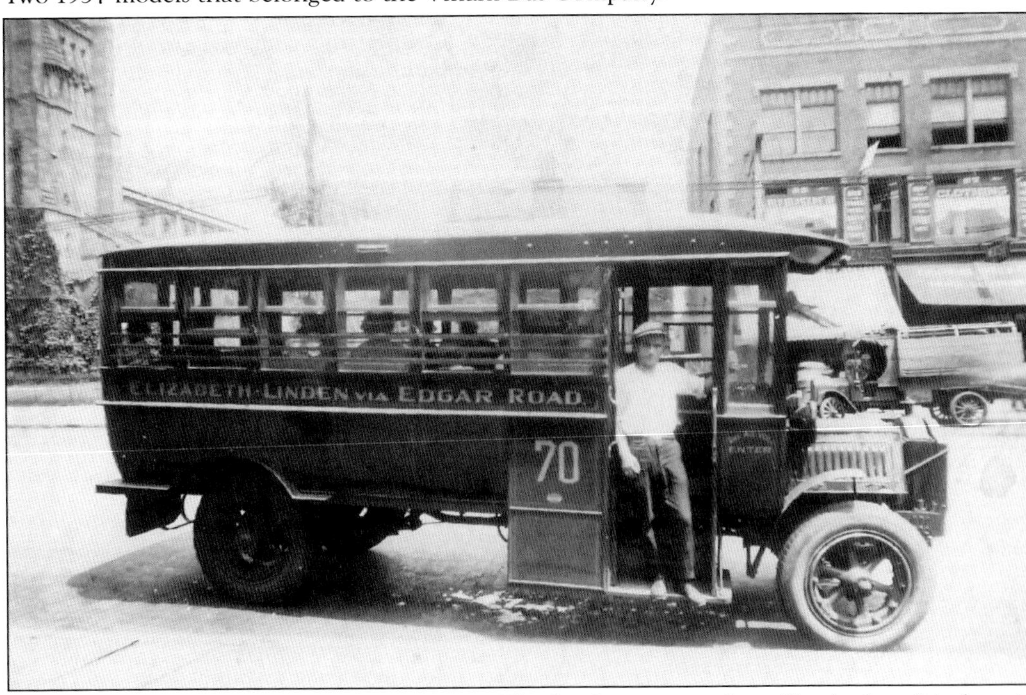

Mr. Frank Villani in front of his bus in 1924. The line's route ran from Elizabeth to Linden via Edgar Road. This stop was in Elizabeth.

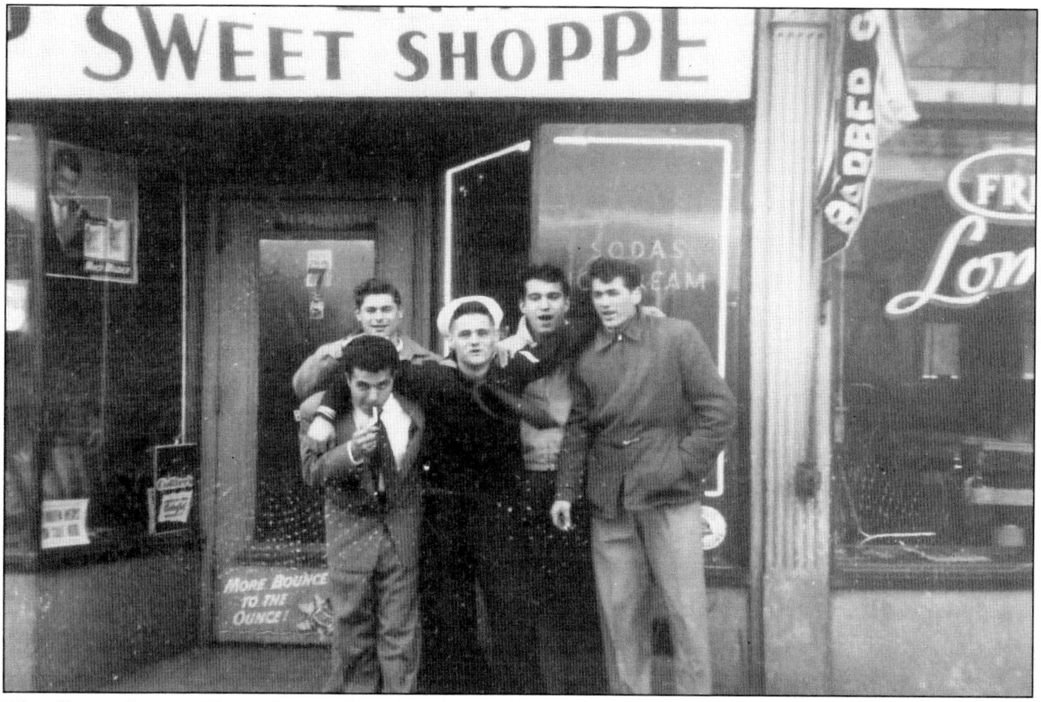

The Penn Sweet Shop, located across from the train station. From left to right are Charlie Venditto, Joe Bruno, Alfred "Bo" Botelho, John Wadiack, and Ed Corduan.

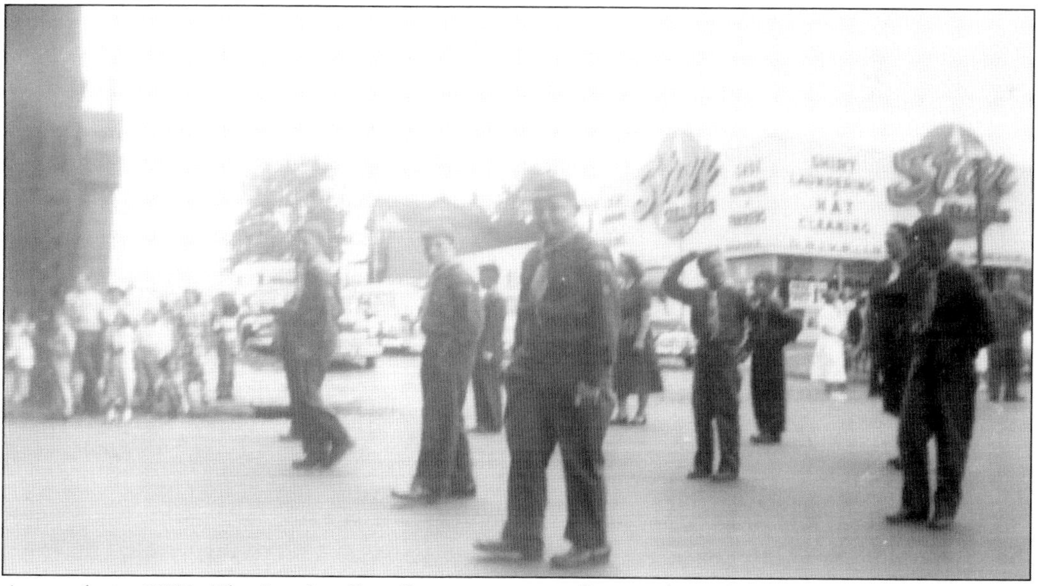

A parade in 1950. The Linden Boy Scouts are proudly marching by Pennsylvania Avenue on South Wood Avenue. The boy in the middle is Ed Hance. Pennsylvania Avenue and Star Cleaners can be seen to the rear.

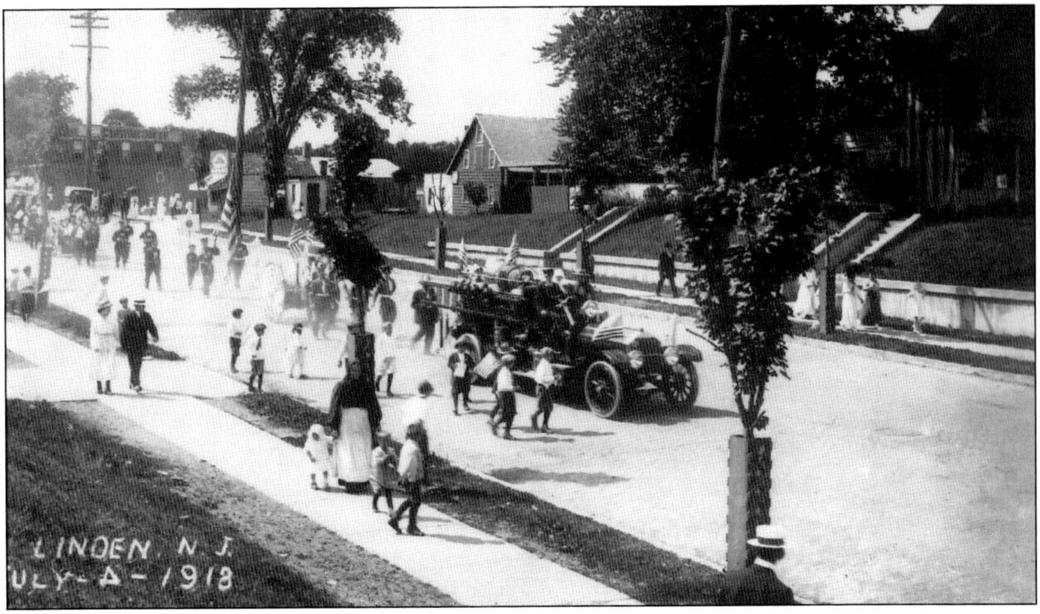

The 1918 Fourth of July Parade. In the foreground is the township of Linden's LaFrance fire engine, followed by a hand-drawn hose cart. The borough also had its own volunteer fire department, but did not acquire an engine until 1920. By this time, Wood Avenue was already depressed to pass under the railroad. Across the street are stairs leading to the Wood Homestead.

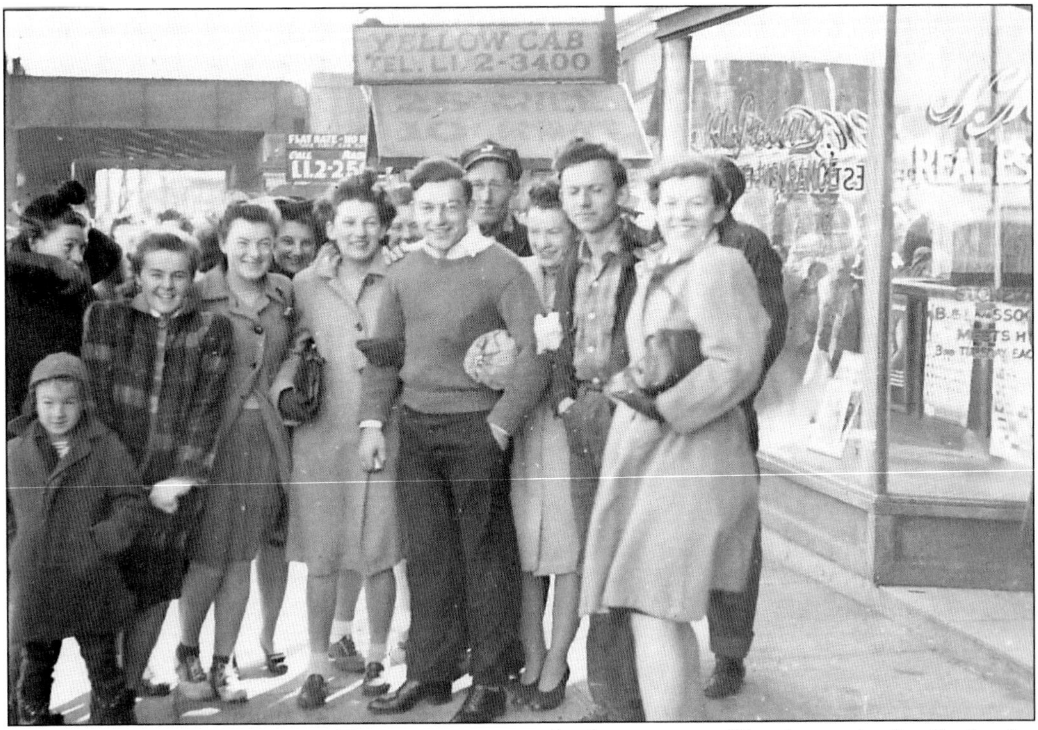

Larry Derrig is leaving for World War II service and is being seen off by the entire family. In the background we can see the Yellow Cab Company and the N.M. Palermo Agency.

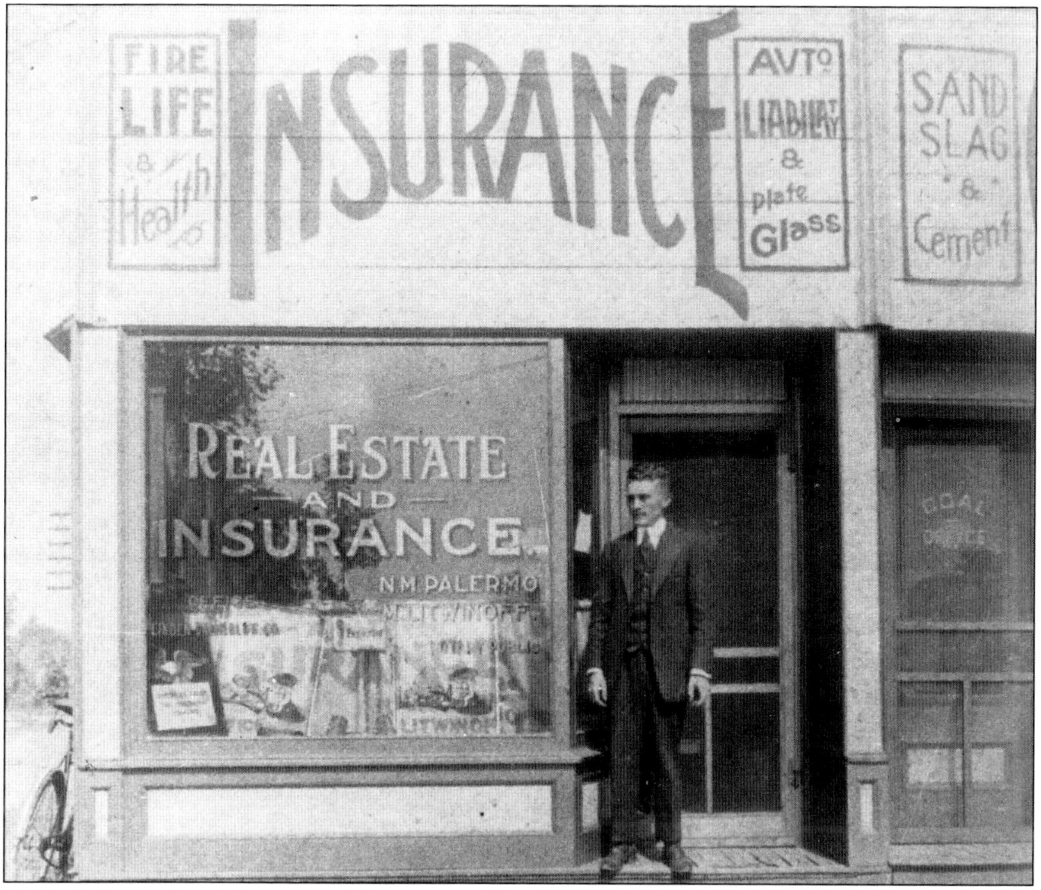

N.M. Palermo Real Estate and Insurance, Wood Avenue. That is Mr. Palermo standing in front. Borough meetings were held here as well.

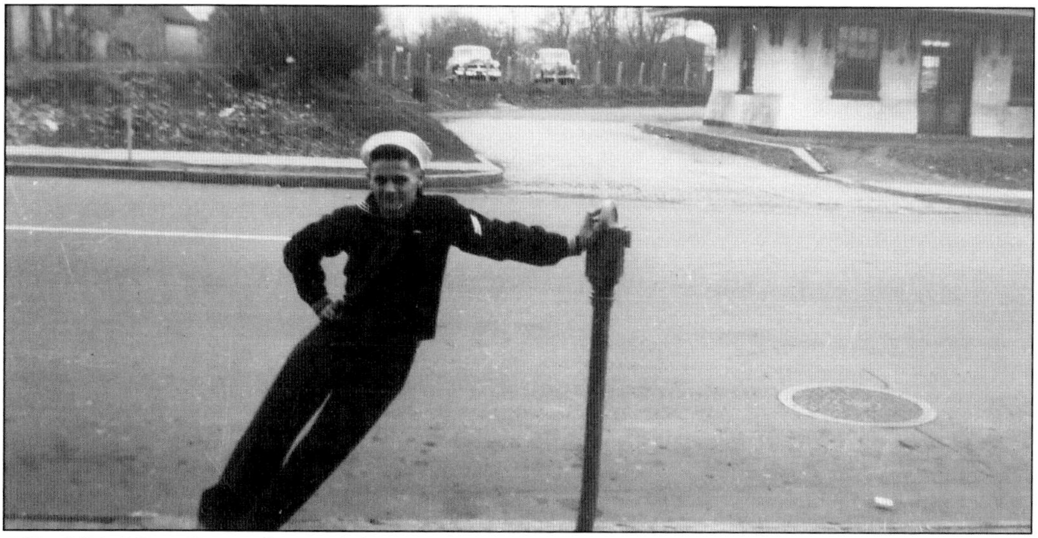

Alfred "Bo" Botelho in front of the Penn Sweet Shop after World War II. The shop was across from the train station on Wood Avenue.

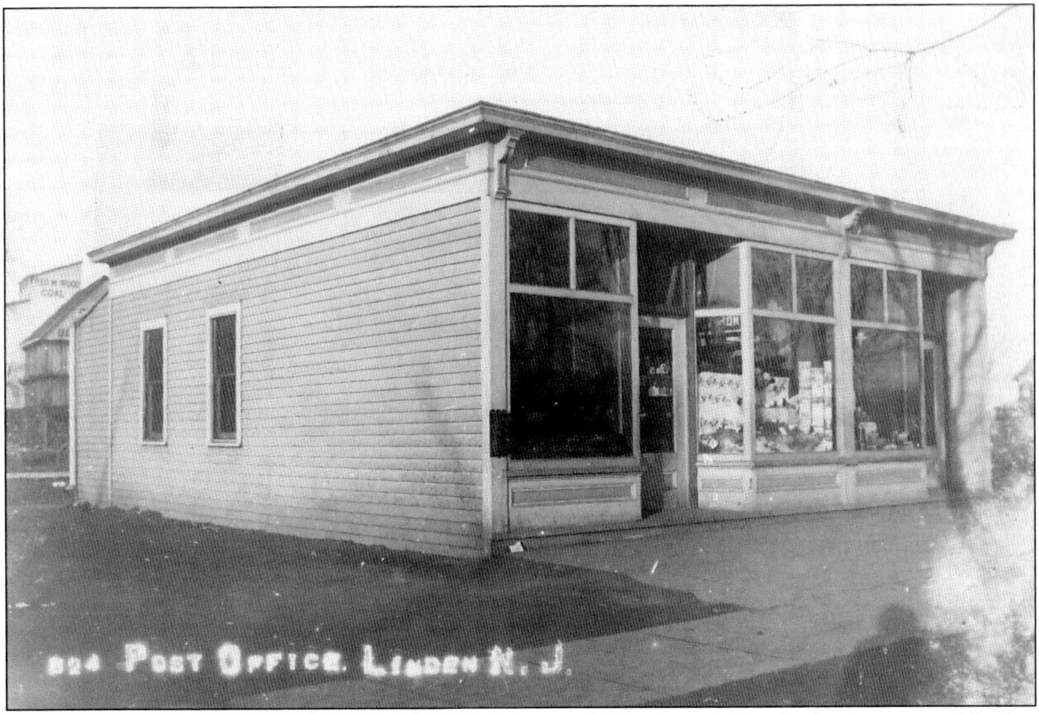

The United States Post Office, southwest corner of Wood and Elizabeth Avenues. Meeker Wood and Susan Winans were the parents of Sadie, the first postmistress of Linden. Together with the veterans, they kept it open despite the government wanting to close it down and give Linden a rural route.

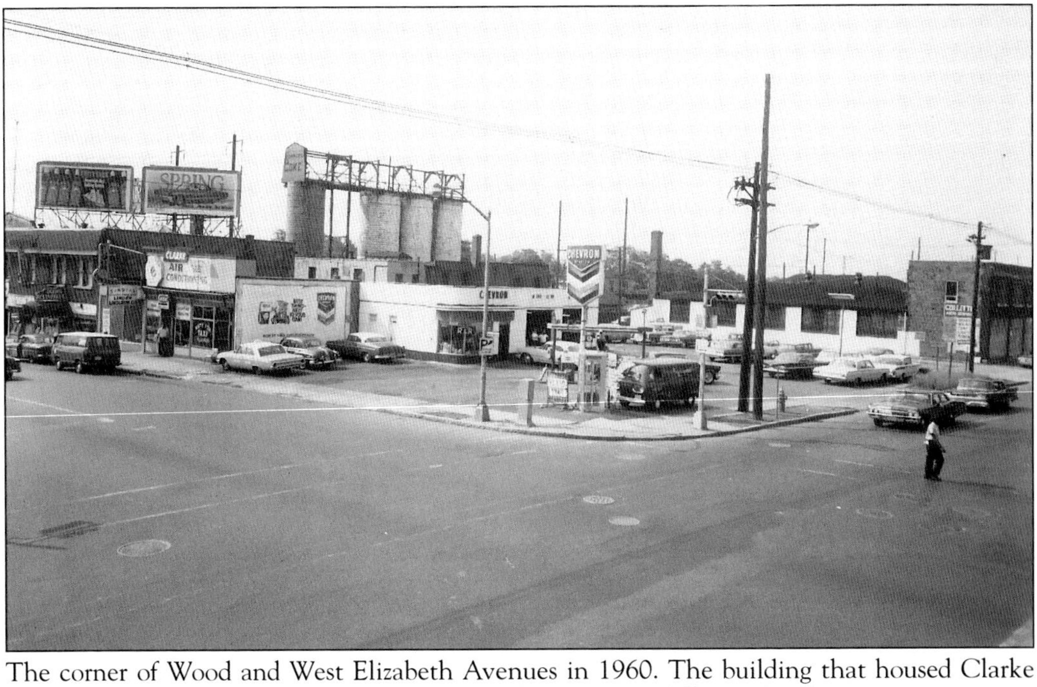

The corner of Wood and West Elizabeth Avenues in 1960. The building that housed Clarke Air Conditioning was originally the first United States Post Office in Linden.

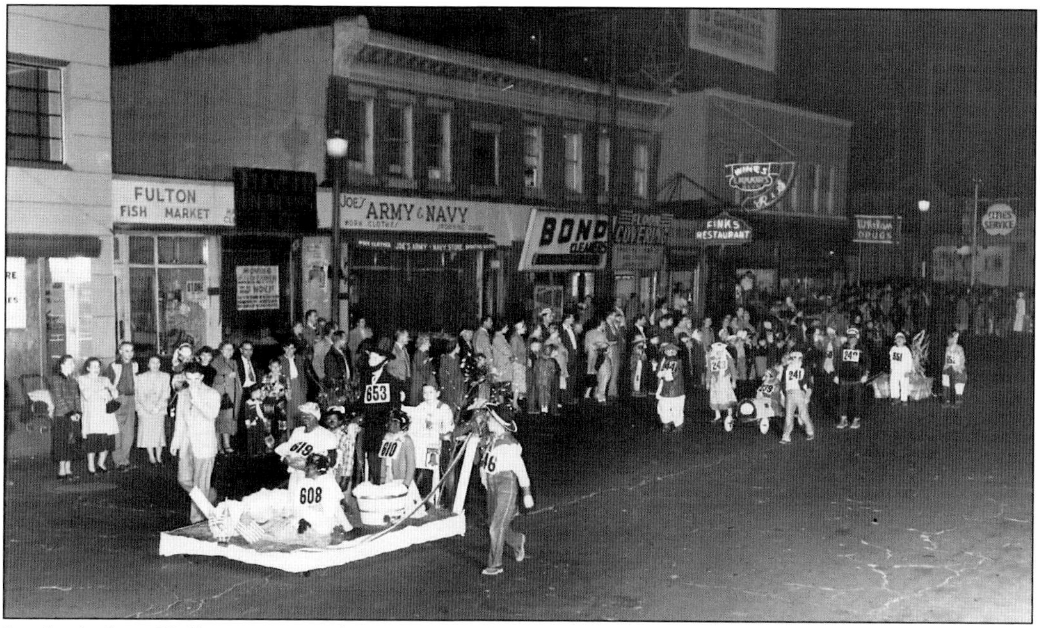

Linden's first Halloween parade in 1950. This float is from St. John's School of Clark, N.J. In the background are Joe's Army-Navy Store, Bond Cleaners, and the Floor Covering Store, all located in the Danninger building. To the right are Fink's Restaurant, Rand's Liquors, and Whalen Drugs. Across Elizabeth Avenue is the Cities Service Gas Station. To the left is Fulton Fish Market.

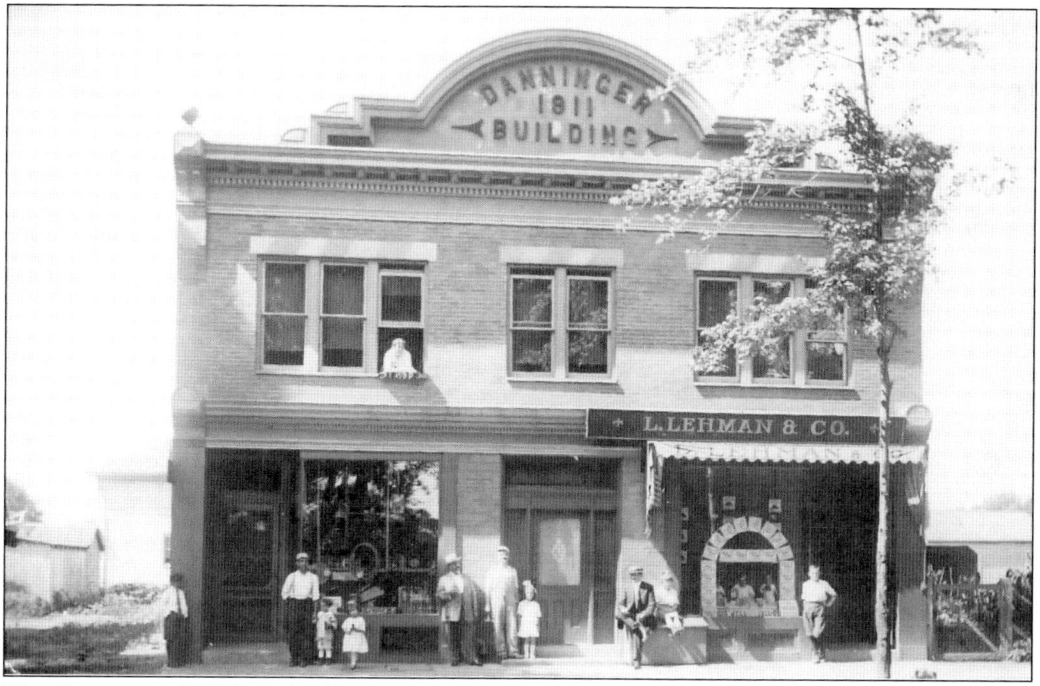

The Danninger building, built in 1911, in the center of the 100 block. Coloman Danninger was the leader of the 1924 movement to consolidate Linden Township and the borough. The building was photographed by H.F. Blancke.

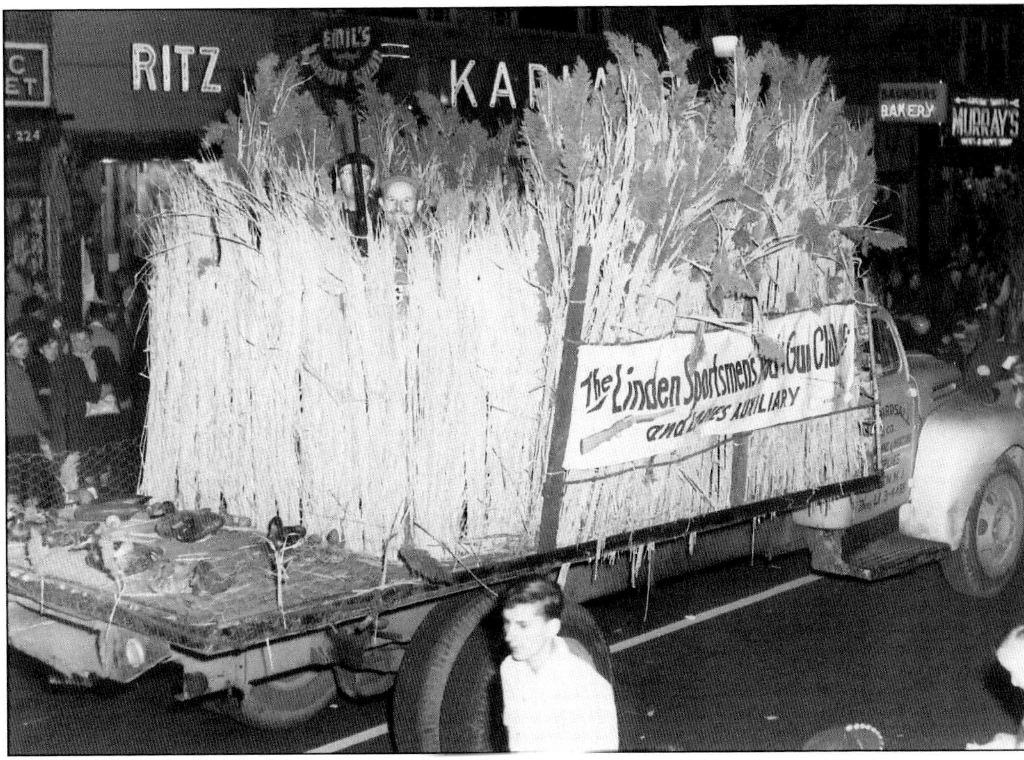

The 1952 Linden Halloween Parade. The Linden Sportsmen's Club and Ladies' Auxiliary Float is shown here. Behind it is the 200 (even numbers) block.

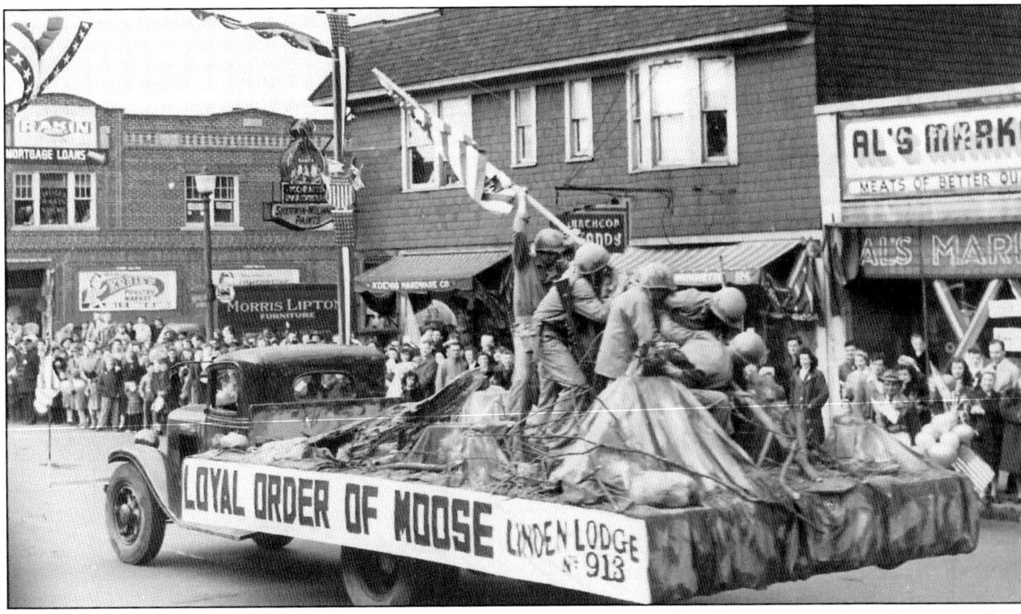

The Victory parade of 1946. The Moose float re-enacts the flag hoisting at Iwo Jima on June 23, 1945. Koenig's Hardware is the corner store. It was started by Charles Koenig in 1910. The business was moved from Wood Avenue in 1989 to West Elizabeth Avenue. After eighty-seven years of business, it closed in August of 1997.

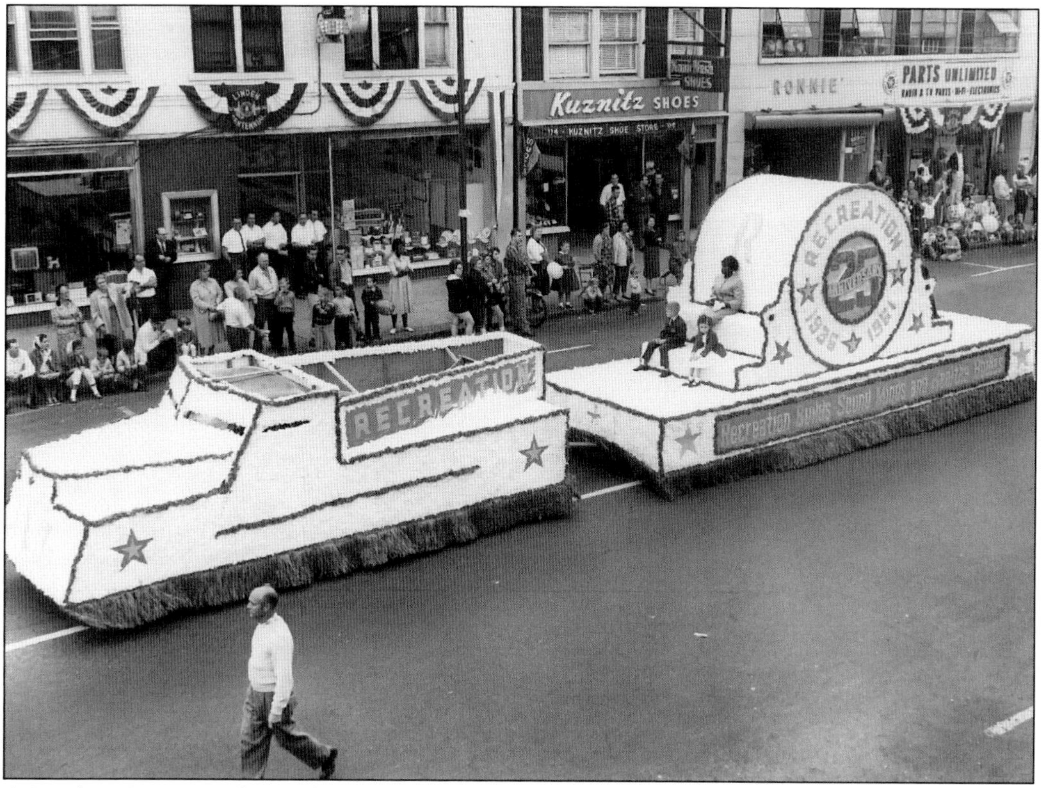

A Linden Centennial Parade float. The parade entry celebrated the 25th anniversary of the Linden Recreation Department in 1961.

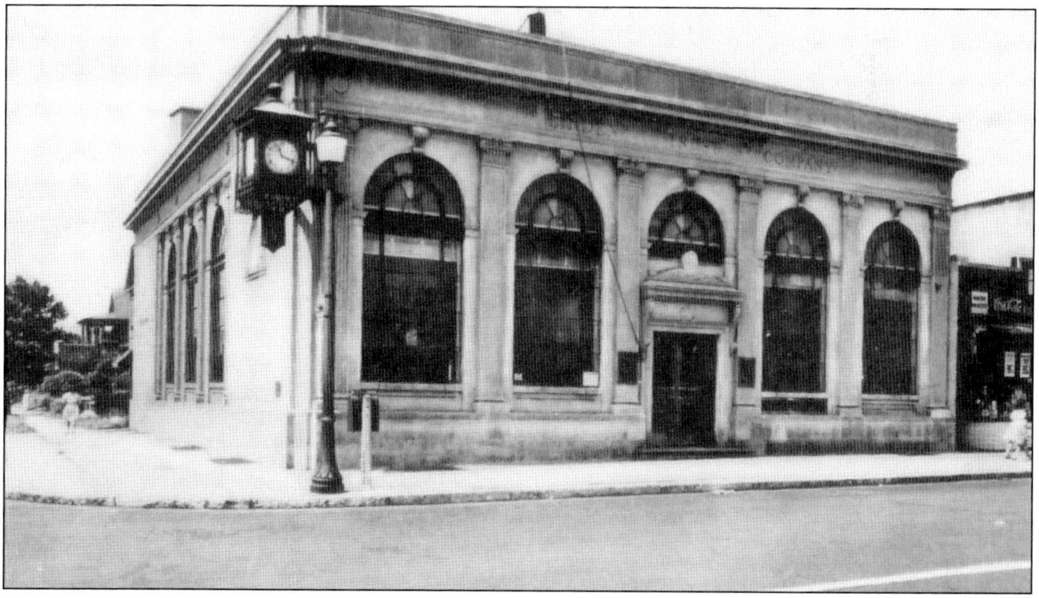

A vintage postcard of the Linden Trust Company, built at the corner of Price Street and Wood Avenue. The clock is still working today.

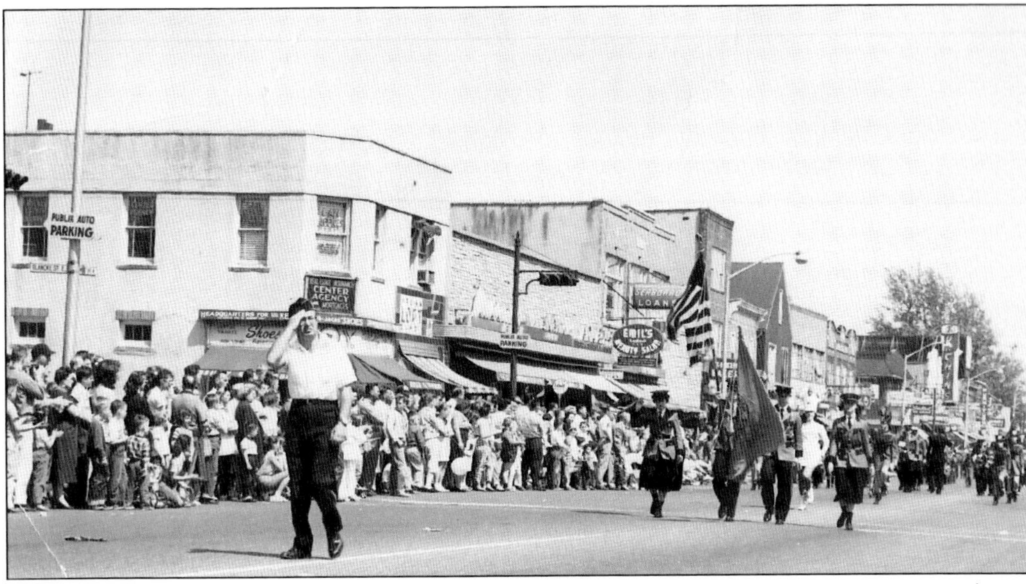

The 1959 Memorial Day Parade at the corner of Blancke Street and Wood Avenue. Saluting the city hall flag is William Weisbrot. He is followed by the Linden High School Honor Guard and Band.

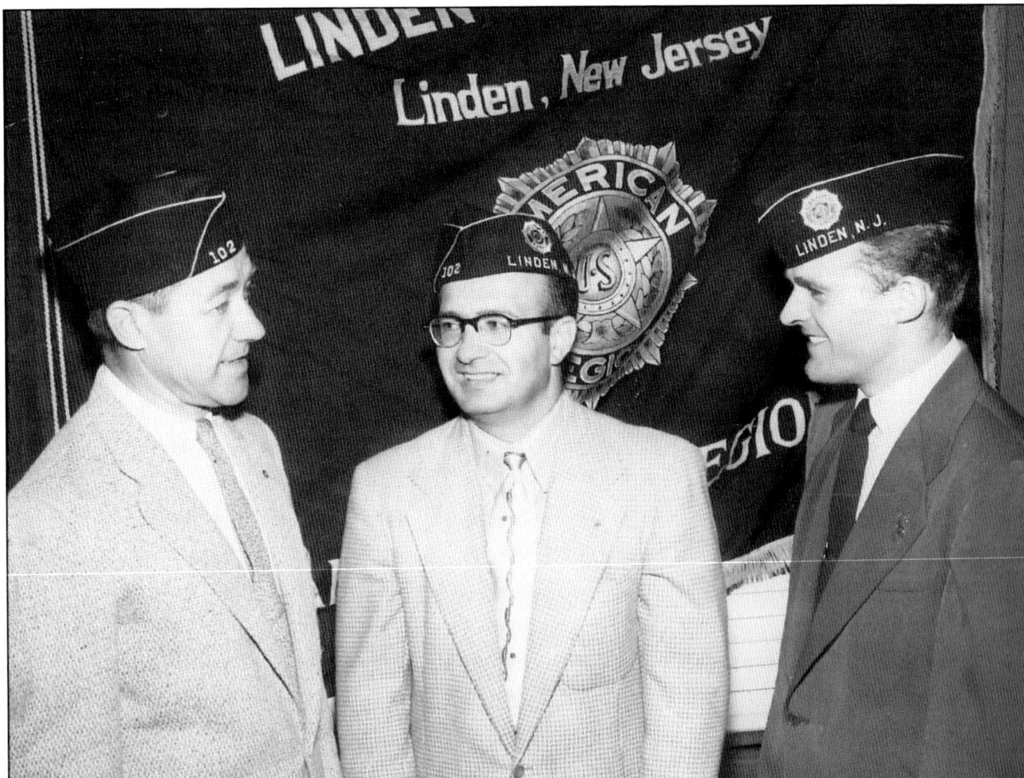

Frank Krysiak, William W. Weisbrot, and American Legion Commander James Cochinour photographed in front of the American Legion flag.

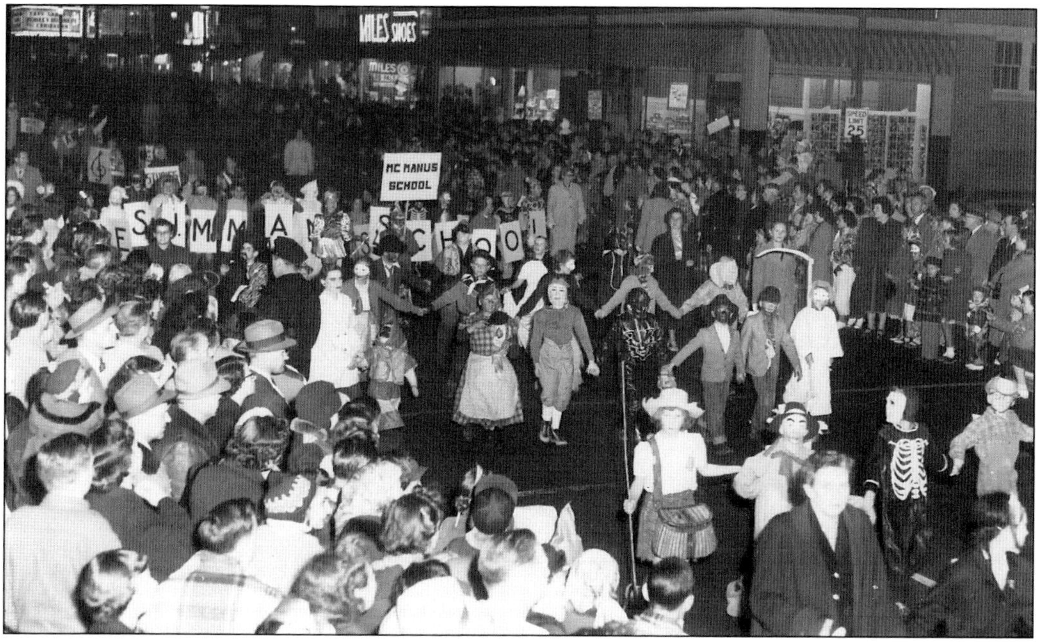

Notice the direction of marchers in the 1952 Halloween Parade. In the background is the 300 block of Wood Avenue. Woolworths, located in the grand Lottery Building, has a window on Blancke Street. Woolworths closed the entire chain of stores in 1997. To the far left is the Plaza Theater showing *Monkey Business* and *Caribbean*.

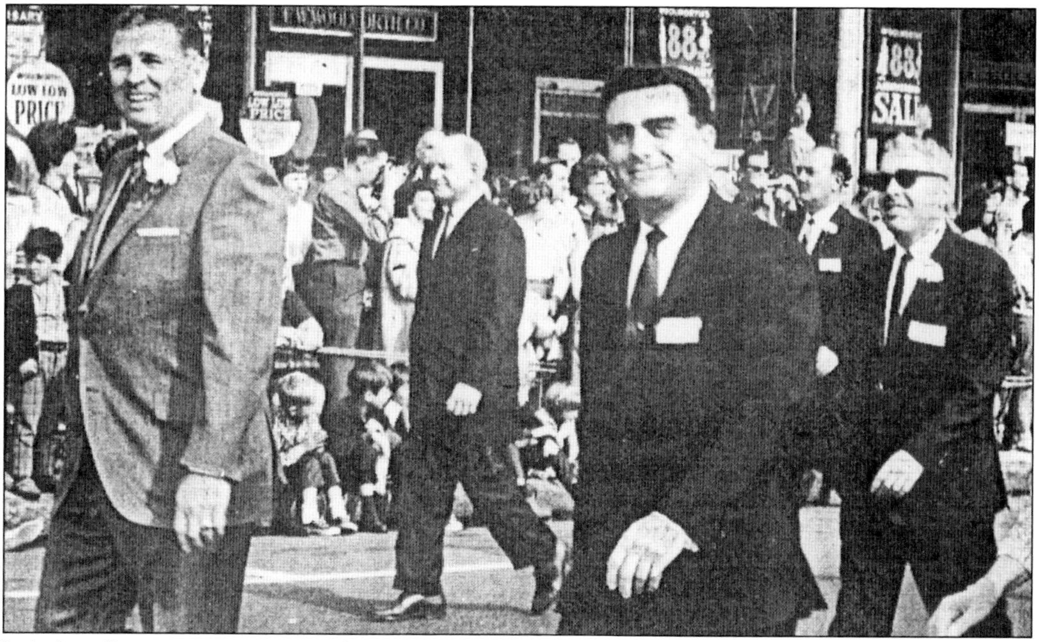

I pledge allegiance . . . Among the marchers renewing their pledge of allegiance to their flag and country during the Linden Loyalty Day Parade were, from left to right, (front row) Assemblyman Henry Gavan and Mayor John T. Gregorio; (back row) Councilman Joseph Bartus and candidate for State Senator Lester Weiner. Ten thousand strong turned out as spectators to cheer the marchers and support Loyalty Day in 1970.

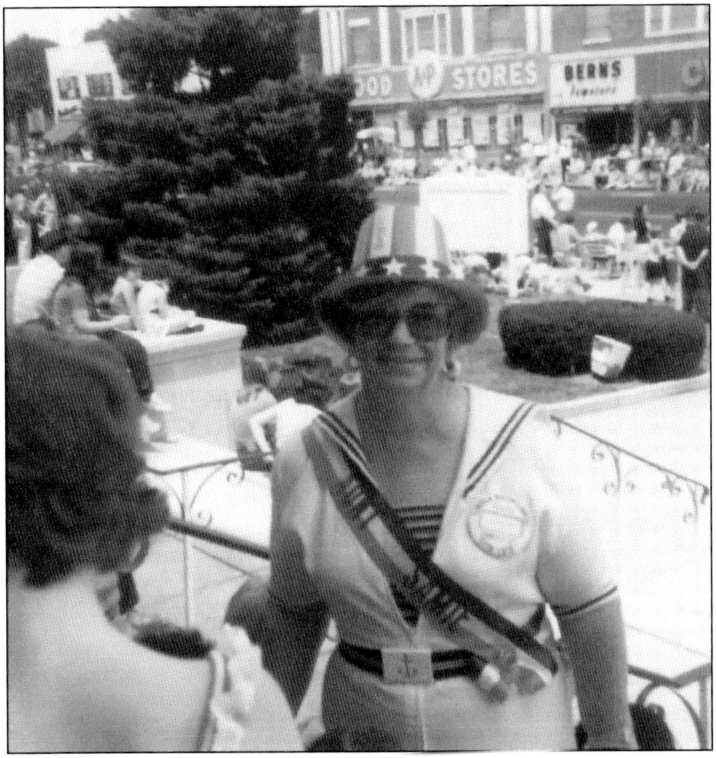

Rae Silverman on the steps of city hall at the Bicentennial Parade. In the background are the A&P Supermarket, CVS, Berns Jewelers, and Palmers Men's Store.

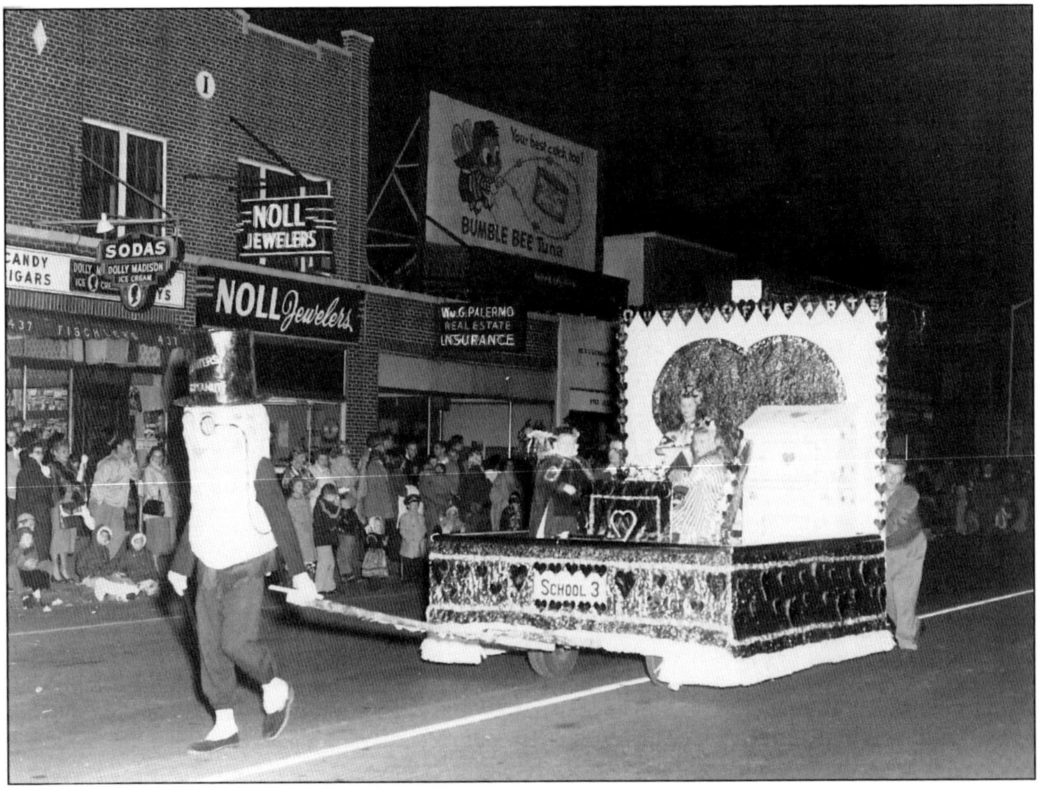

The October 1955 Halloween parade showing the School No. 3 float. In the background are Fischlers, Noll Jewelers, Wm. G. Palermo Real Estate and Insurance, an optometrist's office, and the Rosen Agency.

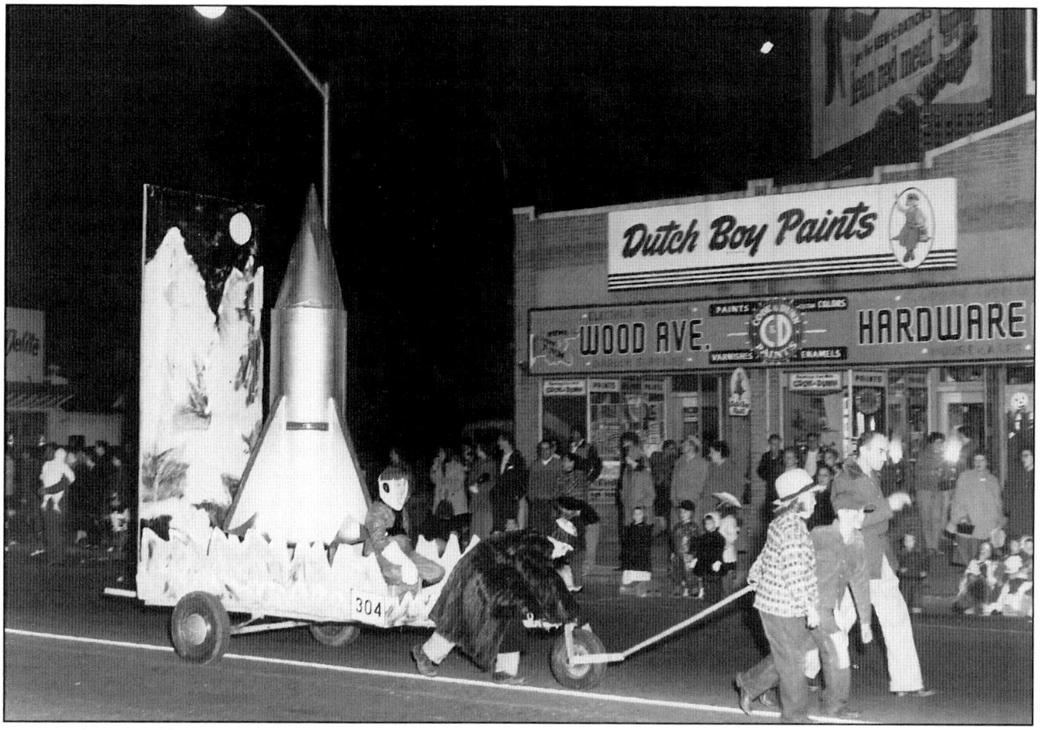

A Linden Halloween parade mini-float in front of the original location of Wood Avenue Hardware. This building was the second home of the library (see below) during the early 1930s. Dairy Delight is to the left in the background.

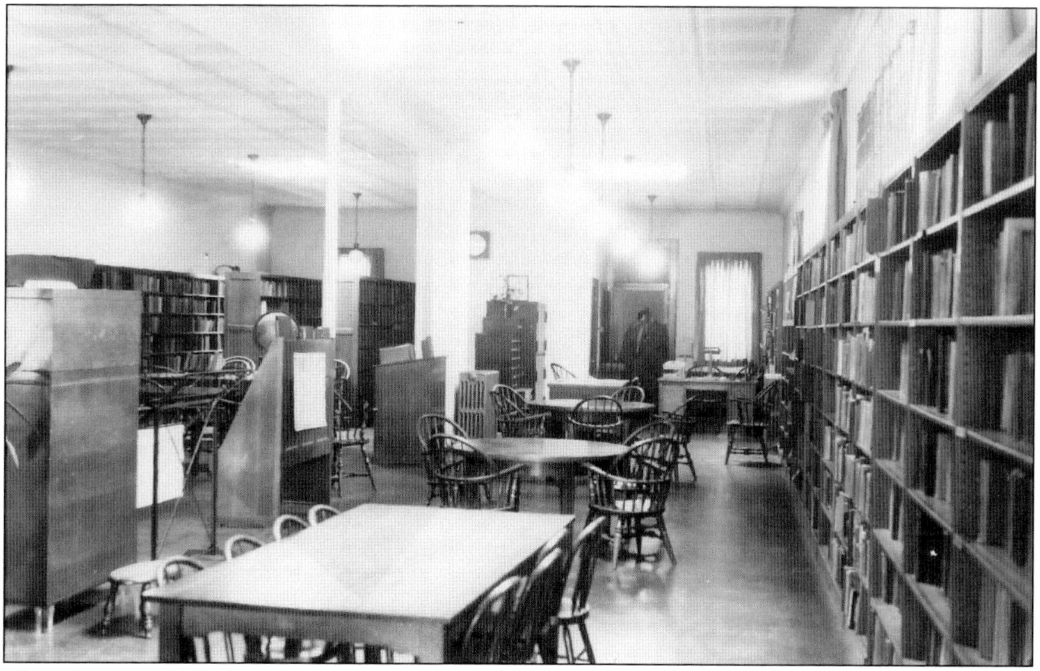

The library's second home at 428 North Wood Avenue in 1931. The storefront later became Hawaiian Palms.

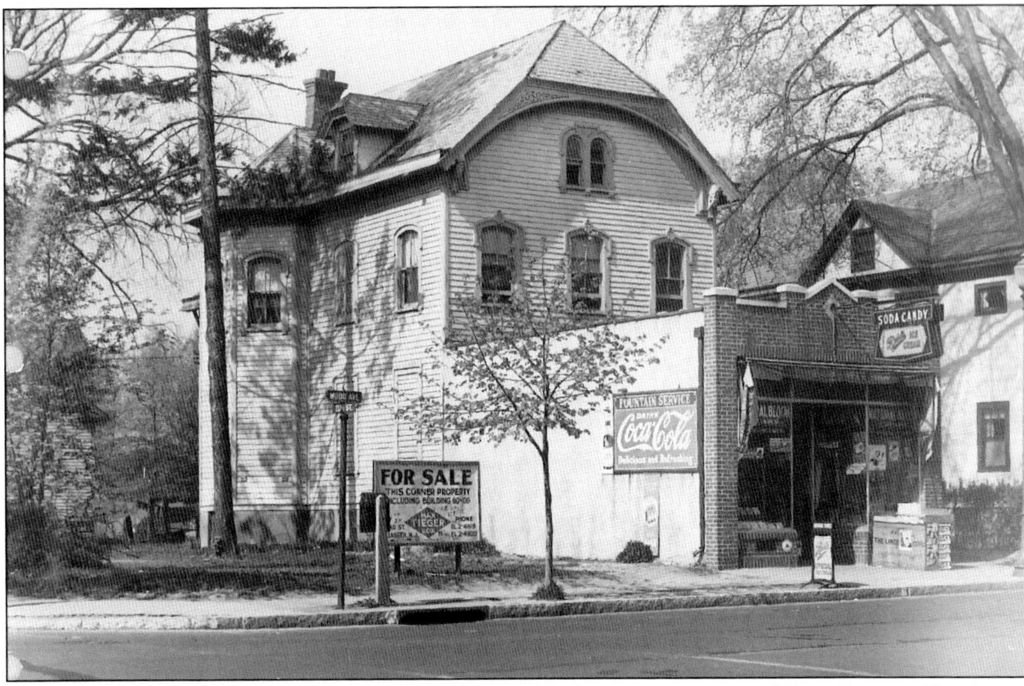

The Elmwood Sweet Shop in 1938. It was razed for the construction of City Savings Bank.

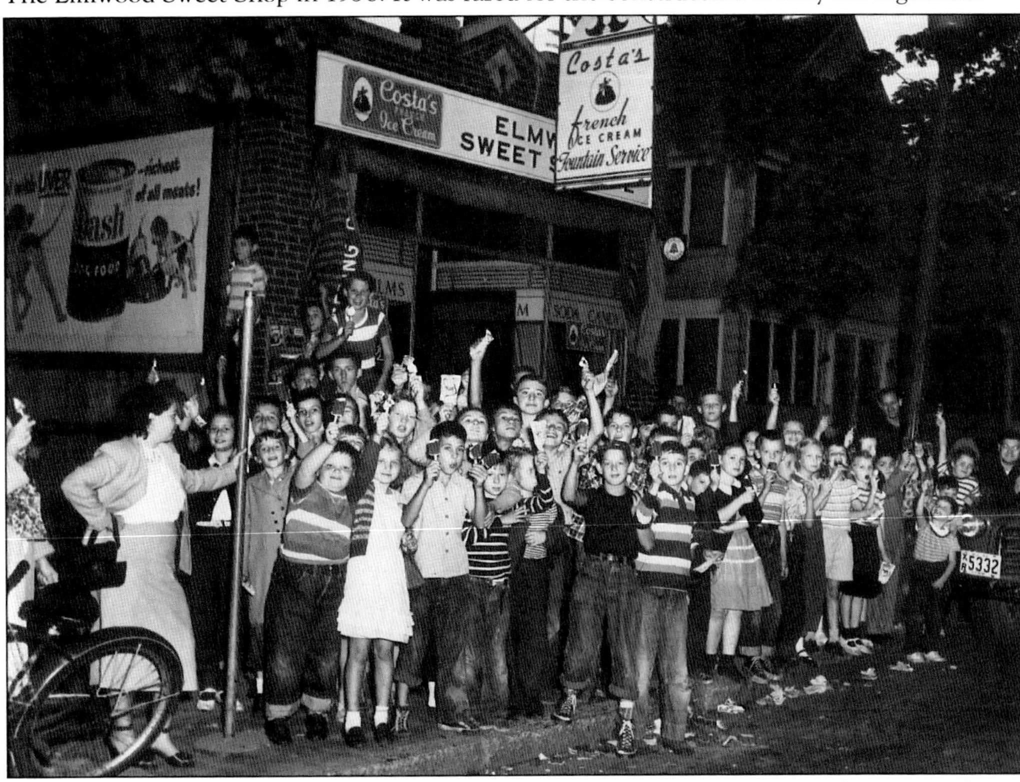

An impressive crowd of onlookers at the 1951 Halloween Parade. The people are standing in front of the Elmwood Sweet Shop holding their ice cream pops high for the camera.

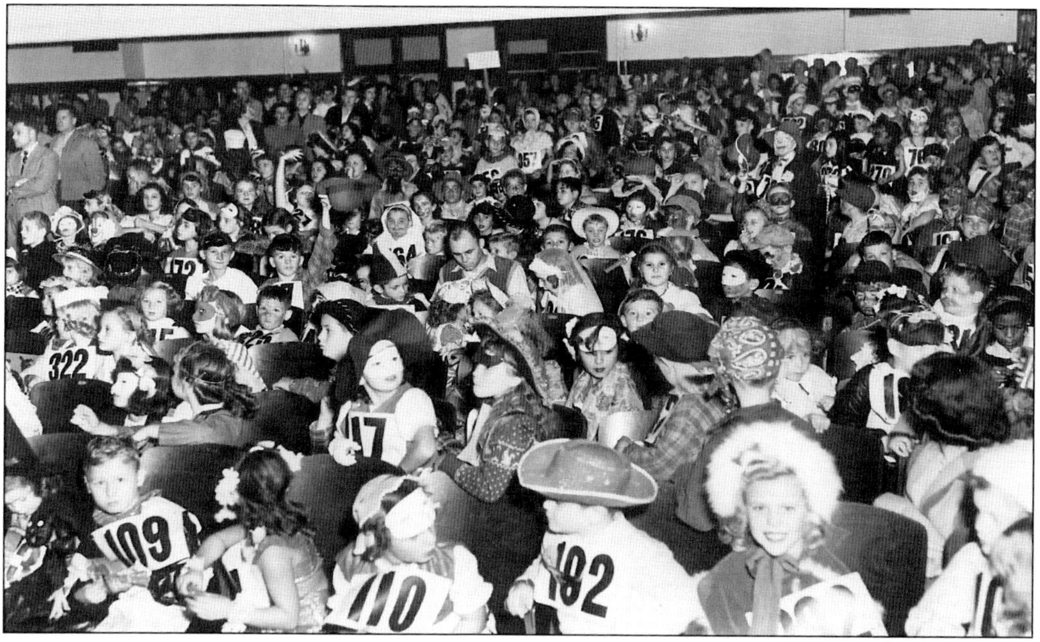

A grammar school and junior high school gathering at the Joseph E. Soehl Junior High School after the Halloween Junior Mummers parade on the night of October 31, 1950.

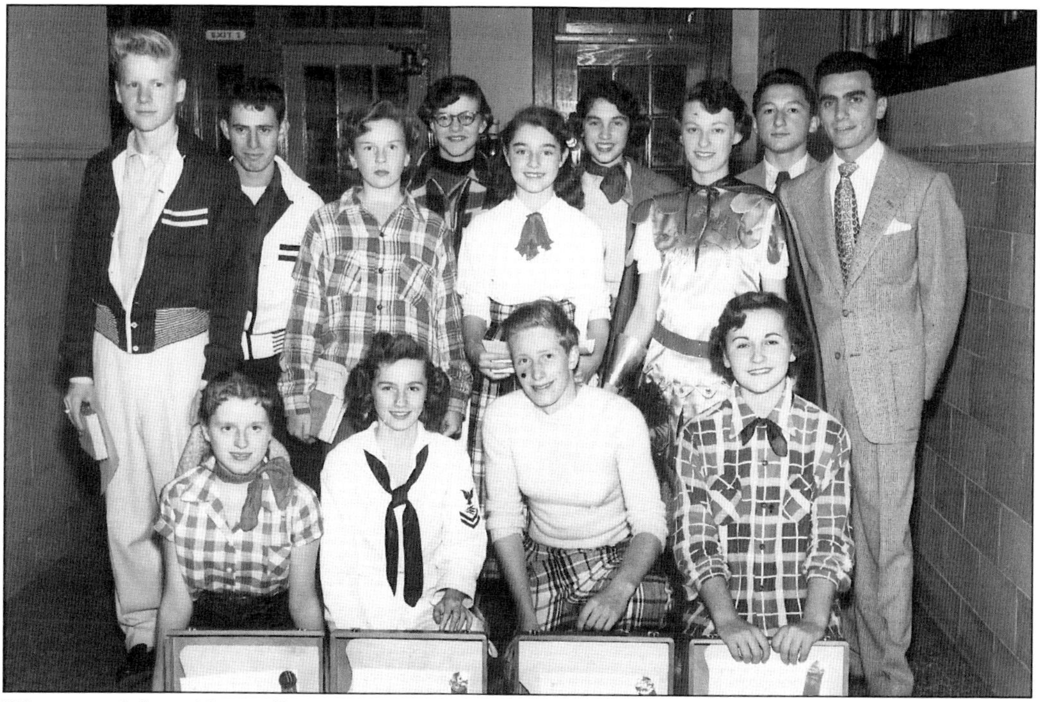

Winners of the 1952 Halloween Window Painting Contest. From left to right are (front row) Pat Brady, Barbara Lehr, Walter Ibach, and Mary Ann Krochak; (middle row) Robert Zakanych, Arlene Stonewski, Mary Jasinoqicz, Joann Reeves, and Mr. John T. Gregorio (owner of House of Flowers and a member of the Linden Halloween Committee); (third row) Lowell Schmidt, Grace Croteau, Carol Yacks, and John Hrehovcik.

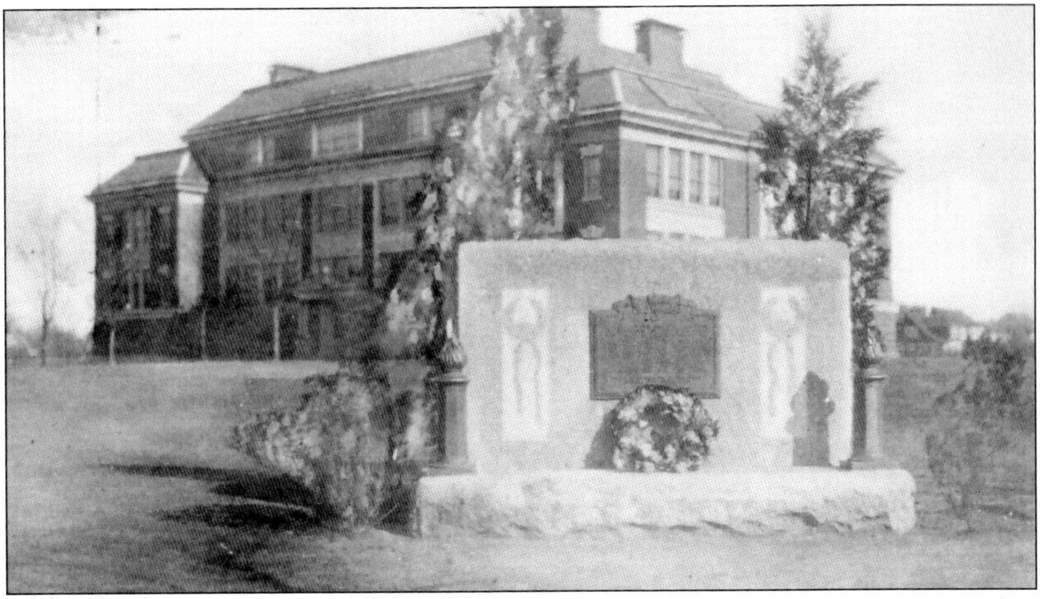

On November 11, 1925, two tablets were unveiled at School No. 1 on Wood Avenue. They were erected in honor of those enlisted as soldiers in World War I. Each stands in its former community: the borough tablet is on the corner of Curtis Street and the township tablet is on the corner of Gibbons Street. This vintage postcard depicts the borough tablet.

The borough list is as follows: George Ashworth, Austin Baldwin, Clifford Baldwin, Charles Beetle, Robert Beetle, Spurgeon Beetle Jr., C. Dudley Blancke, Herbert Bundy, Roy Bundy, Joseph Casino, Robert Eaton, William Gourley, Henry Hardenburg Jr., William Hartman, Anthony Koch, Joseph Koch, Matthew Koch, Daniel Kluge, William Kluge, John Lambert, Harold MacDowell, Stephen Mannuzza, Vincent Mannuzza, Leo McDonagh, George Miller, Ernest Miller, Edward Mitchell Jr., John Monsoon Jr., Andrew More Jr., Leonard A. More (died in the service), Joseph Modrak, Henry Opple, George Paye, Lloyd Roll, Sigmund Schafanovich, Dominic Valvano, Frank Villani, Harry Wagner, and Harry Weitzman.

The township list includes the following: Joseph Angelo, Frank Barr, William Berlinski, John Byko, Percy Carkuff, Anthony Cook, Edward Dillon, Martin Derrig, John Dobosiewicz, Seare Dougherty, John Feehan, Ida Feinberg, Samuel Feinberg (died in the service), Joseph Gabrick, Joseph Gaydos, Elmer Gibbs, Nathan Gushin, Fred Haefner, Romain Harris, Andrew Hicky, Harry Hickman, Roy Hickman, Michael Hudak, William Hurst, Charles Jacob, John Jacobi, Alexander Jagodinski, Oscar Kaplan, James Kenworthy, Henry Klubenspies, William Kraemer, William Krasnowski, George Leyerle, Fred Lichti, Thomas Lichti, William Lindsay, Theodore Lodge, Joseph Loitch, Ernest Mahar, John Mahar, Philip Marshefsky, Garrett Maye, James Maye, Sam Mehrman, John Miller, Leonard Moore, Peter Murin, William Niemeck, Edward Nusse, John Oriechowski, Edward Pellinger, Walter Perkins (died in the service), Walter Pfitzzenmayer, Elmer Pierce, Henry Potter, Ferdinand Rechinitzer, Walter H. Roll, Marion Romanowski, James Runyon, Edward Sanford, William Semlar, Charles Smith, Richard Smith, Rolland Smith, John Steffen, Joseph Urbaowitz, Robert Walker, George Walsko, Bert Walters, Albert Weber, Hugo Wendel, John Russell Wheeler (died in the service), Albert Wilke, John Willick, Bernard Wosniak, Charles Wosniak, Charles Zbranek, and Boleslaw Zygmant (died in the service). This was a dividing line of both from 1892 to consolidation in 1925.

Four

Linden: Gateway to the World's Market

From 1865 to the end of the century was a busy time for industry. Because of this, the population of Linden grew quickly. In 1872, two industries came to Linden's Tremley Point district in Linden and the area has been growing ever since.

The location of our city was as important in the past as it is today. Linden is central to the Jersey shore and the mountains. Newark International Airport is just a short drive away on U.S. Route No. 1. The Garden State Parkway and New Jersey Turnpike are on either side of the city. The railroad station is in the center of the city, traveling north to New York City and south to Trenton, our state capitol. One-fourth of Linden's physical boundary is on the Arthur Kill where waterfront docks are deep enough for ocean vessels. Its location gives Linden a great diversity of business and residents. This chapter features some of the businesses and employees that made their home in Linden, N.J.

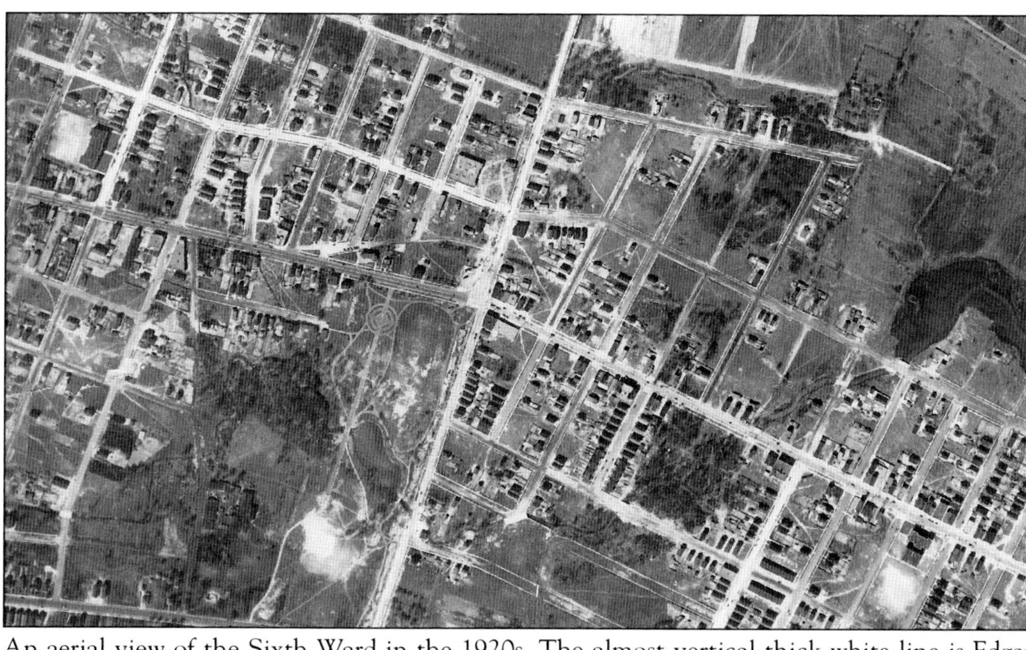

An aerial view of the Sixth Ward in the 1920s. The almost vertical thick white line is Edgar Road. The thick white line starting in the lower right area is Wood Avenue.

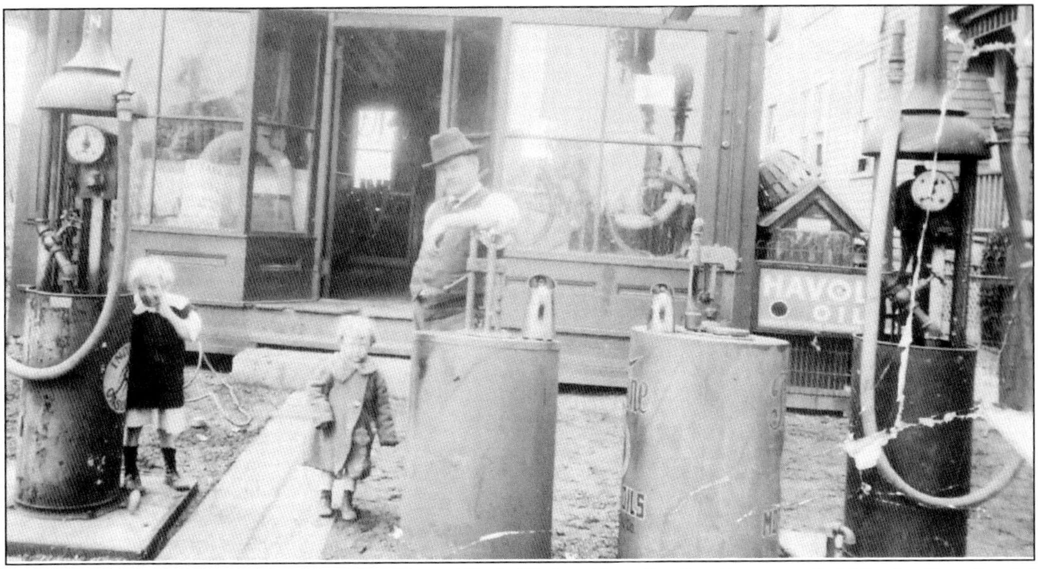

Clinton Street and 43 East Edgar Road in 1921. Helen Gondrecki Crane and Alfreda Gondrecki Markowski are in the front playing while John Gondrecki looks on.

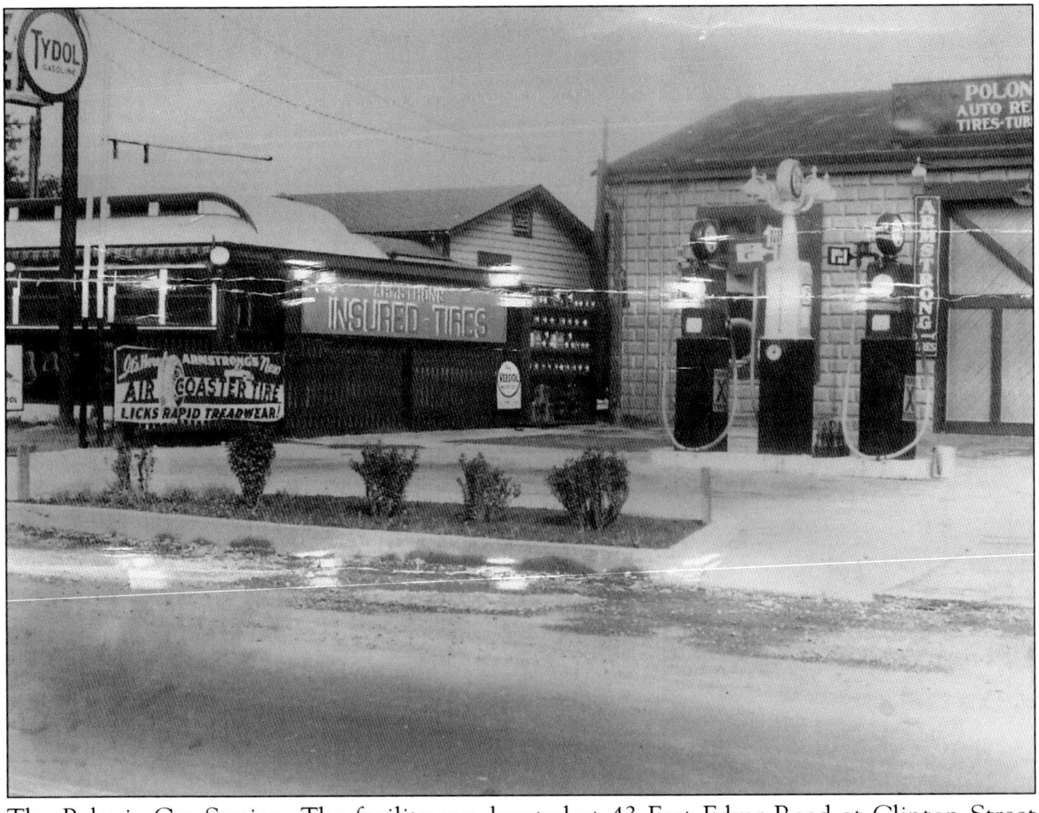

The Polonia Gas Station. The facility was located at 43 East Edgar Road at Clinton Street in 1936. Tydol gasoline was sold here and repairs were made to vehicles as well. Note the neighboring diner.

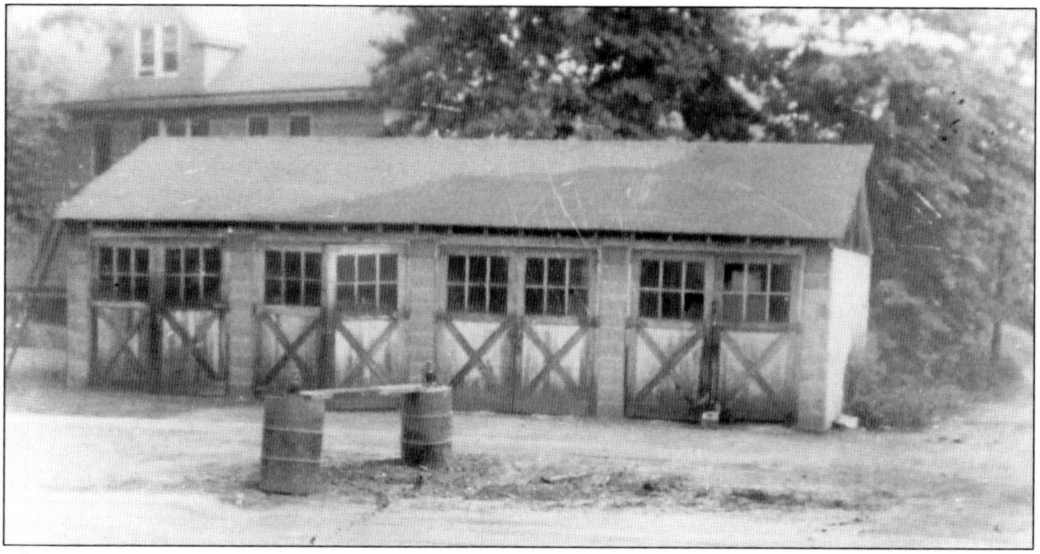

This garage was used for storage by Stella and George Kushner, proprietors of the Clinton Florist. It would later become home to Blue Ribbon Pools with the official address of 102 Edgar Road. It is located at the corner of Clinton Street and East Edgar Road.

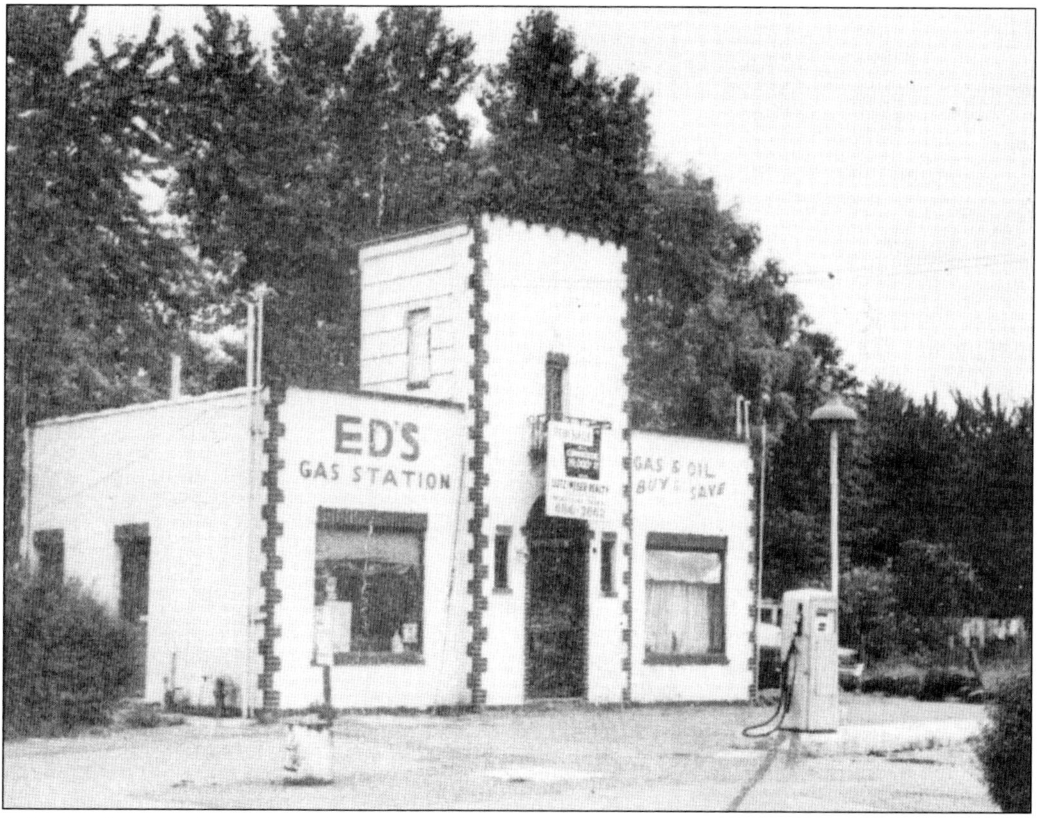

Ed's Gas Station, located at the corner of Woodlawn Avenue and Edgar Road. Gas was 19.9¢ per gallon when the building was purchased by Allie Motors, 176 East Edgar Road. This building is now their offices.

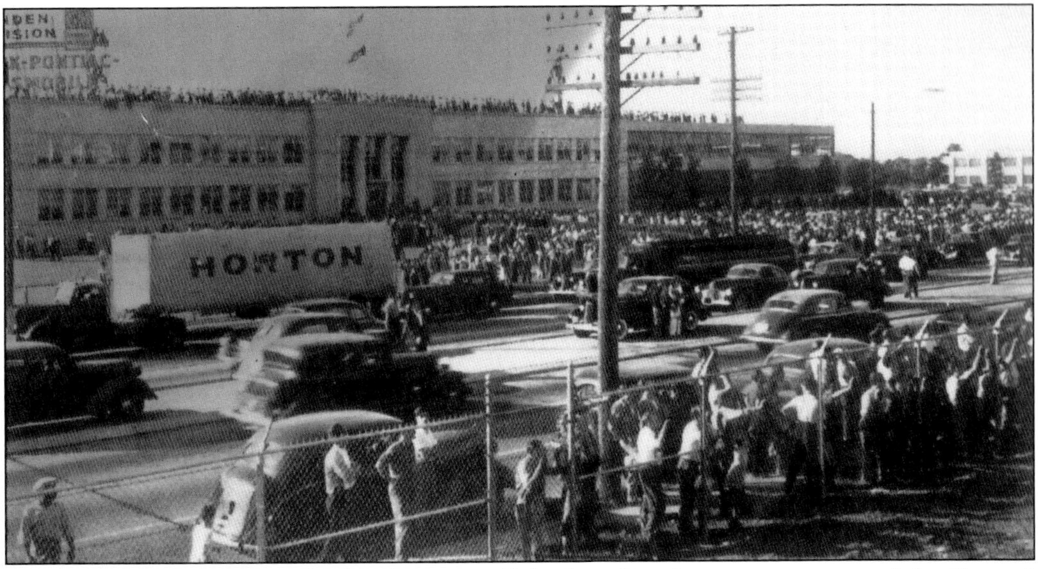

The whole city turning out for the first ones off the line. People are even on top of the General Motors building. The people in the foreground are looking through the fence to see the planes still on the ground awaiting takeoff from the airport.

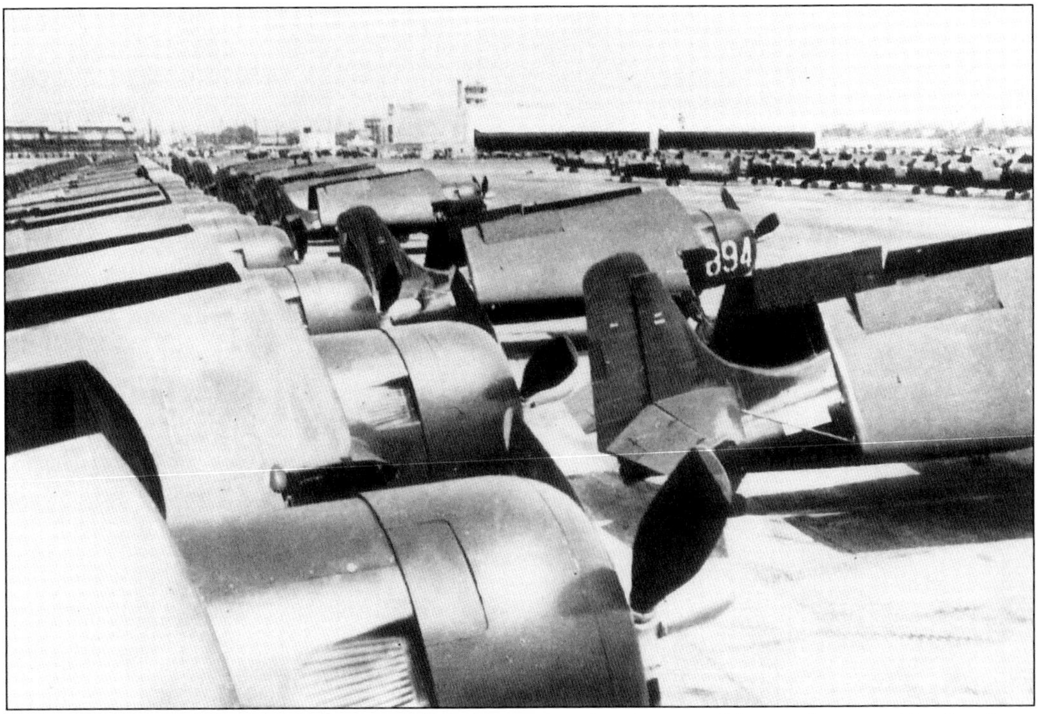

The Wildcats! The finished planes are lined up at Linden Airport. Navy pilots would take them up for test flights before they were put onto aircraft carriers for combat in World War II.

Major William Silverman, commander of the civil air patrol, standing by a plane that was reconstructed from its frame in 1962. It was the 1-2-3 Piper Cub, and was flown from 1962 to 1971 for rescue missions in New Jersey.

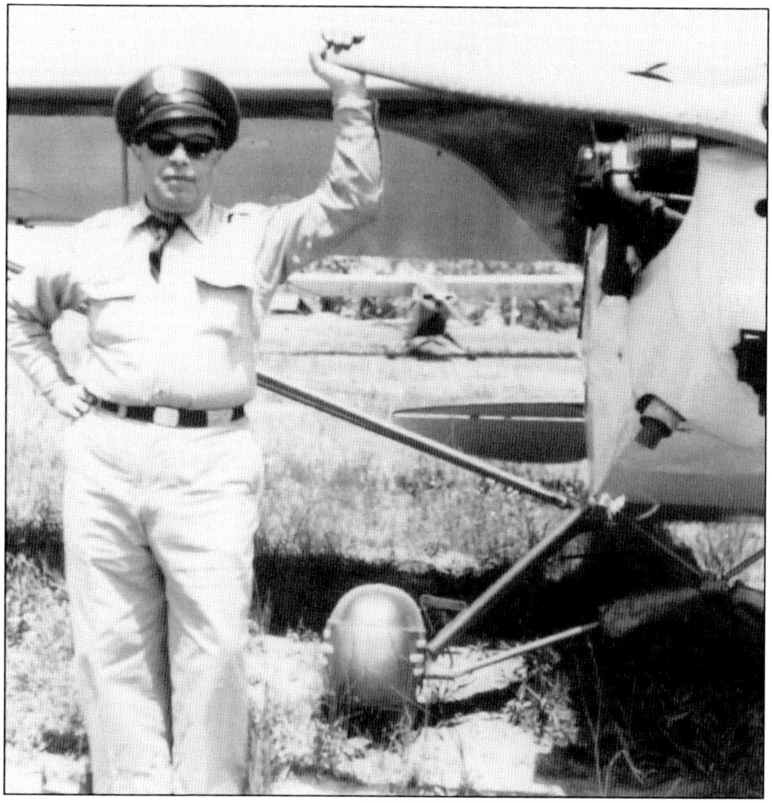

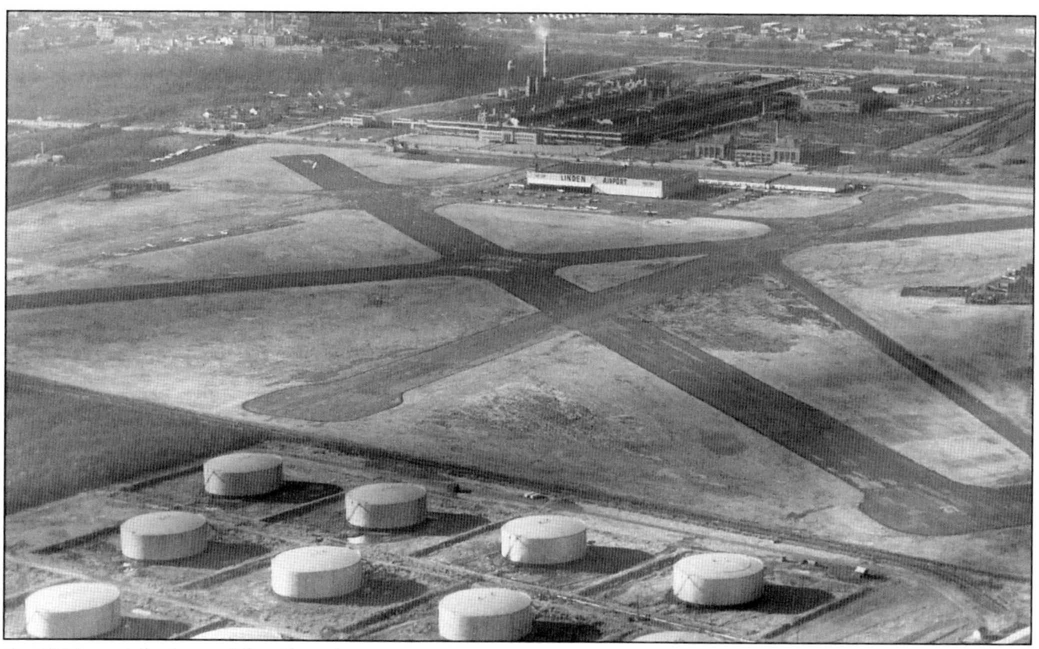

A 1948 aerial view of Linden Airport.

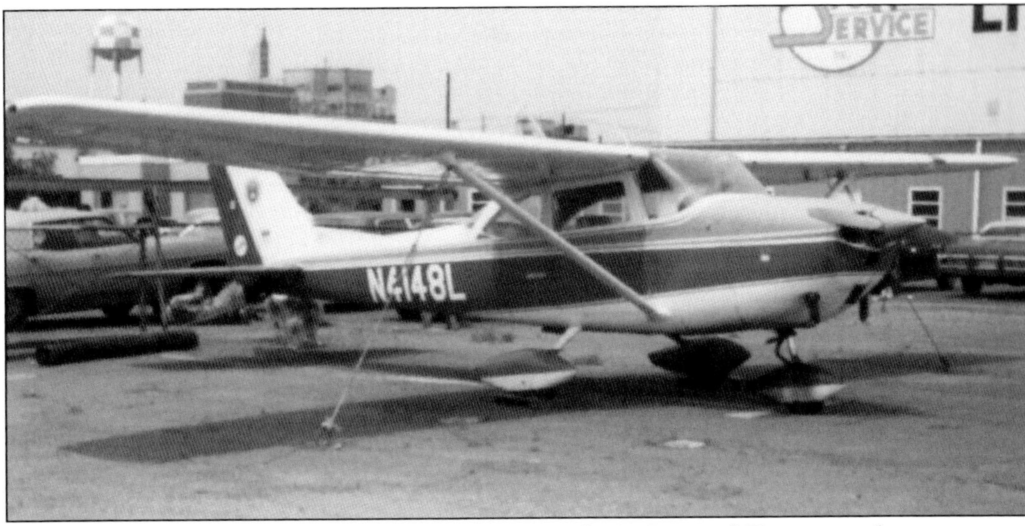

Plane No. N4148L parked at Linden Airport. Gordon's Gin and Tenco can be seen across Edgar Road.

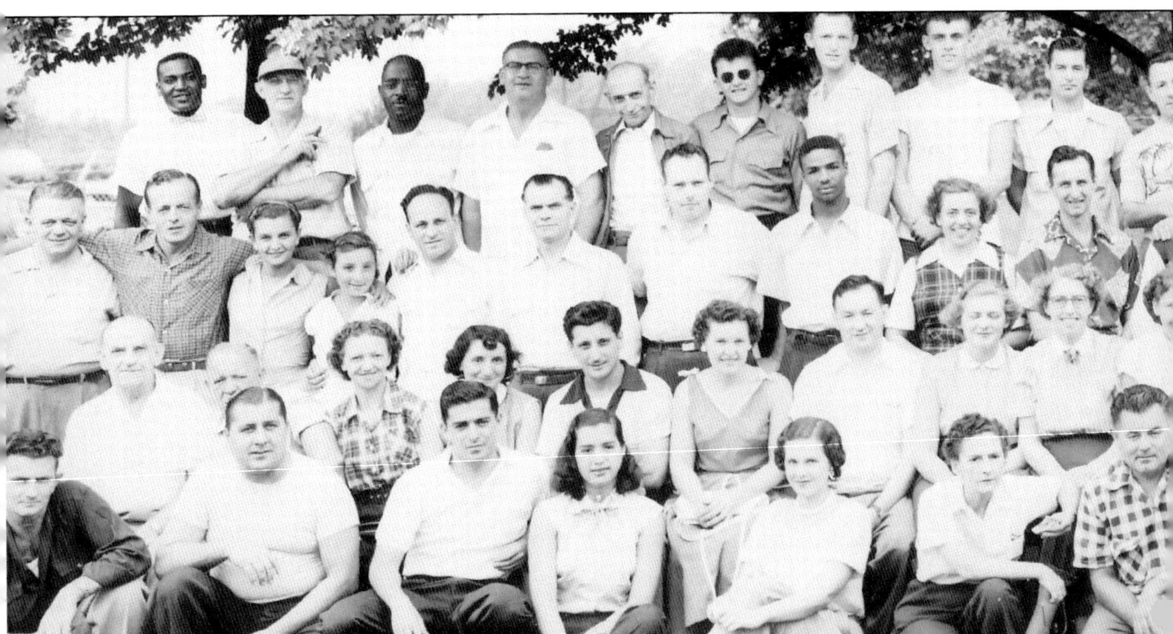

A Volupte employee outing. Pictured on August 9, 1952, are members of the Local 44, AF of L.

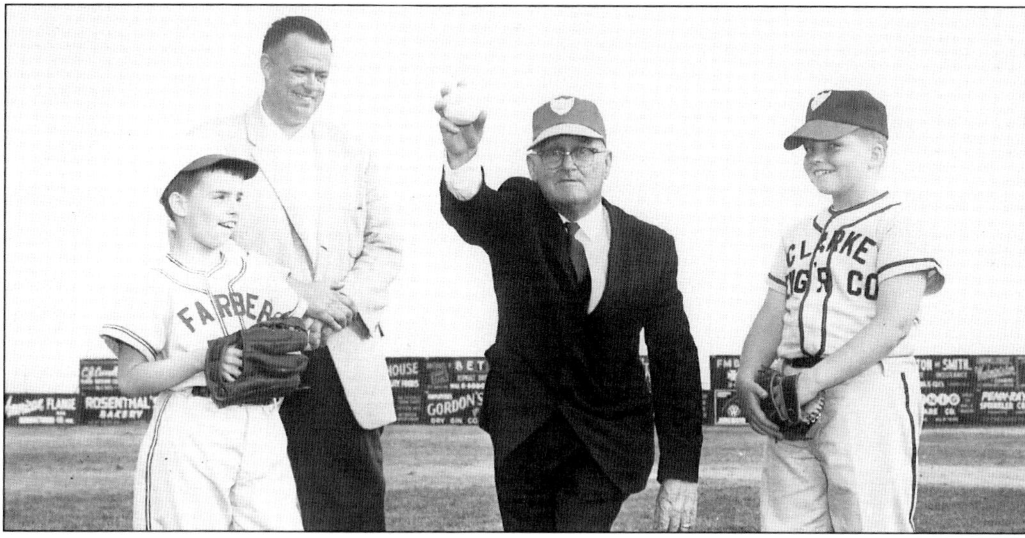

The opening of the Little League field, June 6, 1961. Edward Kreig, Edward Flanagan Sr., Mayor Hurst, and Frederick Kaufman are pictured. The field was located on South Stiles Street. Just beyond the fence is Linden Airport. Local businesses sponsored teams that played. Sponsors also advertised on the fence around the field.

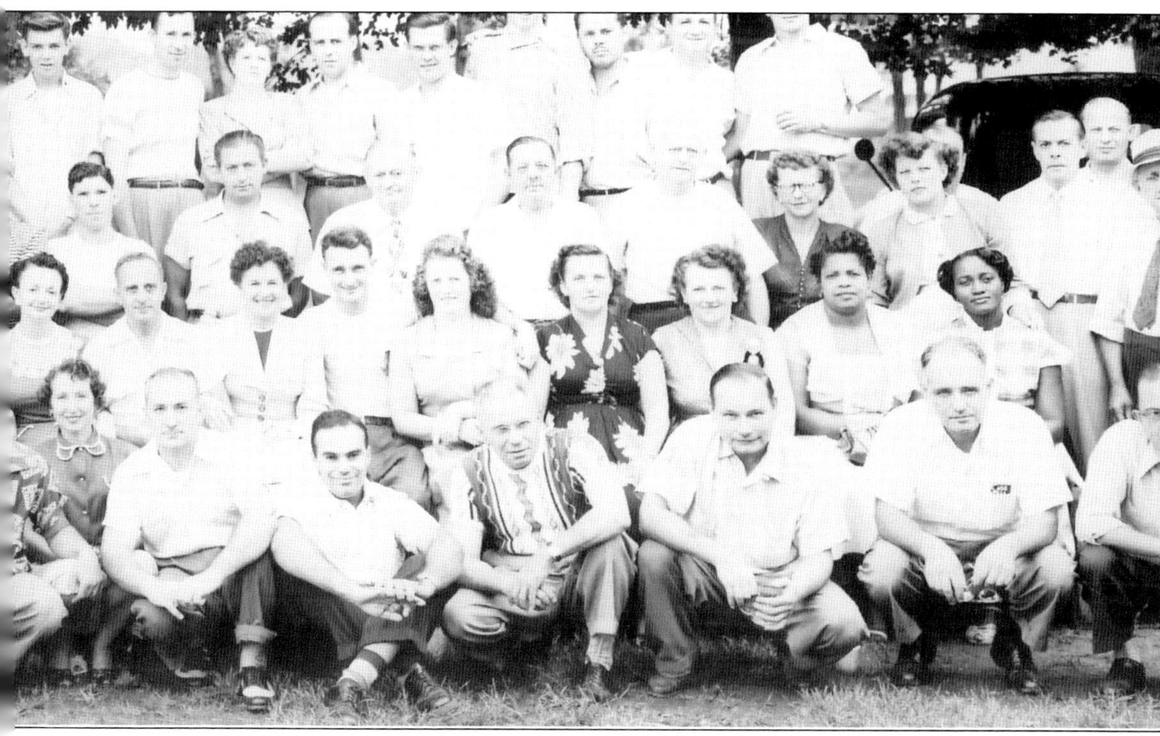

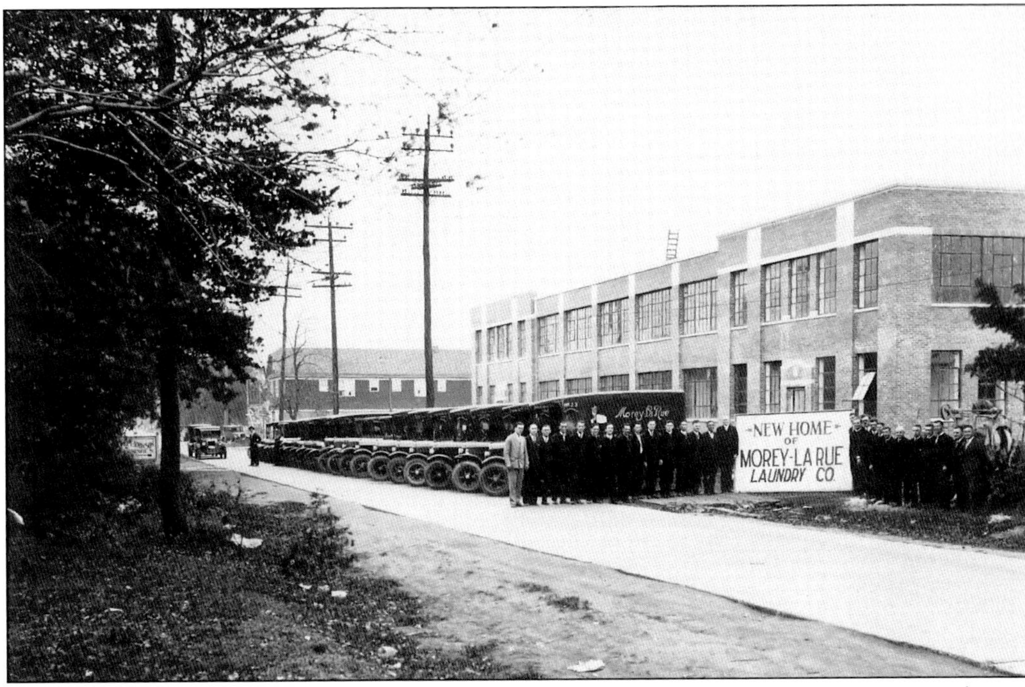

The Morey La Rue Laundry. My parents met here as many other couples did, according to Mahlon Scott, the present owner. The laundry has been a family-owned business and has made Linden its home since 1928.

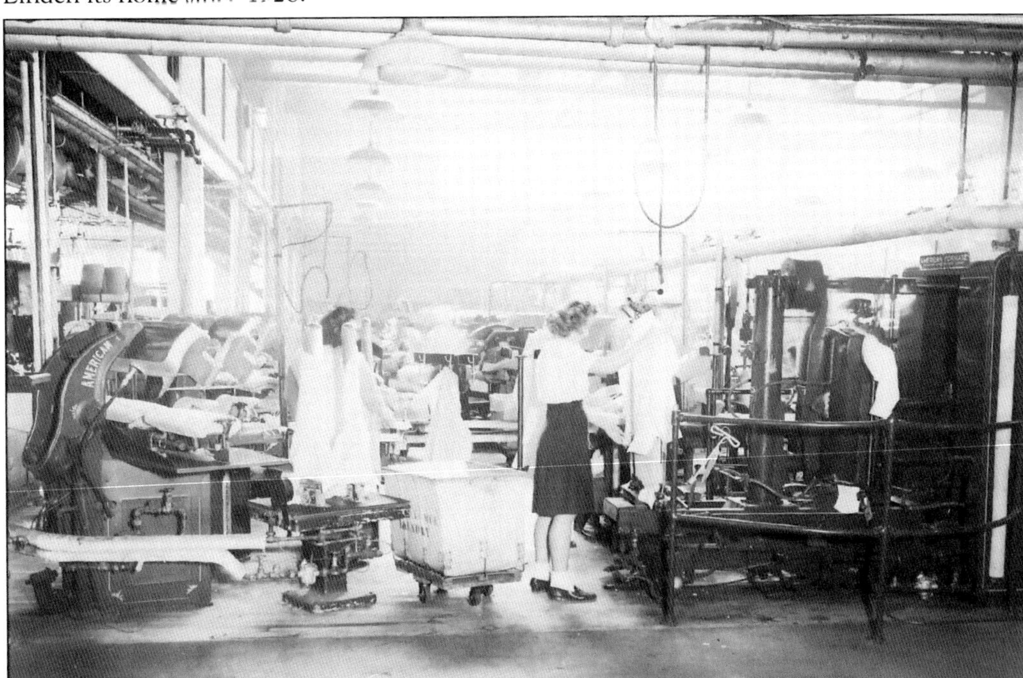

The interior of the pressroom of the Morey La Rue Laundry in 1947. The woman in this image is Mildred Pedersen Genz.

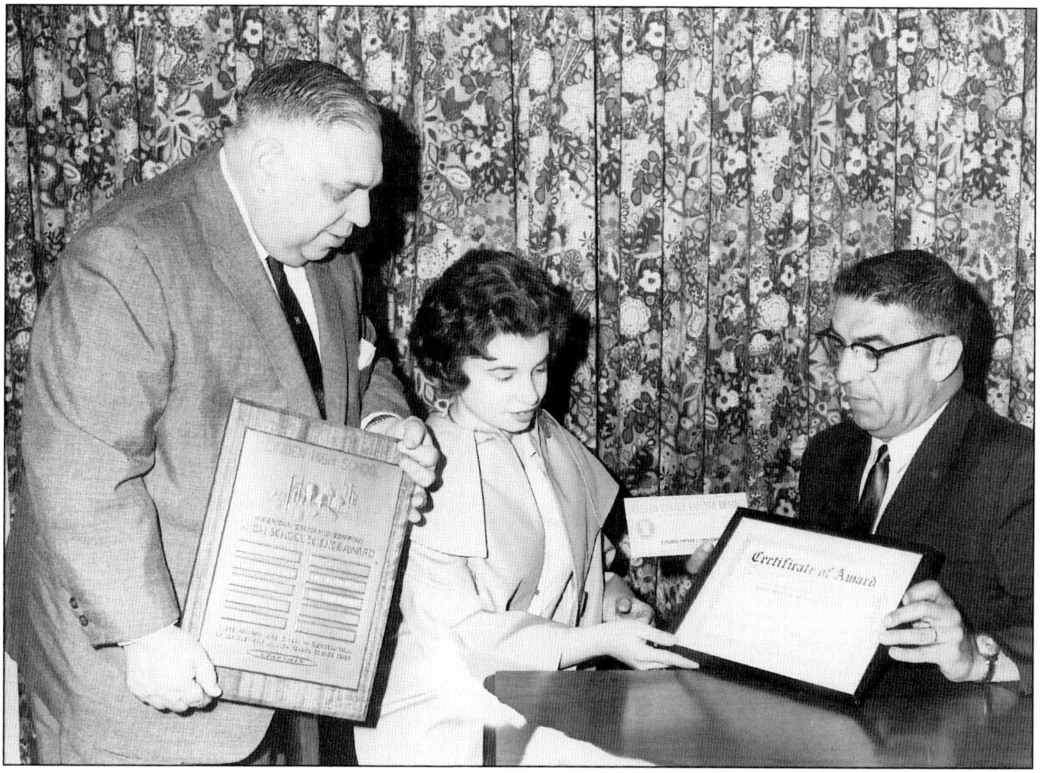

The 1962 American Cyanamid Award recipient. The award was given to Linden High School student Jane Bedrick. Her father Emanuel Bedrick, superintendent of schools, looks on. Many industries have given awards and scholarships to deserving students each year. Jane is now a pediatrician.

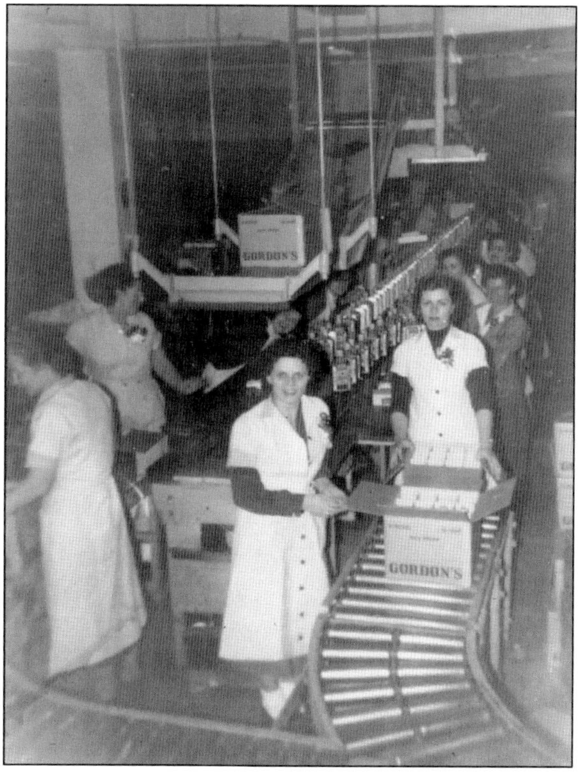

On the line at Gordon's Gin, which was located on Edgar Road for many years.

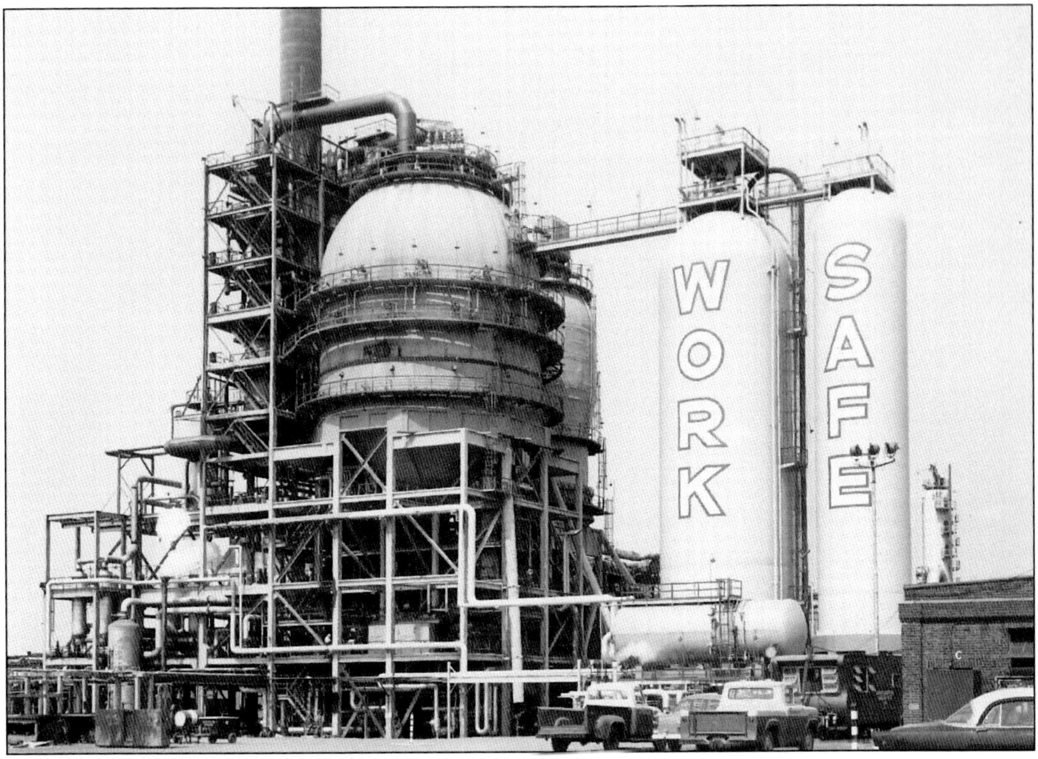

The Fluid Catalytic Cracking Unit, 1949. In 1997 the unit was deemed the largest in the world in the *Guinness Book of World Records*.

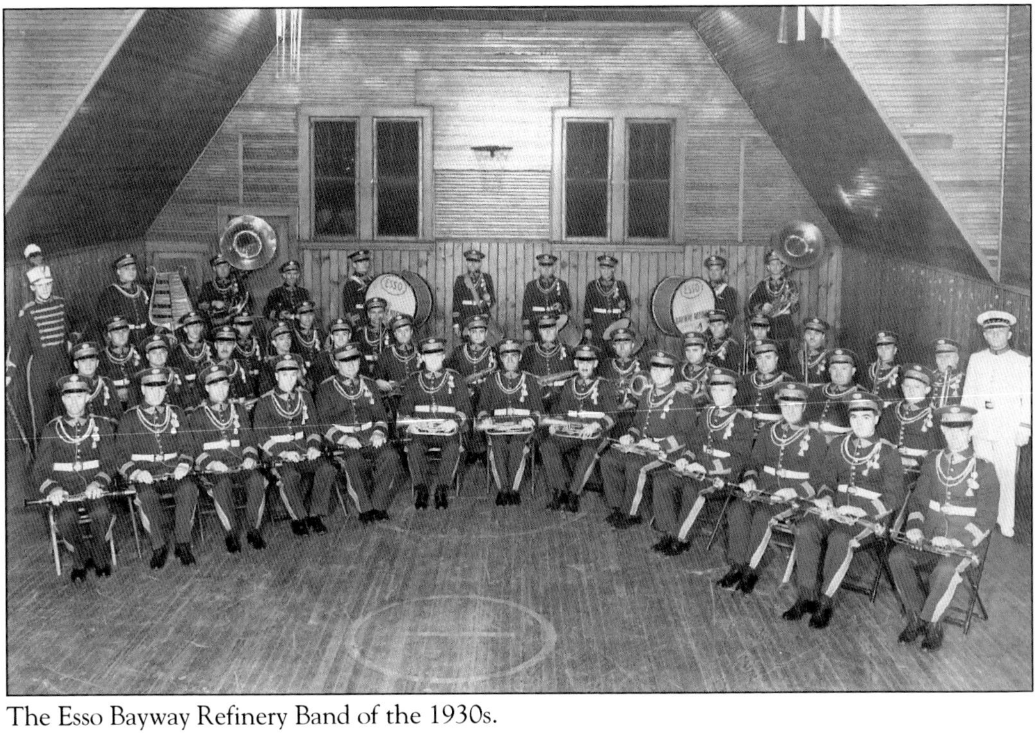

The Esso Bayway Refinery Band of the 1930s.

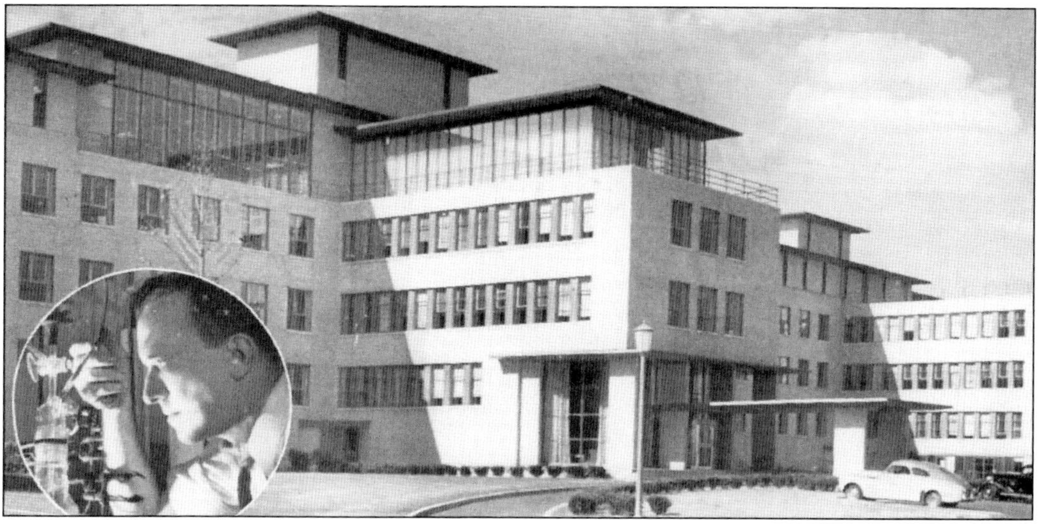

The Esso Research Facility. This laboratory, pictured here on a 1949 postcard, was erected on the former site of the dog track.

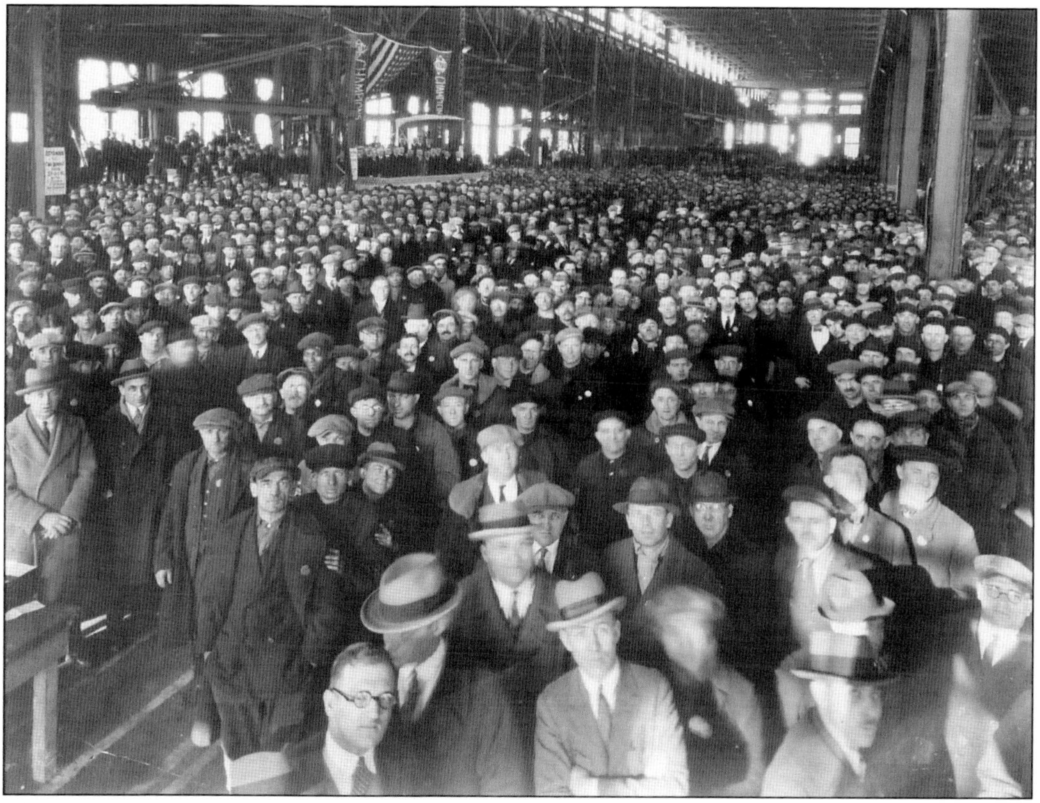

This was a large Esso Standard Oil company meeting in the early 1920s. Proudly displayed are their championship banners.

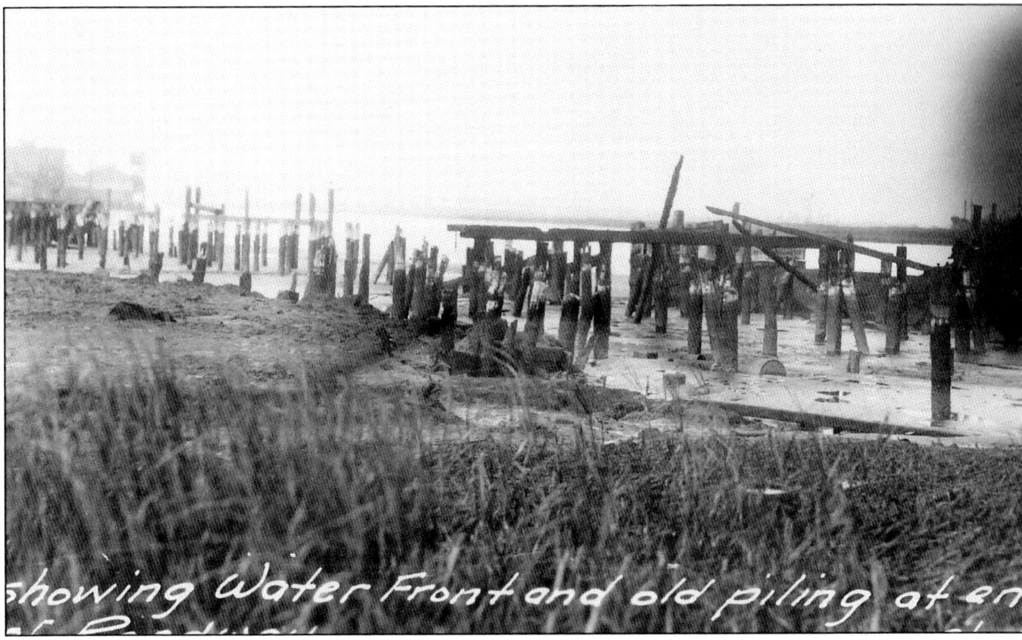

The waterfront and old piling at the end of Warner Quinlan's private roadway, 1931.

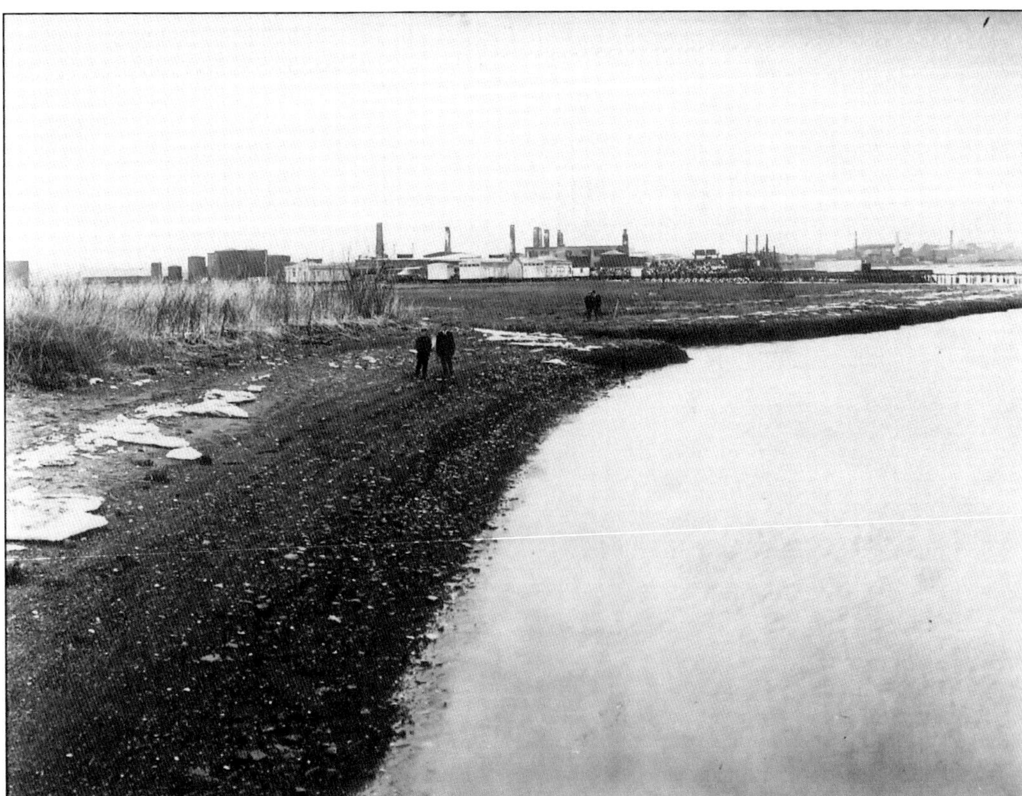

The Esso waterfront property in 1909.

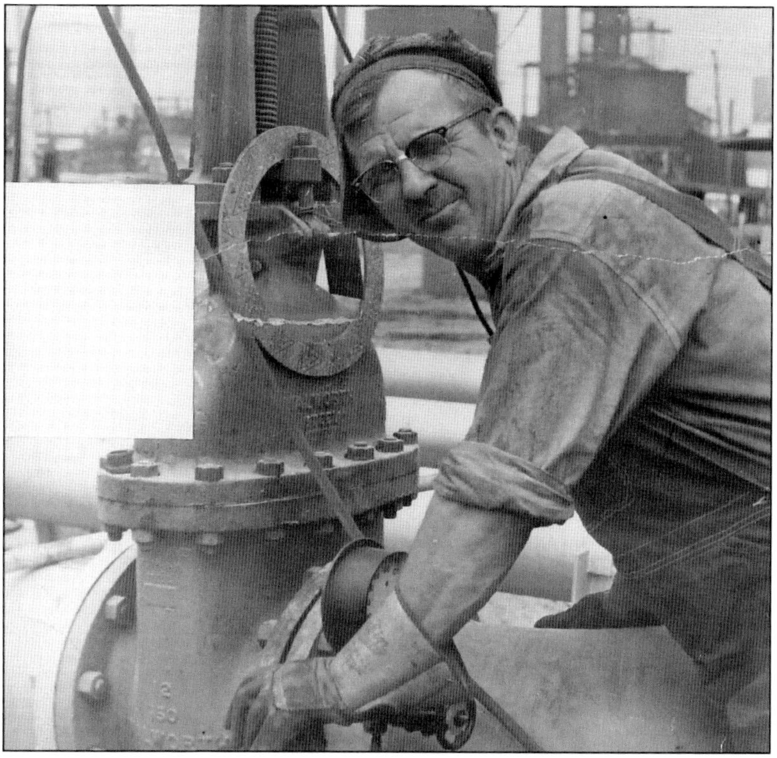

John Dobosiewicz at work at the refinery of Cities Service.

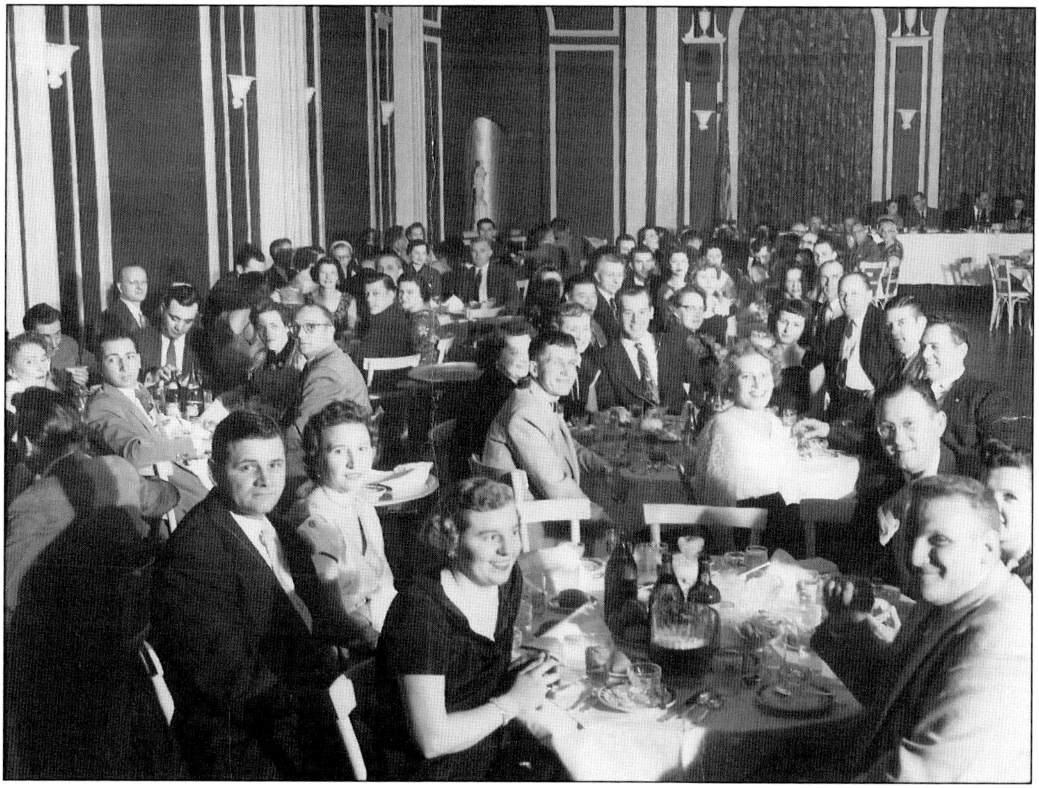

An annual presentation dinner sponsored by the Doherty Fraternity Chapter 106 of the employees of the Cities Service Oil Company on February 27, 1954.

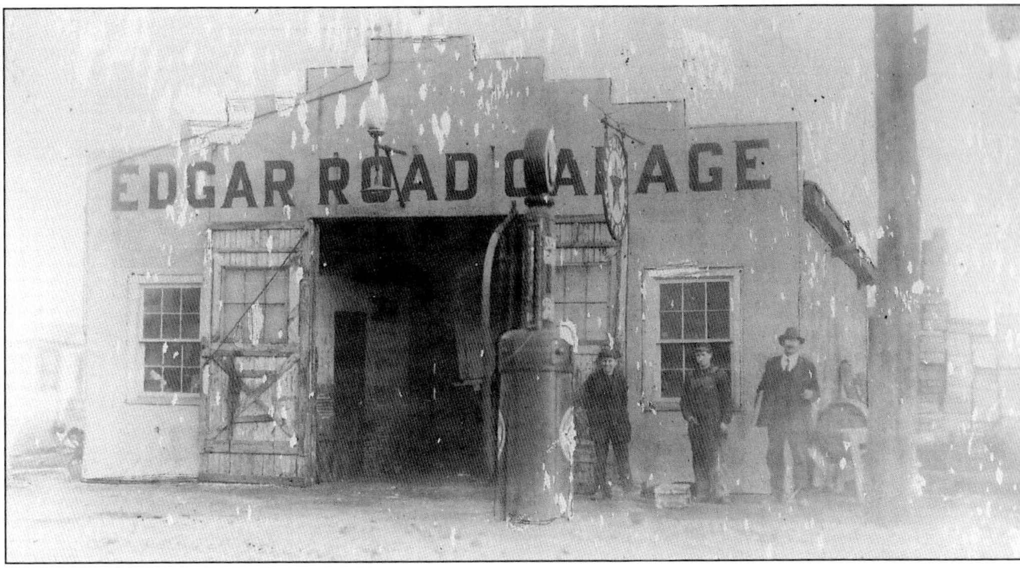

A 1923 photograph of the first home of the Edgar Road Garage. It has been a family-owned business since then, with Bernie Plungis now the owner. It is now located at 1636 East Edgar Road.

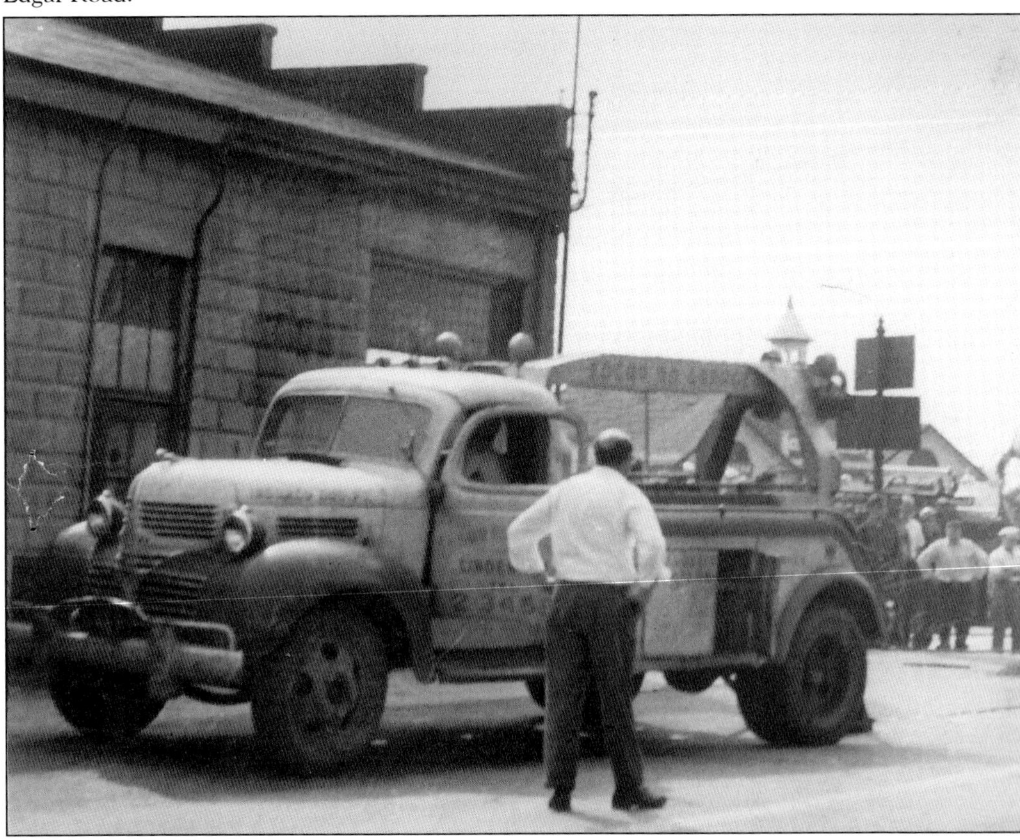

Another view of the Edgar Road Garage. The steeple in the background belongs to the dog track.

Five

Leisure at Its Best

For many years recreational life centered around the Linden Country Club, which disbanded in 1930. Most of the Sunnyside area became a golf course. There was the Suburban Club and during the late 1800s there was a horse track, later replaced by a dog track. There were areas that people would set up as racetracks for their cars, too.

The recreation department of the city of Linden was organized in 1935. They now have a total of thirty-six parks with sixteen of them having playground areas. The recreation department offers a wide variety of services to the community for all age groups.

Lindenites have made the best of their free time but not with just one organization. There were many opportunities for activities around the city. This chapter will show you some of those activities.

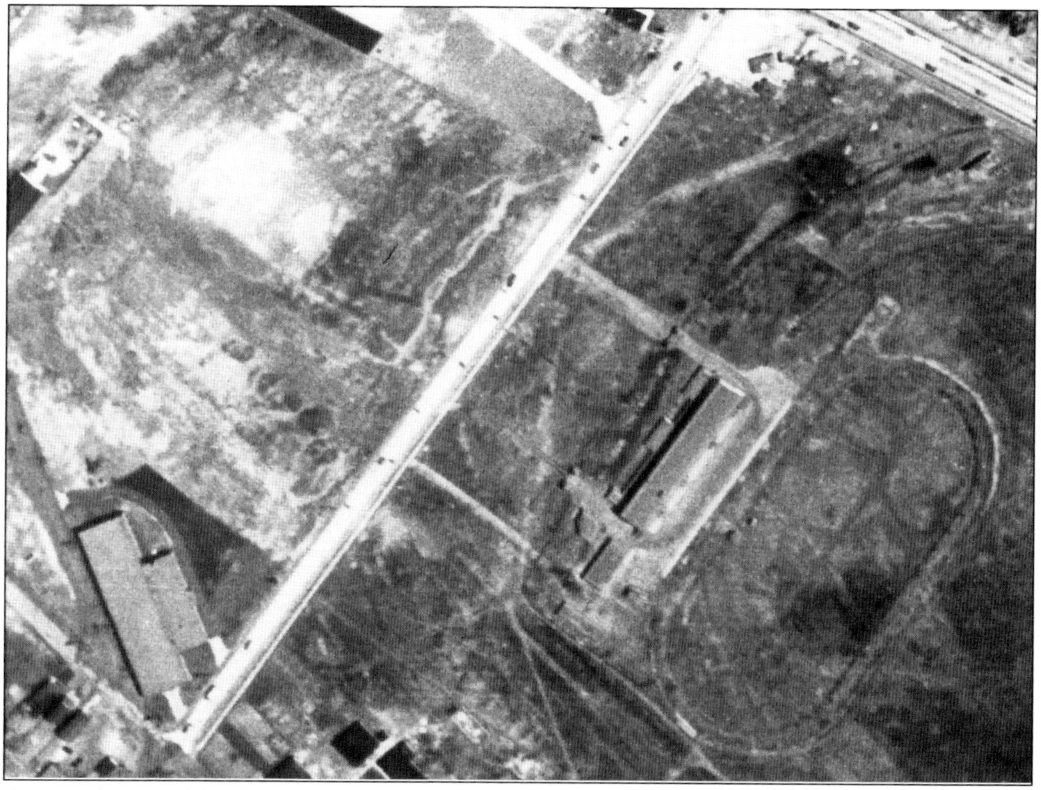

An aerial view of the dog track in Linden. Edgar Road is a four-lane highway with a grass median at the top and Park Avenue is to the left. The land became the home of Esso Research.

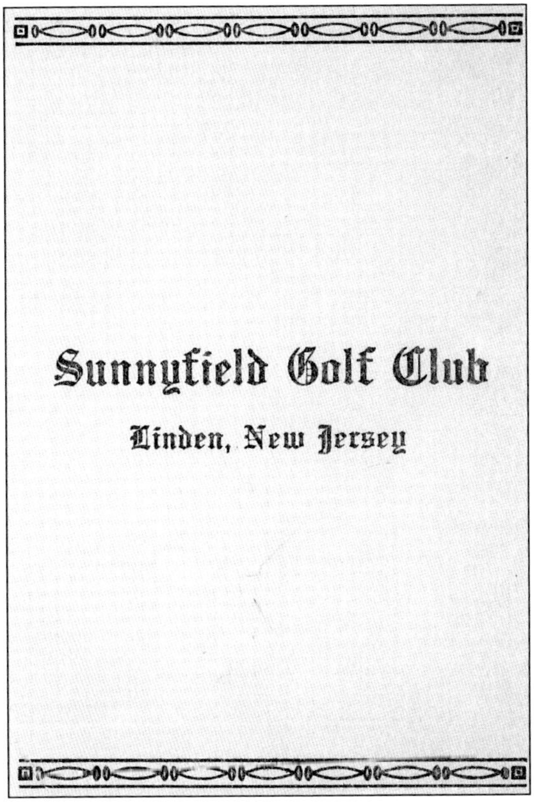
Sunnyfield Golf Club
Linden, New Jersey

A scorecard from the Sunnyfield Golf Club. The course became a community of split level and ranch-style houses after World War II.

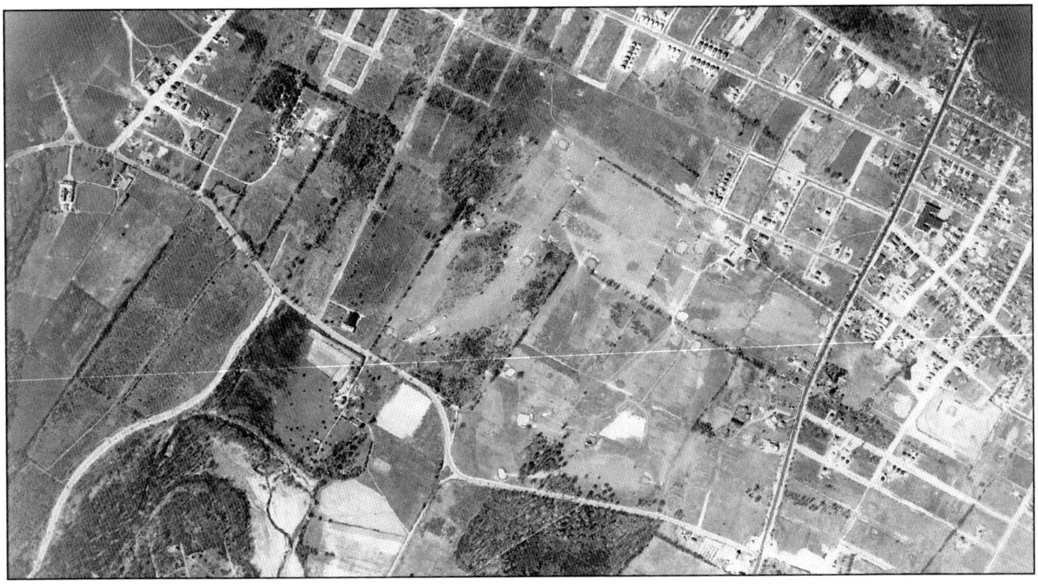

An aerial view of the Sunnyfield Golf Course. The course is the large, light gray area in the center, which was later cut through to make streets. It became the major portion of the Sunnyside area of Linden, as you will see on the next page.

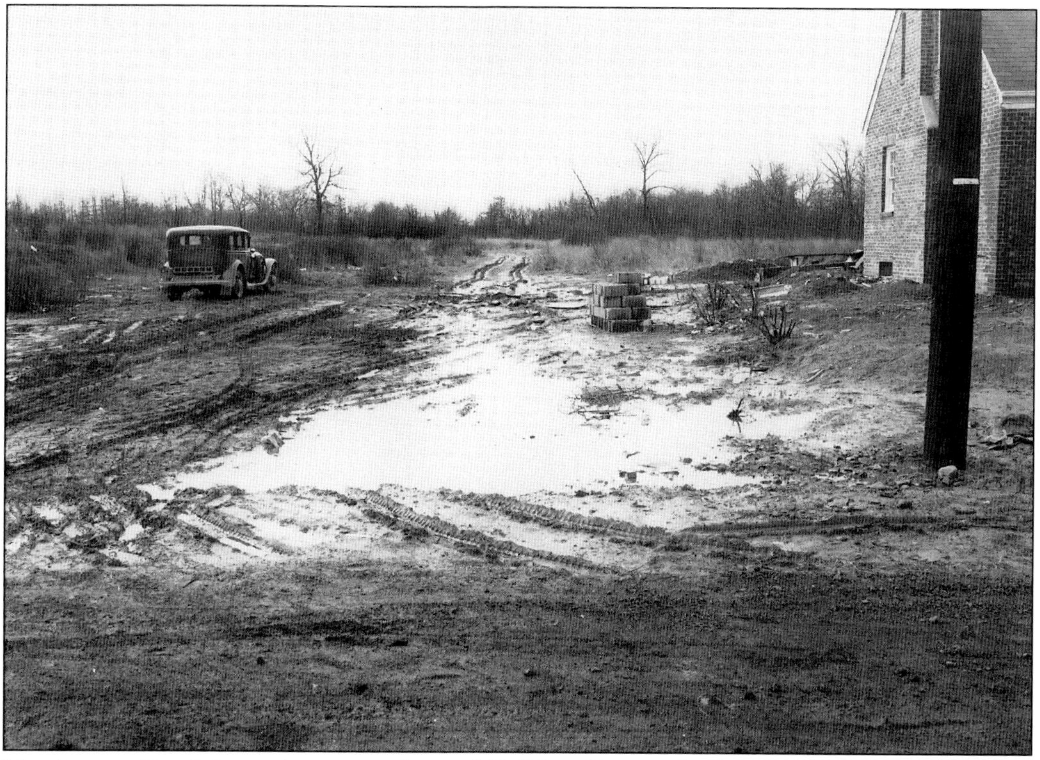

Morristown Road from the center line of DeWitt Terrace looking west. At the time this photograph was taken—February 12, 1940—the road was being cut through to Stiles Street.

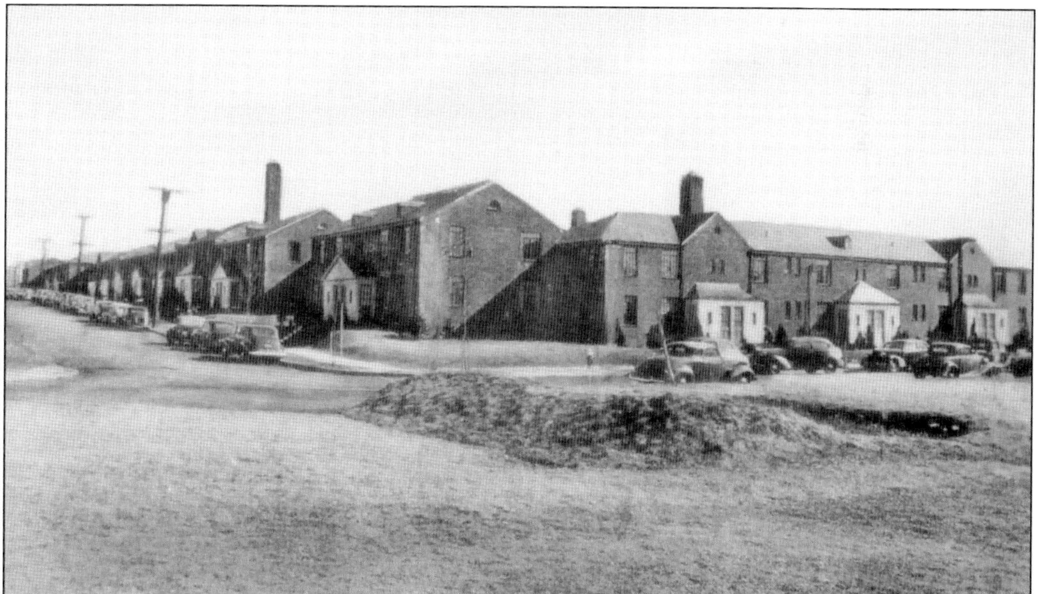

A postcard view of the Lindcrest Apartments. This card was published by the Mayrose Company of Linden *c.* 1930s. There were no houses on the lots around the apartments when this image was taken.

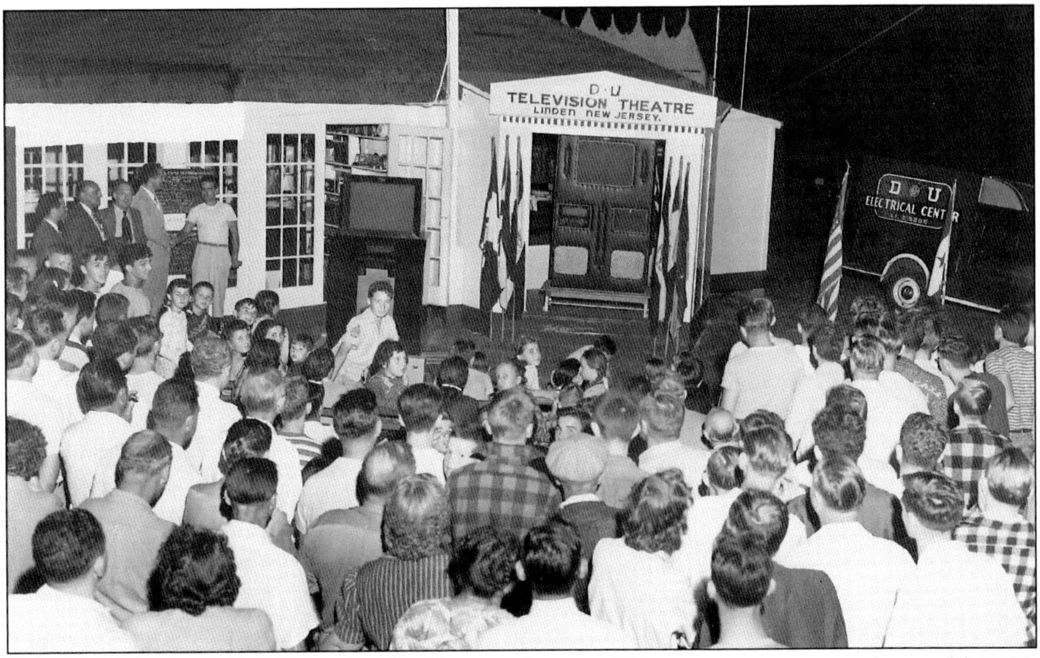

D.U. Electric, located at 140 West St. George Avenue. Television was new to the world. D.U. Electric sponsored "Television Theater" for the public's nighttime entertainment at 140 West St. Georges Avenue.

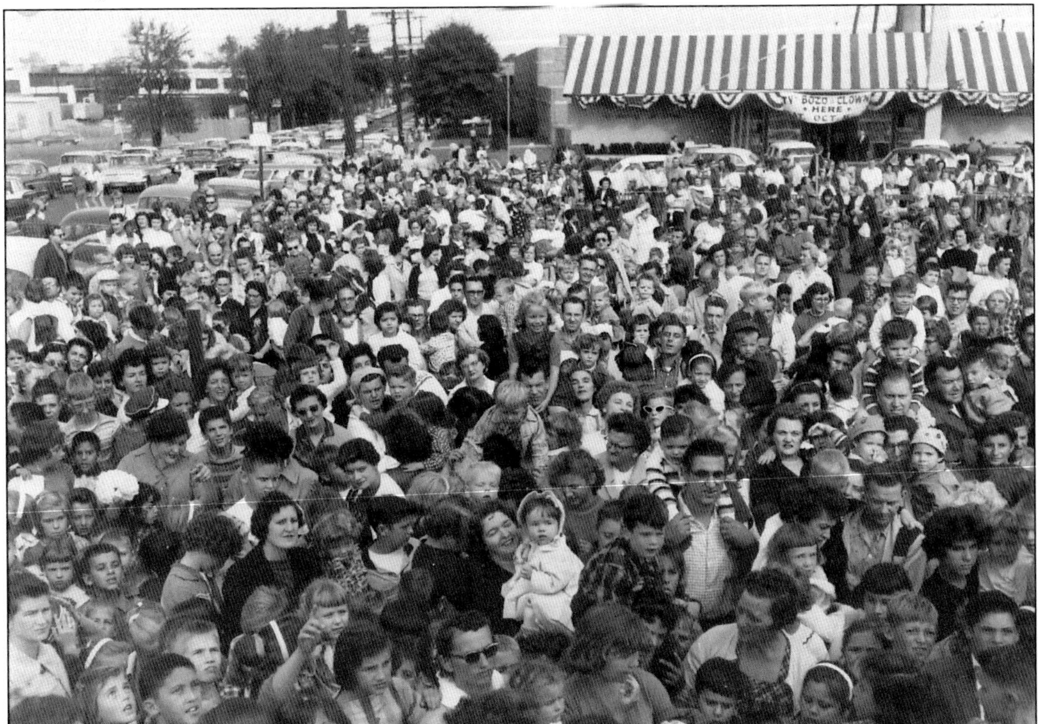

A monumental attraction. There was a huge turnout when Bozo the Clown made an appearance at Morey La Rue.

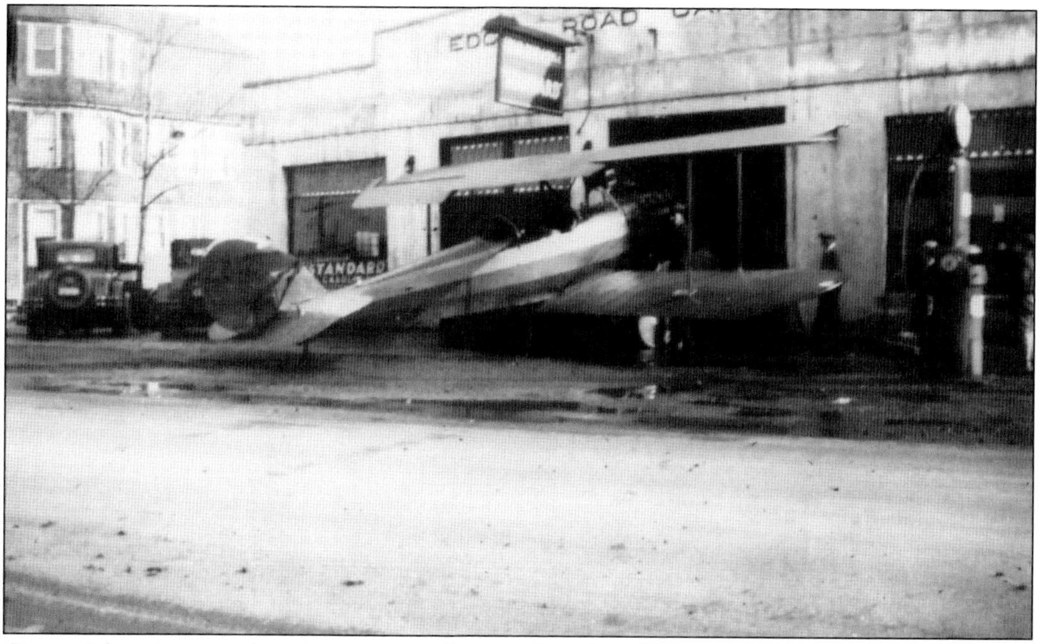

George Plungis, an early aviator, is seen here parking his Waco-Nine airplane in the driveway of the Edgar Road Garage. He delighted neighborhood children in the 1920s by landing his craft in the infield of an abandoned thoroughbred racing track on the site now occupied by Exxon Research. He was one of the first aviators to fly a plane in Linden.

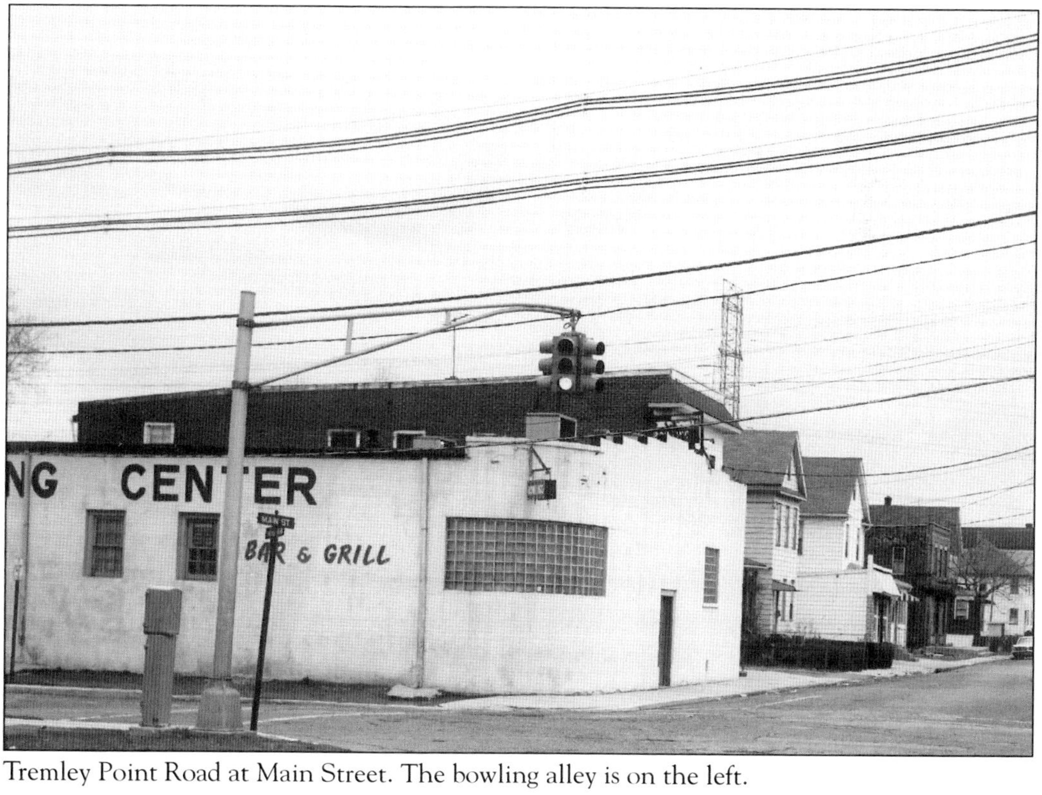

Tremley Point Road at Main Street. The bowling alley is on the left.

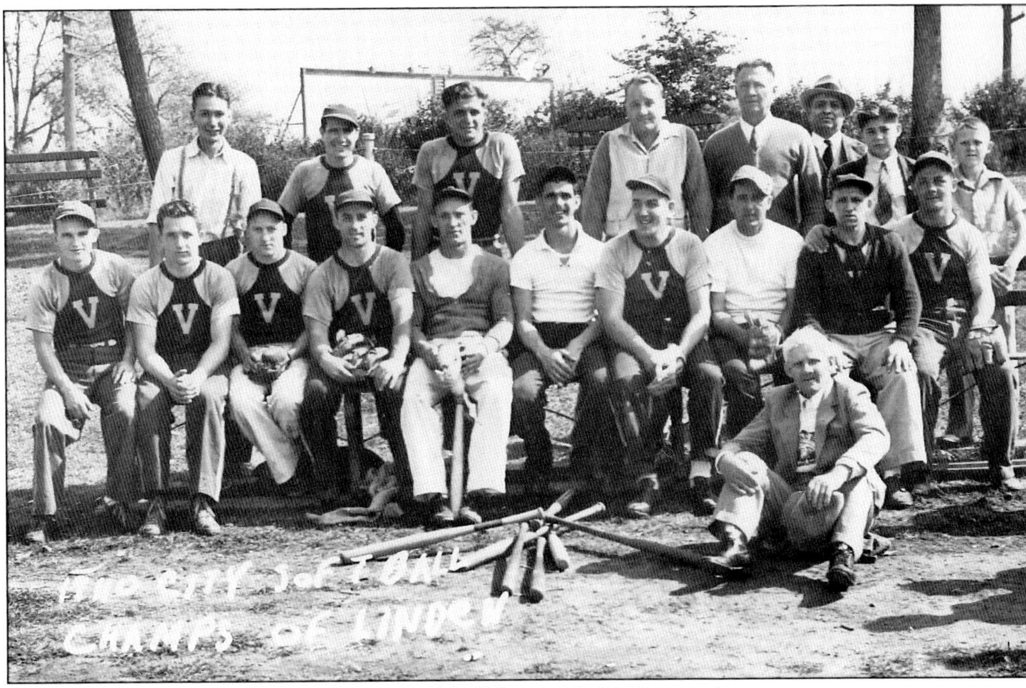

The Linden Recreation Department Softball League's 1940 city champions.

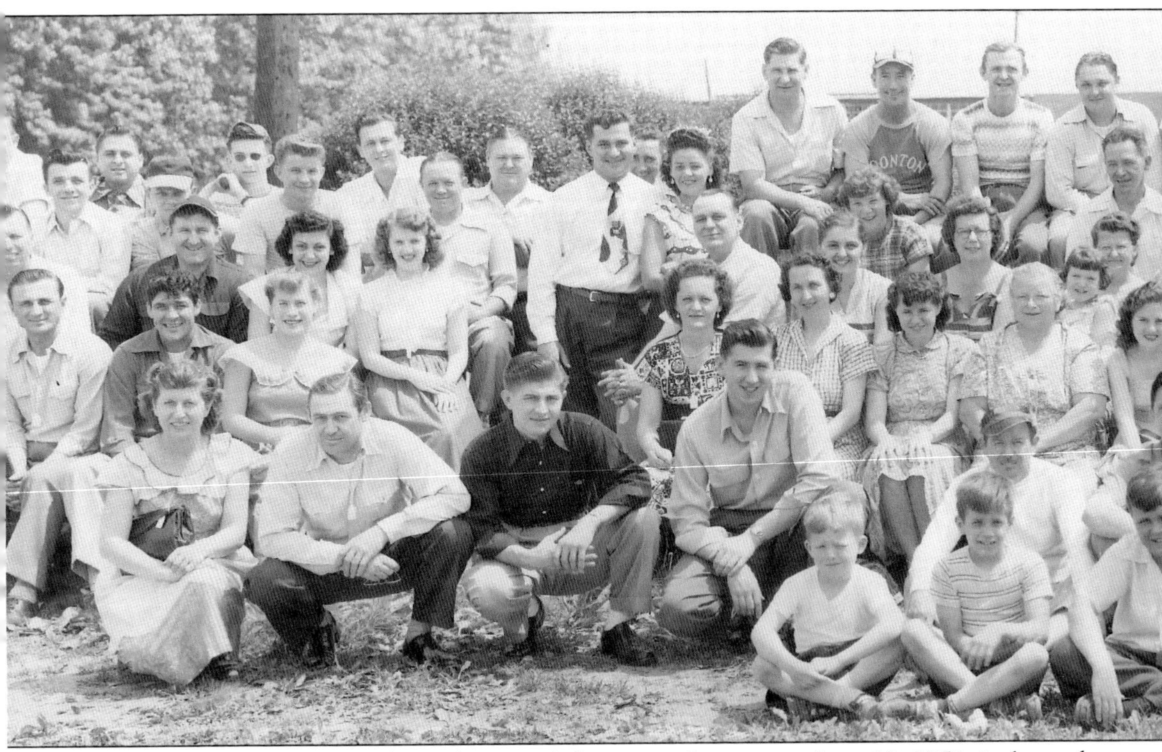

Eighth Ward Linden Cadets. The group's first annual outing on June 17, 1951, is shown here.

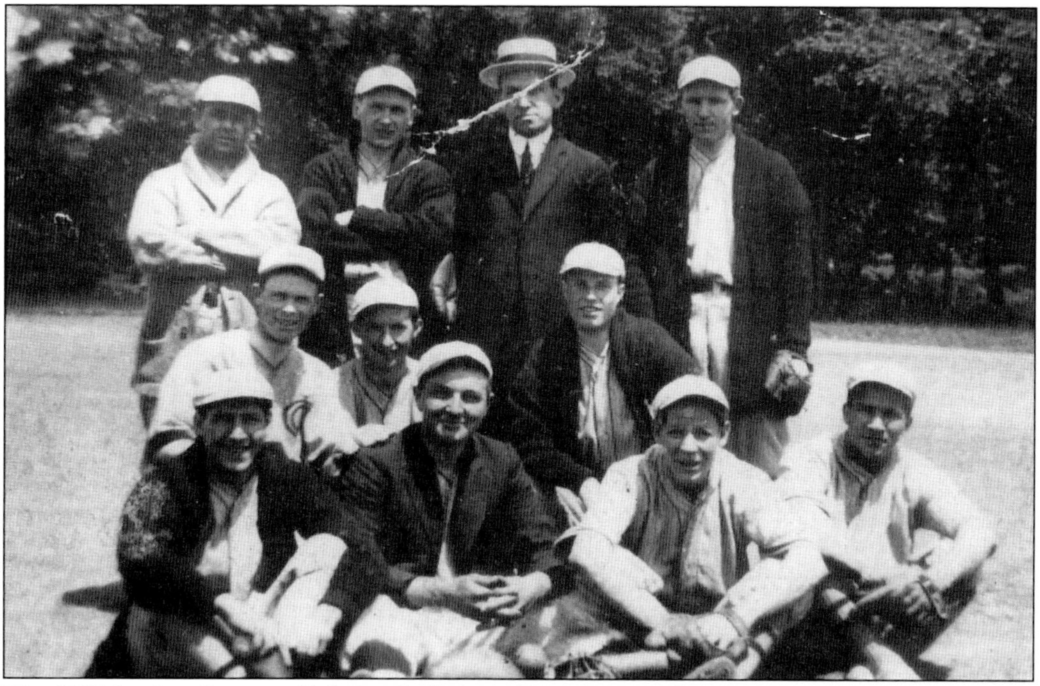

The 1917 Linden Country Club Baseball Team. From left to right on top are Larry Tallon, Joseph Spillinger, Reverend Betterton, Hugo Wendell, Russell Wheeler, Spurgeon Bettle, Arthur J. Mellor, Andrew More, Harold R. "Mac" Nowell, Roy Bundy, and Walter Schordicke.

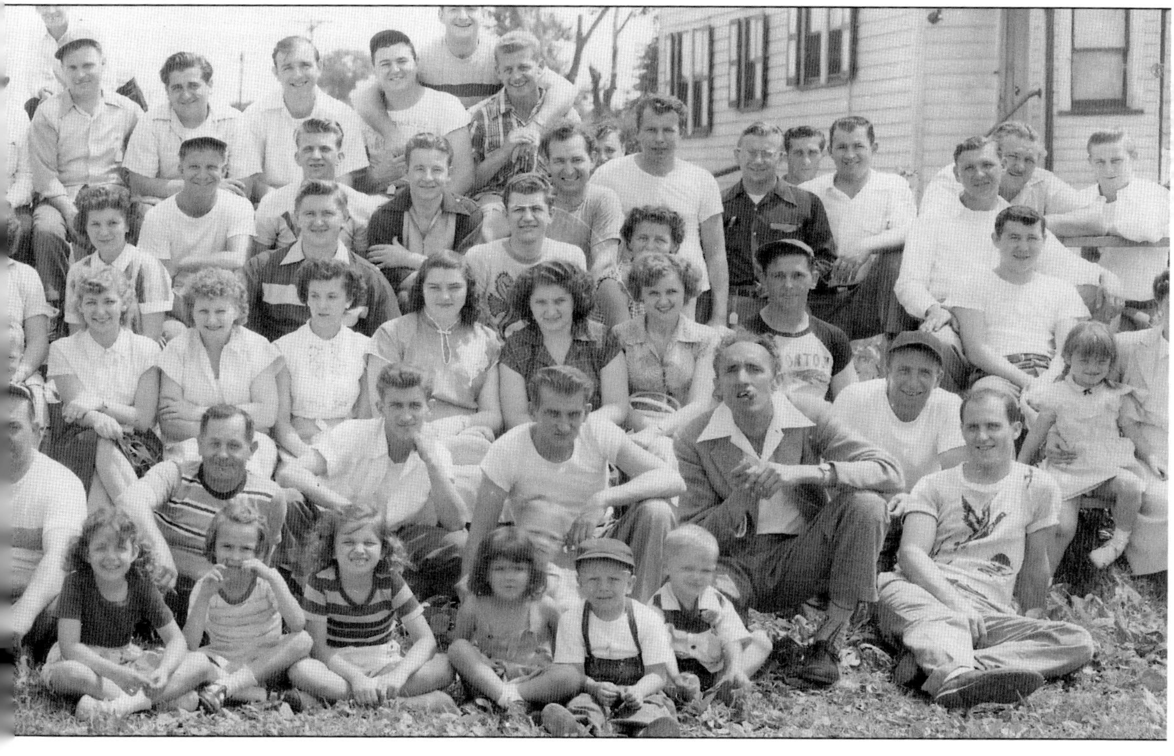

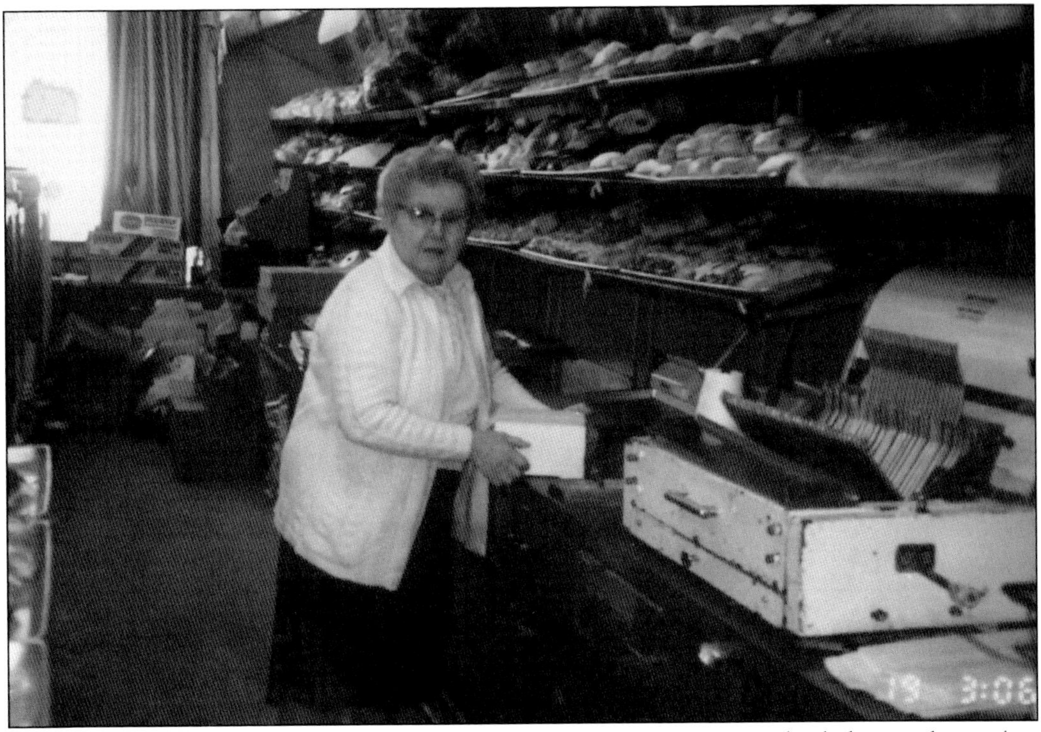

Wanda Knapp has been working for the Village Bakery since 1955. The bakery is located at 1742 East St. Georges Avenue, Linden.

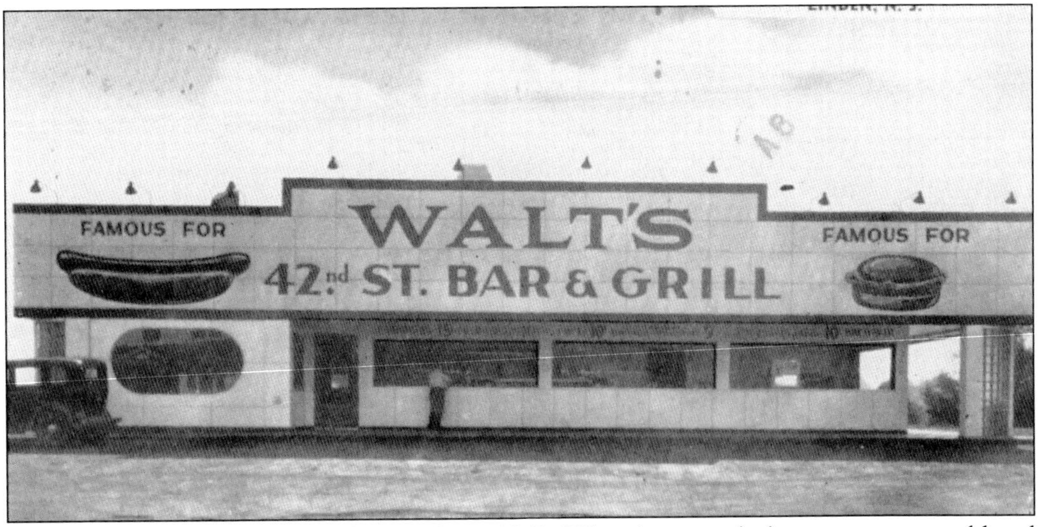

Walter Mrozek operated Walt's from 1930 to 1968. When he retired, the property was sold and became what was the Pathmark Shopping Center. Mrozek's parents, Frank and Mary, purchased the eatery in 1929 when it was called the Broadway and 42nd Street Bar. It had an adjoining gas station and used to be open twenty-four hours a day. The name was changed to Walt's after Prohibition was repealed. The building pictured here was constructed in 1941.

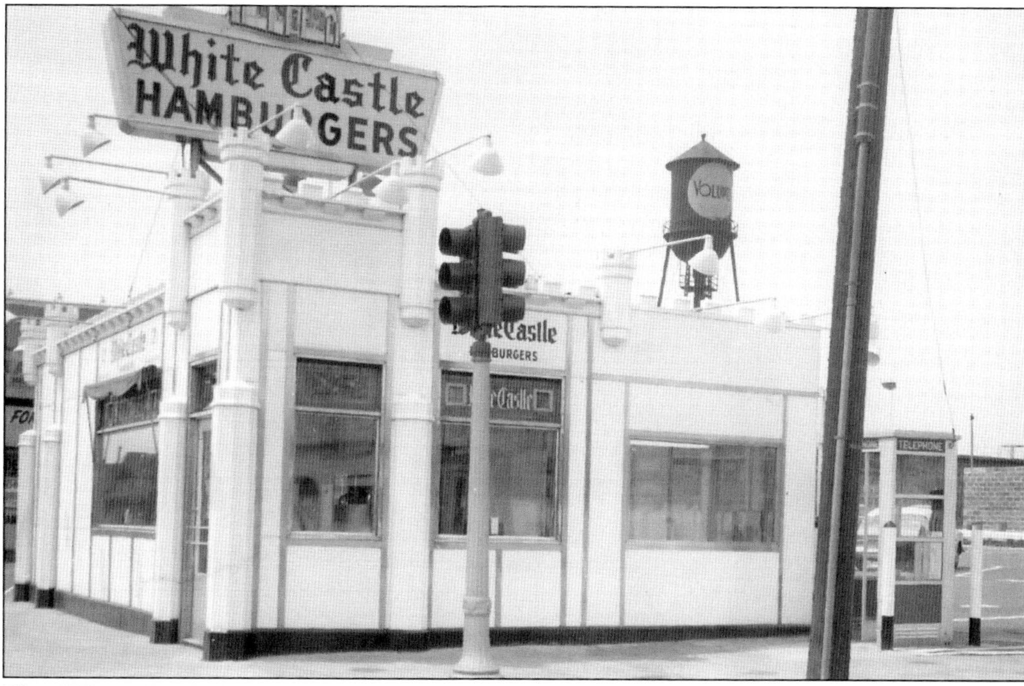

The White Castle Restaurant was modeled after the Chicago Water Tower, whose turrets and battlements were reproduced in white porcelain enamel. The Linden restaurant opened on September 2, 1935, and was the castle of the system with its leading sales. It closed on October 1, 1981.

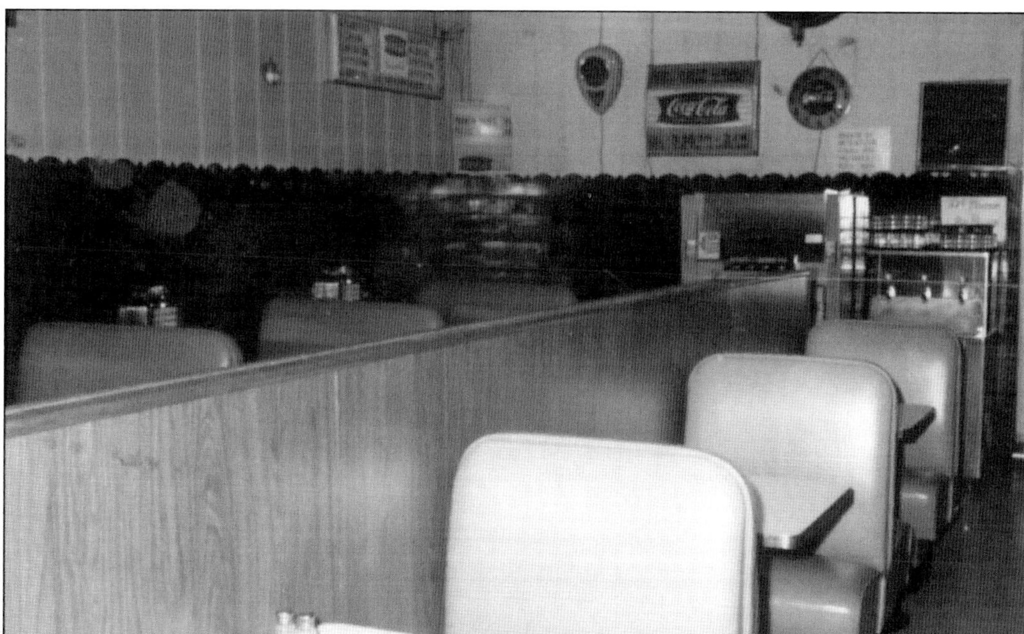

Connie's Pizza on East Edgar Road. The restaurant was purchased in 1955 by the Gant family. Connie's was a landmark that was known for its pleasant dining and the best pizza anywhere around. This is the dining room looking to the front door. The establishment closed in 1981.

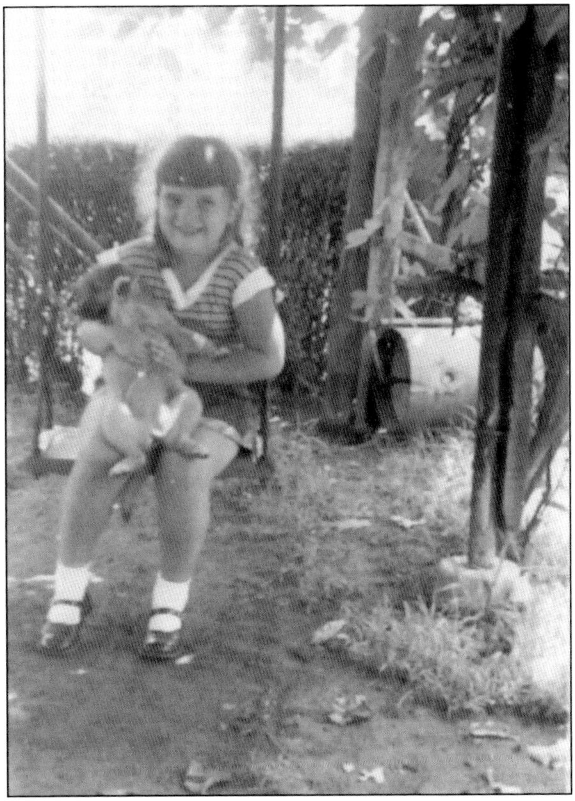

The simple pleasures of life. Jeanne Wade relaxes on a homemade swing under the grapevines of a 16th Street yard. She is holding Butchie, her grandfather's dog.

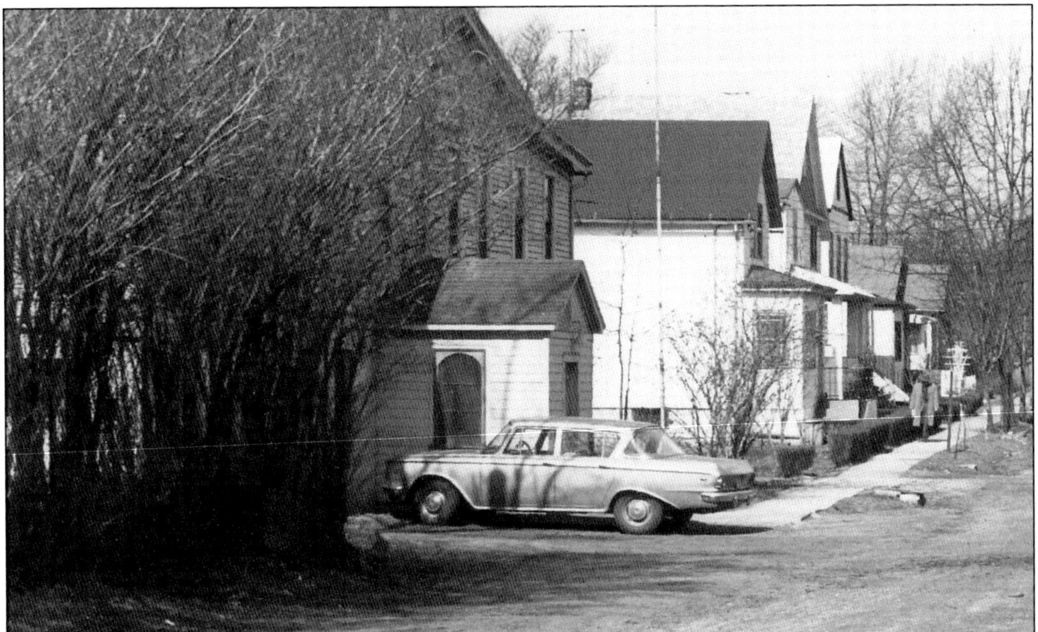

Lithuanian Liberty Hall on Mitchell Avenue was the place to be for picnics and high-spirited entertainment. It was located adjacent to the J. Wheeler Park in the picnic area where bands would play and one could dance the day away on the dance floor of the gazebo.

Six

Dear Old Golden Rule Days . . .

In 1750, the first school was Wheatsheaf, at Old Post Road (St. Georges Avenue) and Roselle Street. In 1820 a new school was erected nearby. In 1866 the school was closed but rented for six months as a private school. In 1895, the Wheatsheaf School belonged to the new borough of Mulford (Roselle).

In 1786, a second school was built in Trembly on Morses Mill Road. By 1825, "The Union Seminary" was erected nearby. It was also known as the "Hog town School."

In 1804, a third school was located opposite Willow Glade Avenue (Mount Calvary Cemetery is now on that site). Later, a replacement was erected for that area on the south side of the Shunpike (Edgar Road). In 1865, the fourth school was built at the corner of Stiles and Blancke Streets by the borough. It later became the first M.E. Church.

In 1871, Linden's first public school was built on Linden Avenue, on land donated by Meeker Wood. It took the place of the Shunpike and Stiles Street schools, which were discontinued by the state creating the public school system.

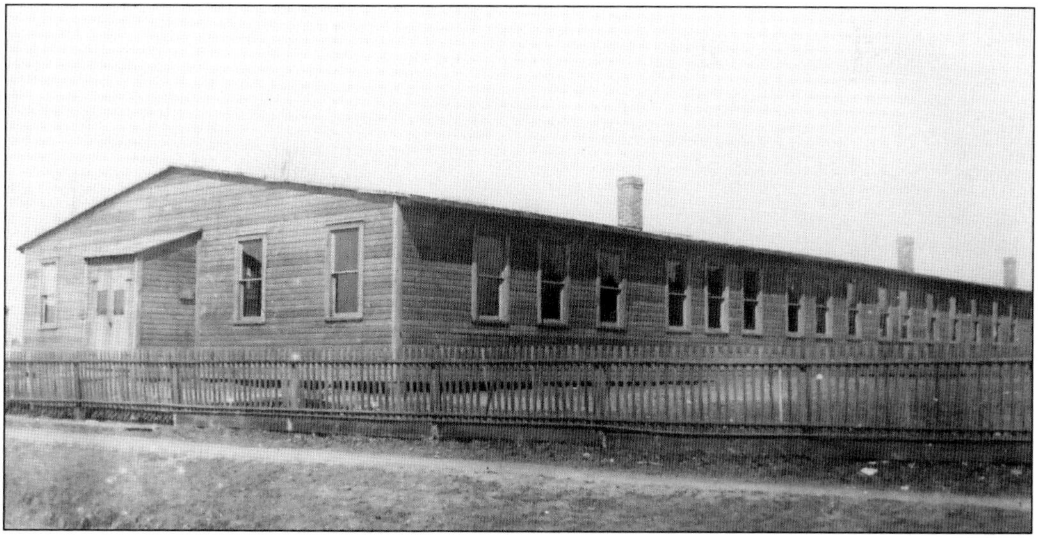

On December 2, 1909, a fire burned down the first public school. Until permanent facilities could be built, a temporary school was built at the corner of Munsell and Wood Avenues. Many of the very early schoolhouses listed above were built like this one.

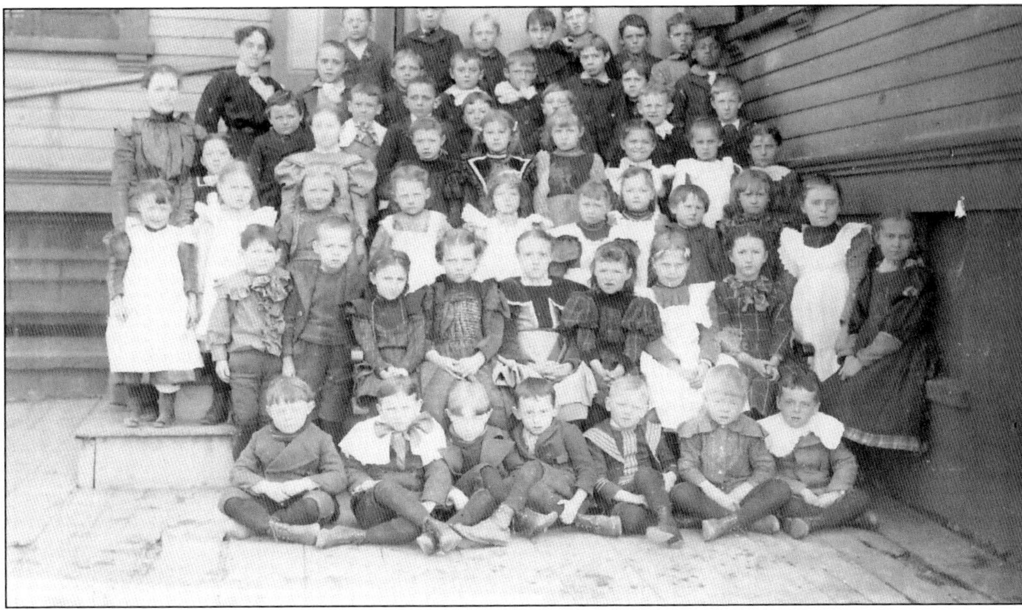

The Linden Public School No. 1 Primary Class of 1899.

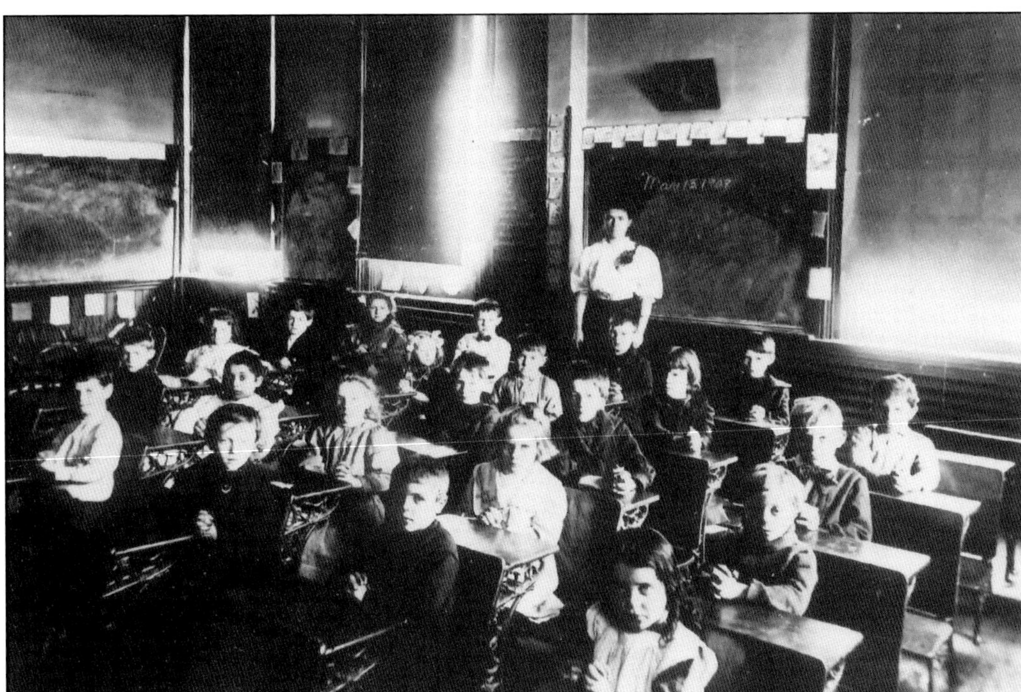

An interior view of Linden Public School No. 1, taken on March 13, 1908.

Happy days at the first public school, erected in 1871. At first the school was known as the Academy, but in 1875 it received the official title of Public School No. 1, Linden, Union County, N.J. By 1907, two years of high school classes had been added. The building burned to the ground on December 2, 1909, and School No. 6 is now located at this site.

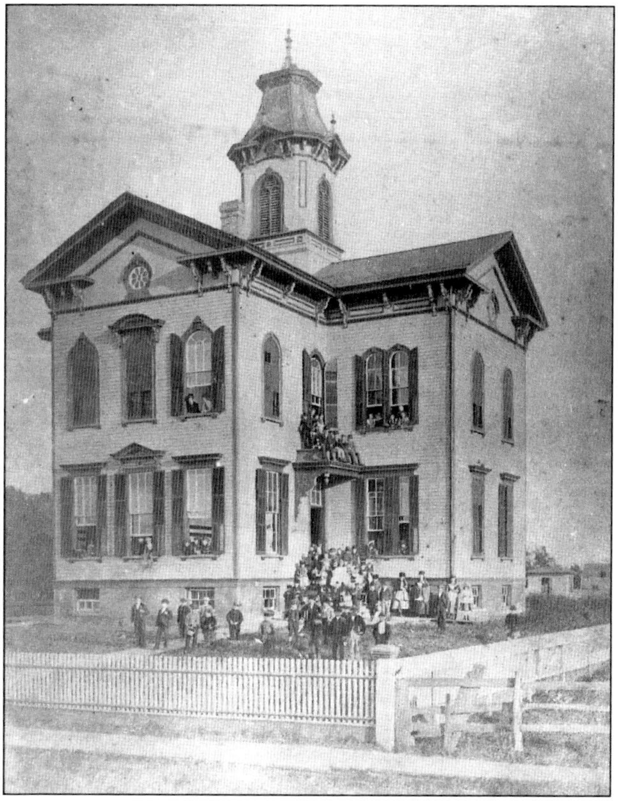

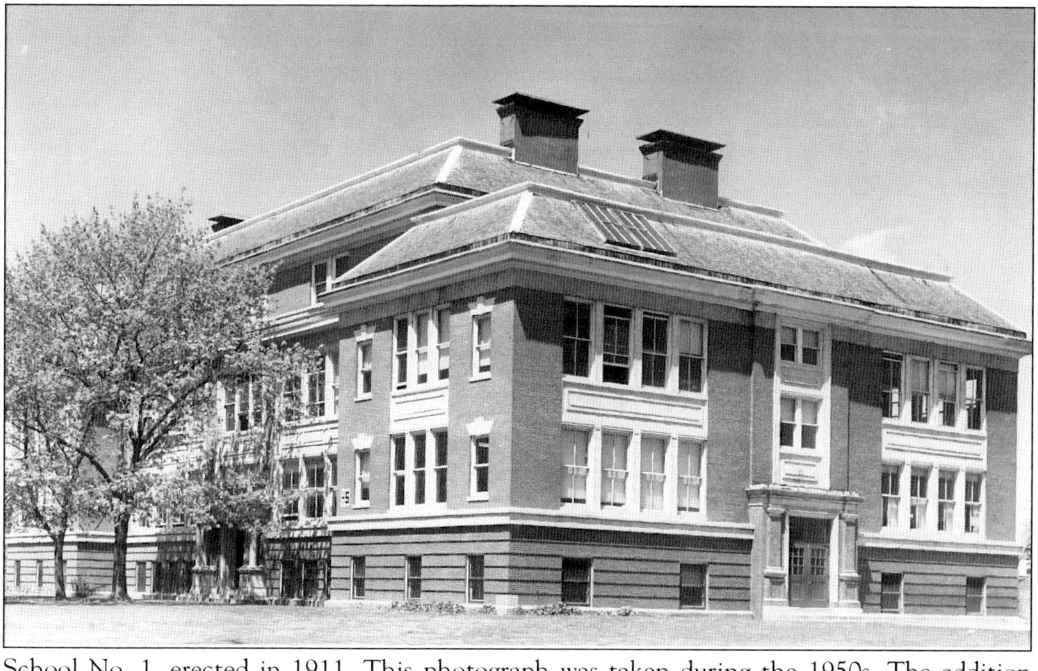

School No. 1, erected in 1911. This photograph was taken during the 1950s. The addition that now houses the board of education was constructed in 1972. It is located at 728 North Wood Avenue.

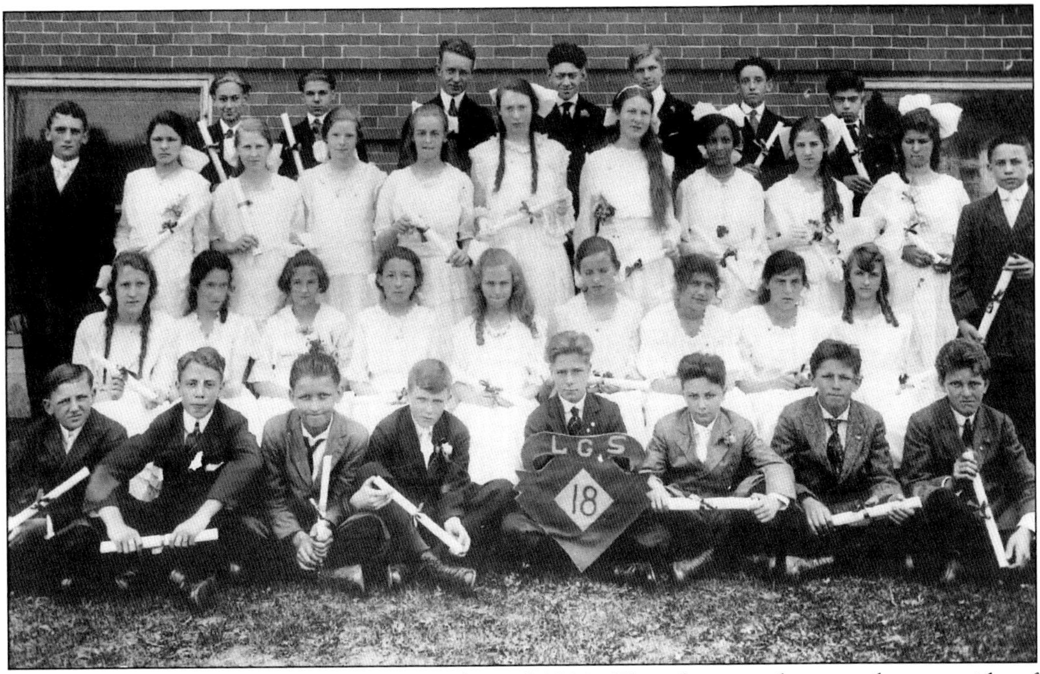

The Linden Grade School graduating Class of 1918. The photograph was taken outside of School No. 1.

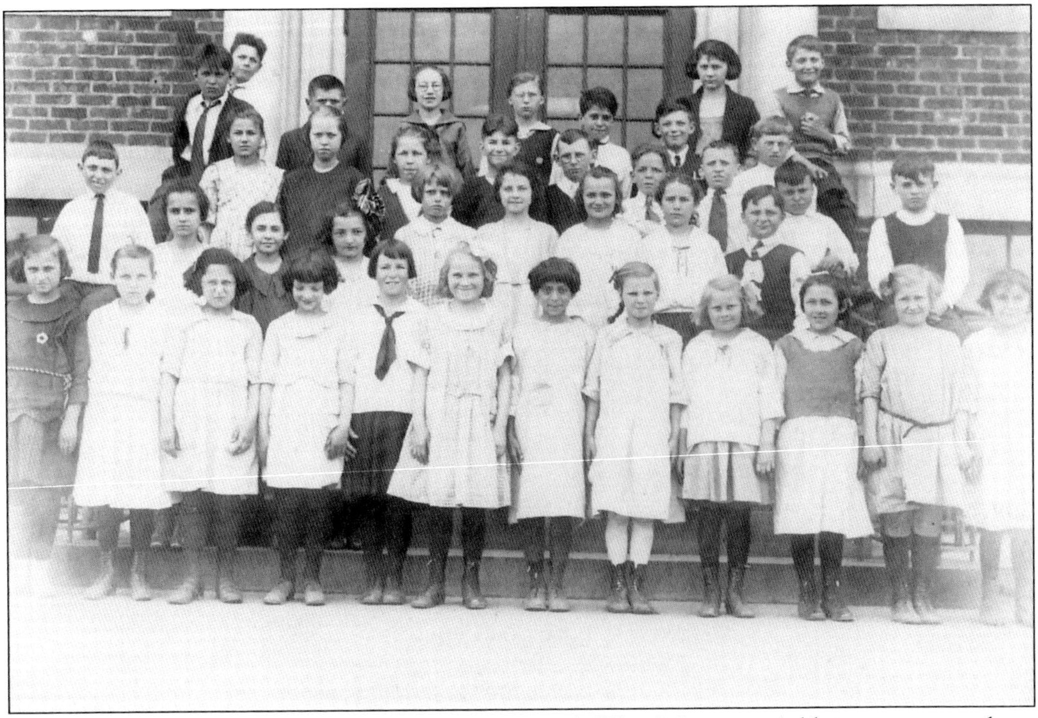

School No. 2 was constructed in 1913 at 1700 South Wood Avenue. Additions were made to the original structure in 1919 and 1967. This is a photograph of the graduating Class of 1925.

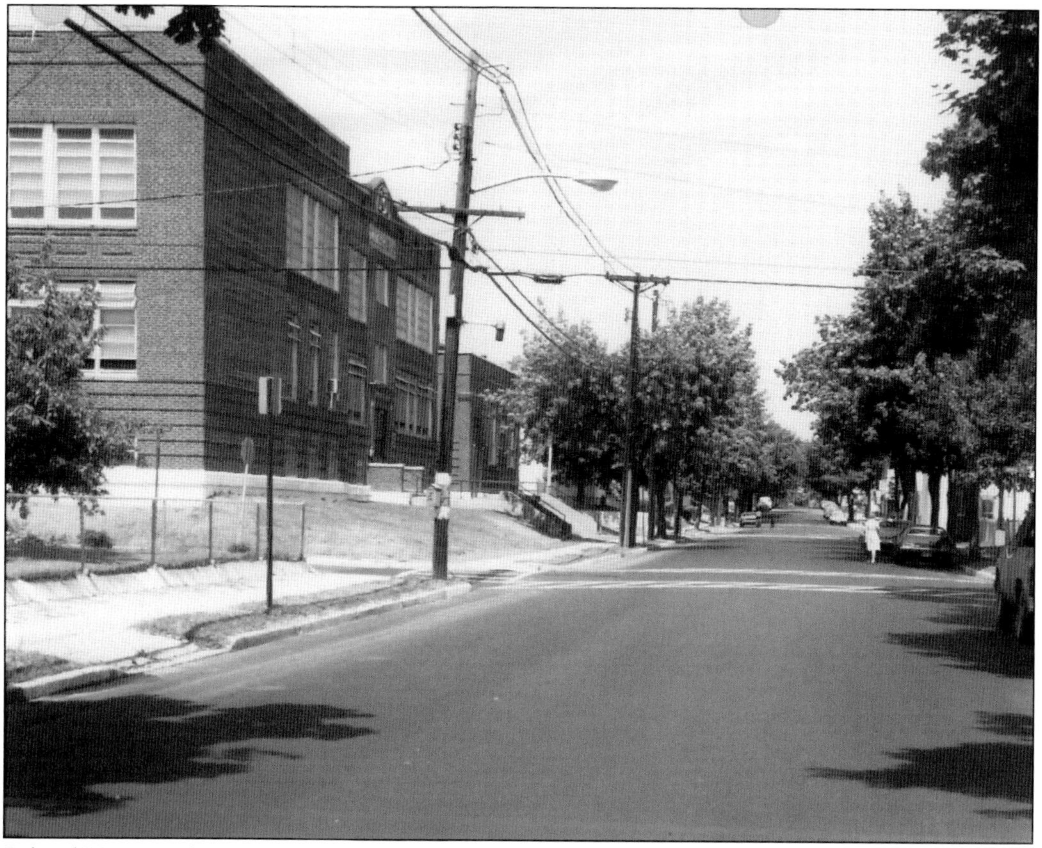

School No. 3 at the corner of Grier Avenue and Dennis Place in 1912. In 1927 an addition was built. The building still exists today but is not used as a public school.

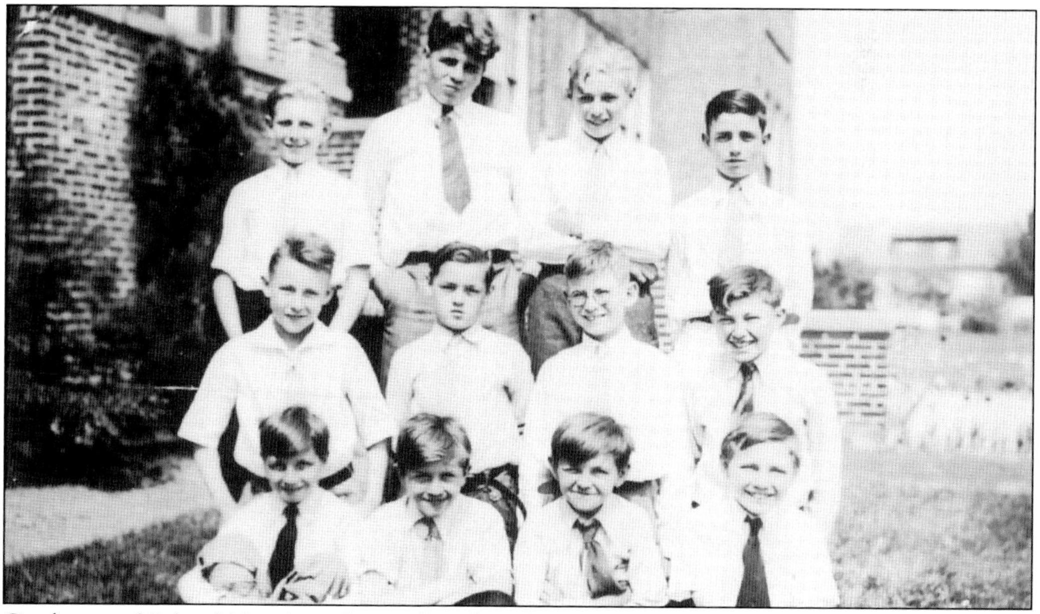

Graduates of School No. 4 are featured in this photograph taken on June 20, 1935.

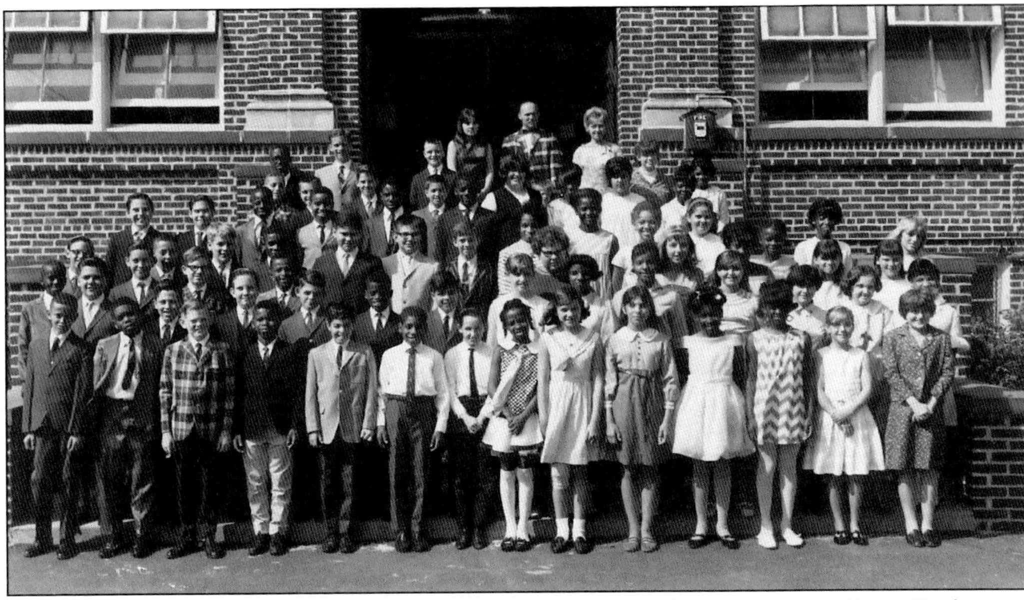

The sixth-grade graduating class of School No. 4 in 1967. The teachers are Rose Gutkin and Jules Leboff.

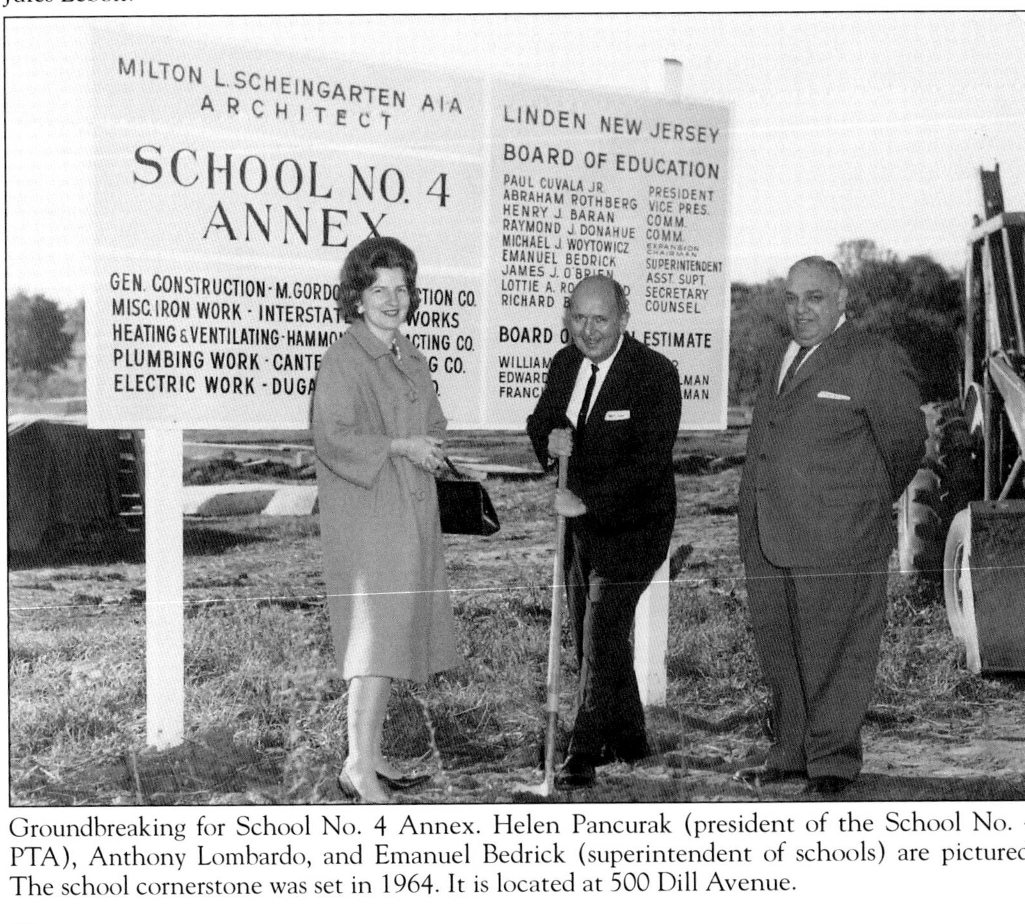

Groundbreaking for School No. 4 Annex. Helen Pancurak (president of the School No. 4 PTA), Anthony Lombardo, and Emanuel Bedrick (superintendent of schools) are pictured. The school cornerstone was set in 1964. It is located at 500 Dill Avenue.

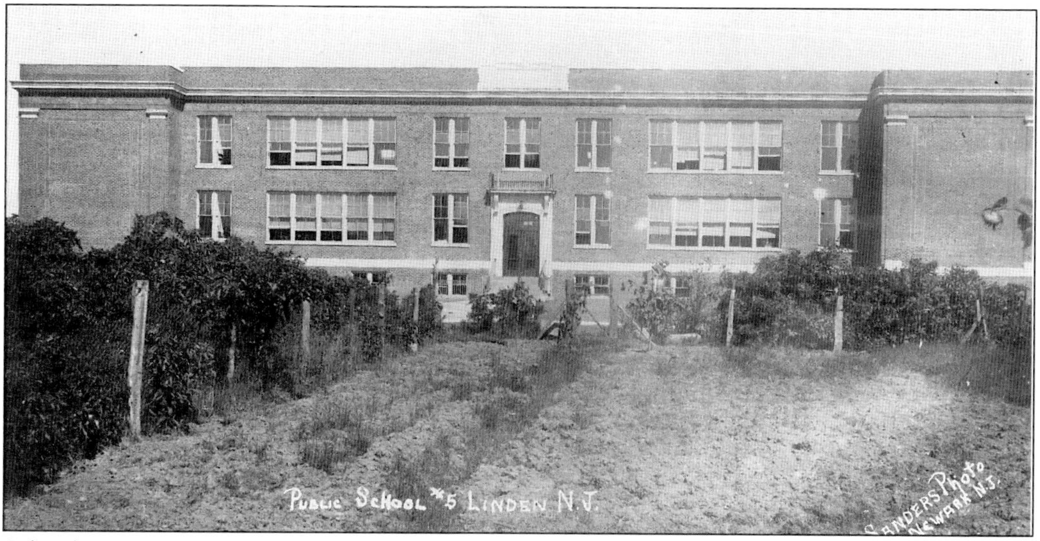

School No. 5, erected in 1921 on Bower Street. An addition was constructed in 1965. This photograph was taken before any buildings were across the street.

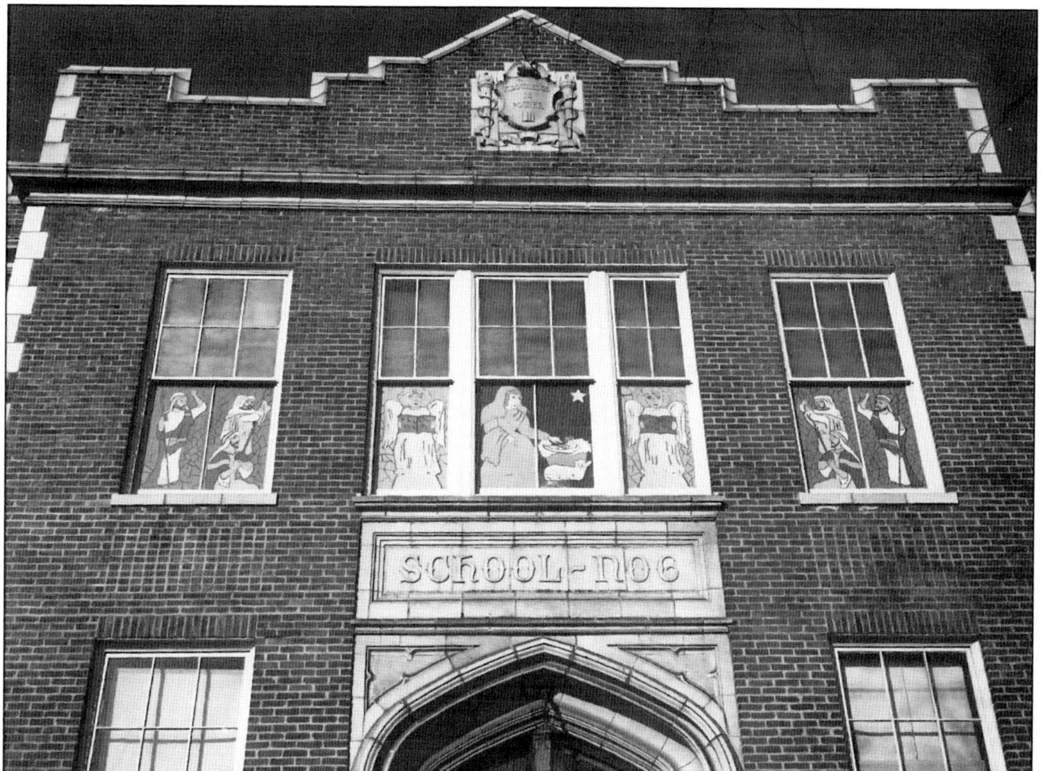

School No. 6, constructed in 1923 at the site of the first public school. It is located at 19 East Morris Avenue. This image depicts the front windows painted by the students at Christmas during the 1960s.

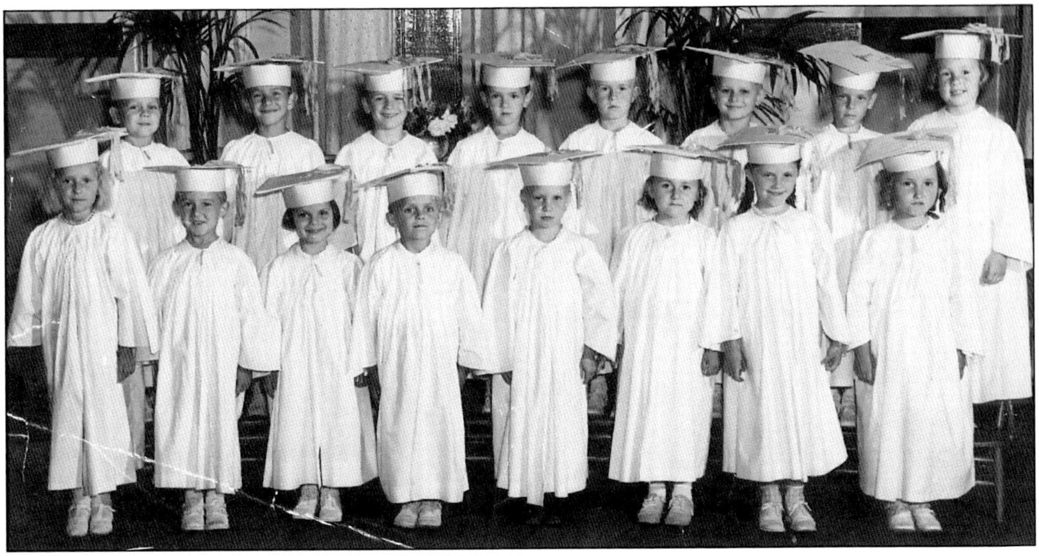

The 1953 kindergarten class from School No. 7.

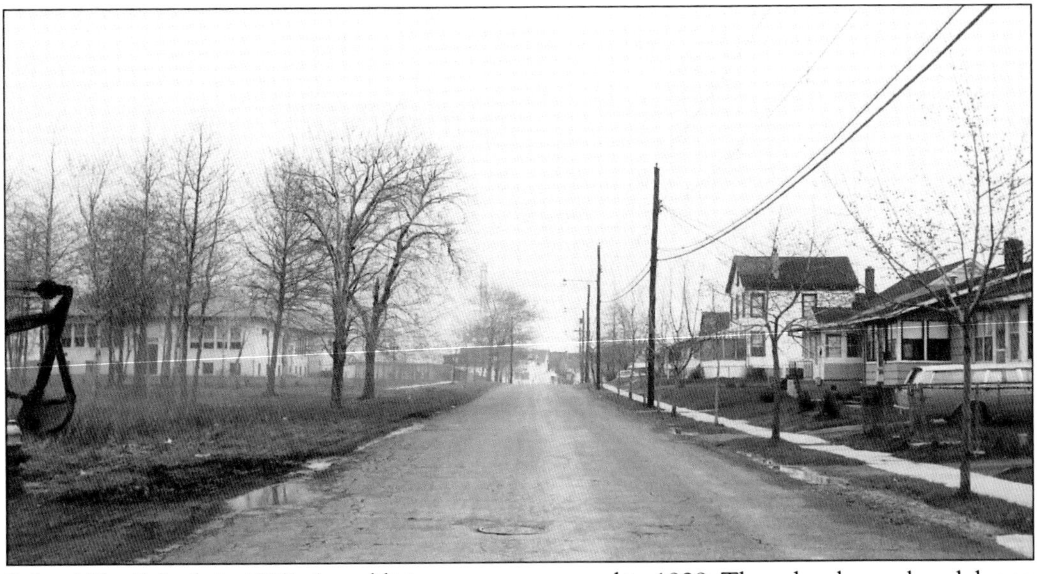

School No. 7, built in 1927. An addition was constructed in 1929. The school was closed due to low enrollment and the need for repairs to update the facility. A city park is now located at the site. This view is from Tremley Point Road. The school is to the left.

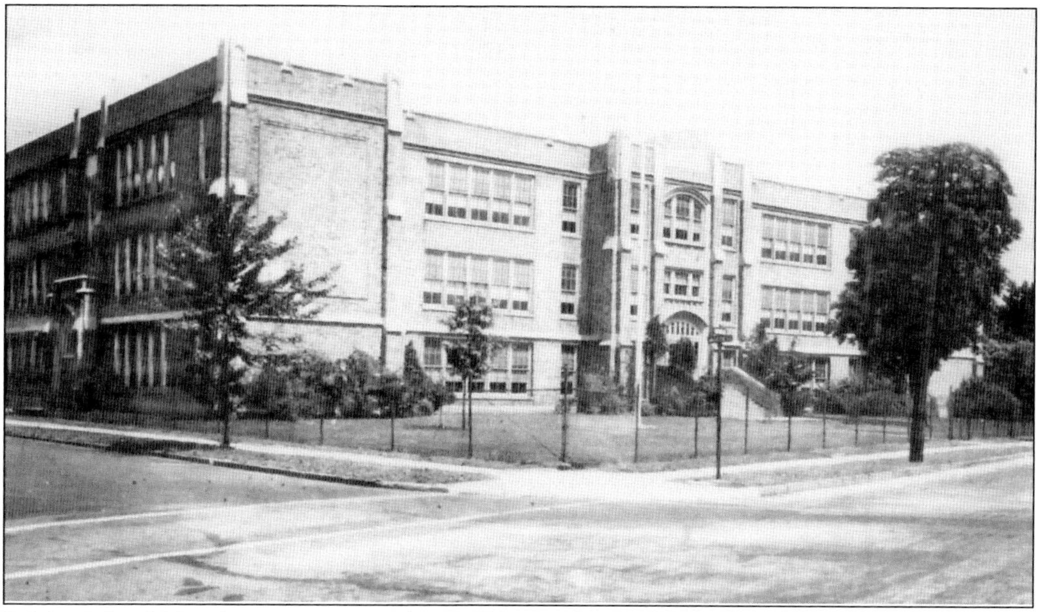

Public School No. 8 was constructed in 1930. It is located at 500 West Blancke Street. This vintage postcard shows a fence that no longer exists.

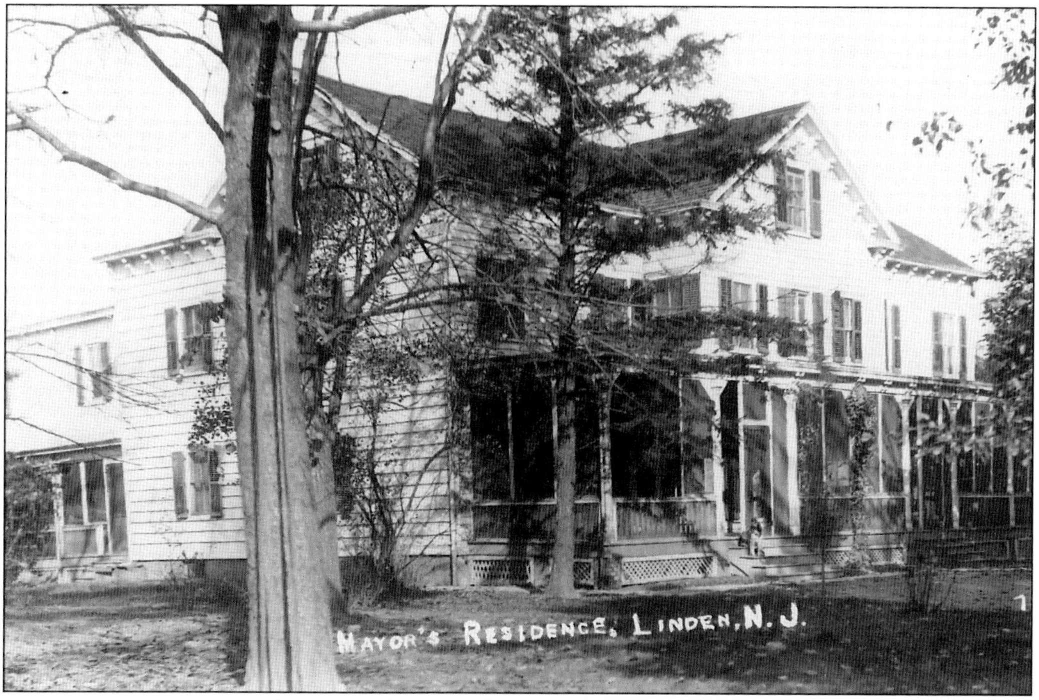

The residence of Mayor H.B. Hardenburg, located on West Blancke Street. Hardenburg was the borough mayor for twenty-one years. He was in favor of consolidating the township and borough in 1925. This was the future site of School No. 8 in 1930.

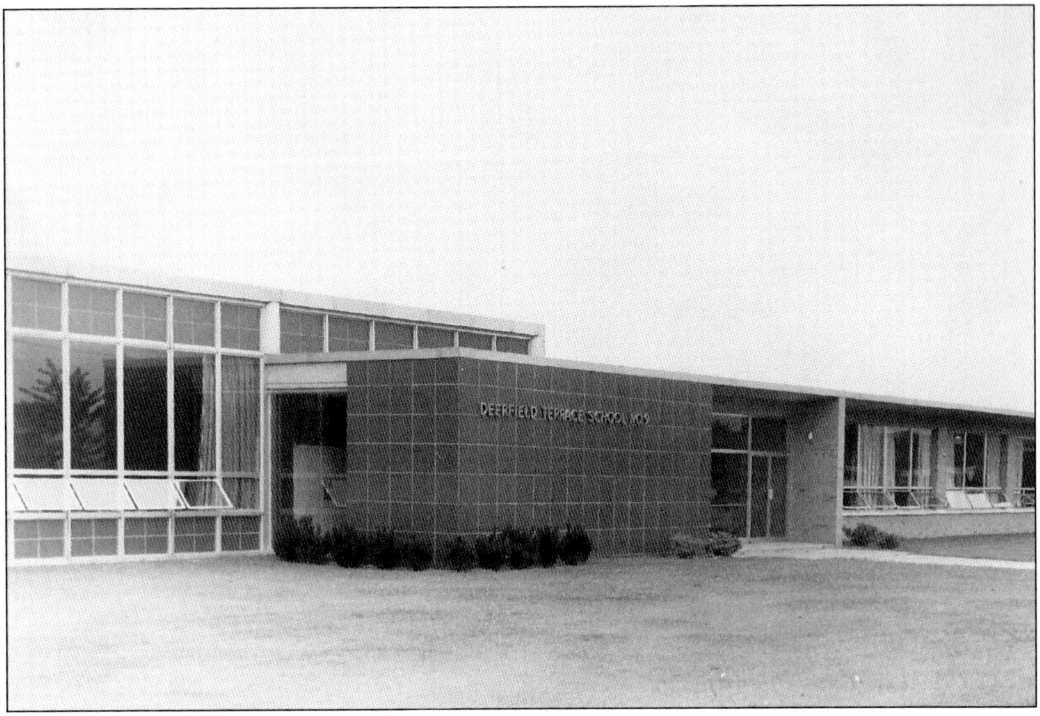

Deerfield Terrace School No. 9 was constructed in 1957.

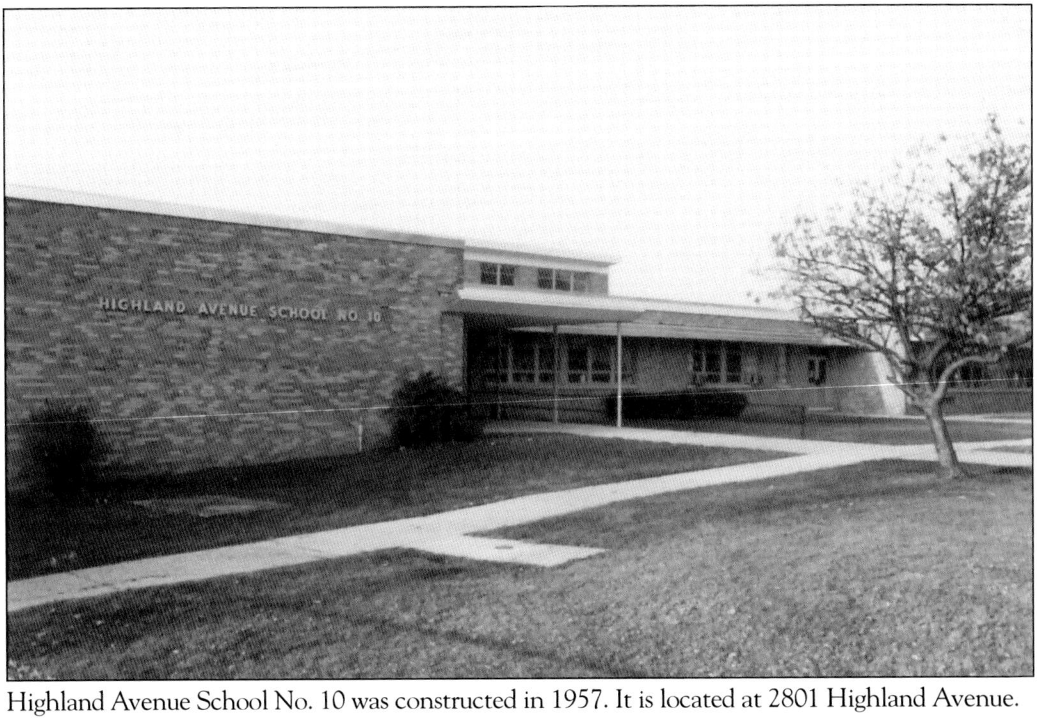

Highland Avenue School No. 10 was constructed in 1957. It is located at 2801 Highland Avenue.

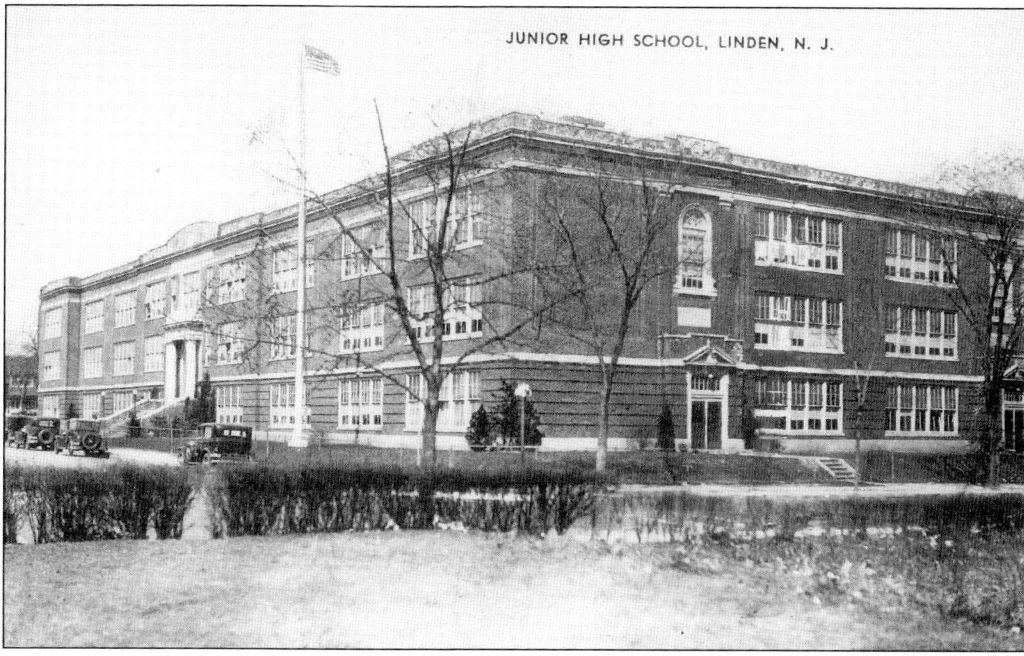

The Joseph E. Soehl Junior High School, built in 1928. It was the only junior high school in Linden until 1957, when Schools No. 9 and No. 10 were built. Additions were constructed in 1958 and 1971. It is a middle school now with grades six through eight enrolled.

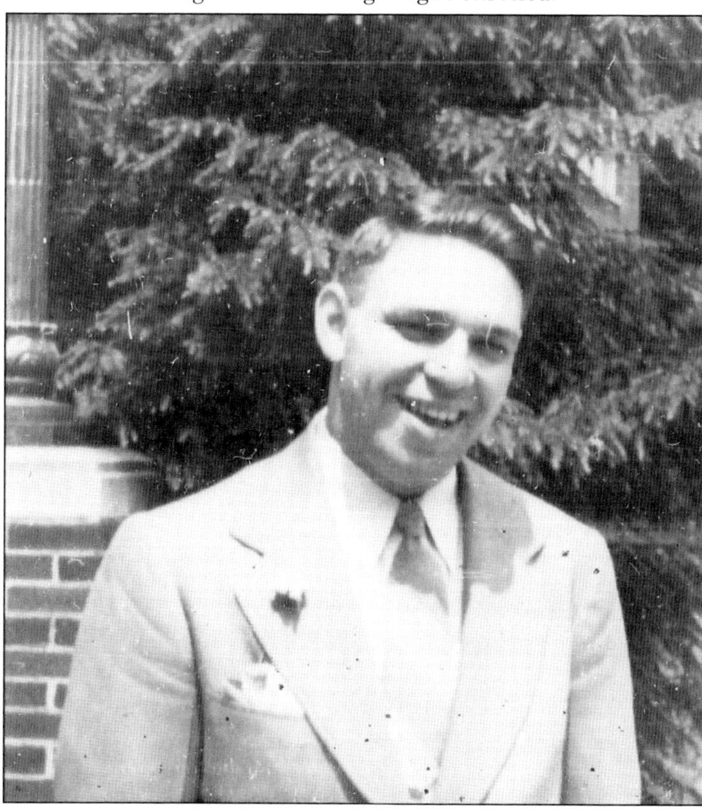

Emanuel Bedrick at the Joseph E. Soehl Junior High School in 1938. At that time, the school was not named for anyone, as it was the only junior high school.

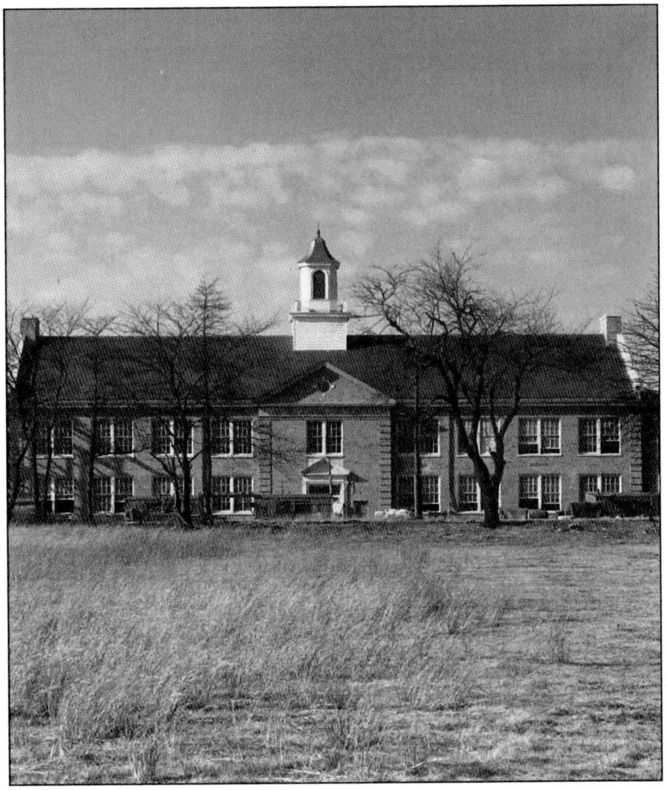

The Myles J. McManus School, built in 1950 as an elementary school. Additions were made in 1958 that assisted its transition to a junior high school when Schools No. 9 and No. 10 were built in 1957. The school is much longer on each side than it appears in this photograph. This is the main entrance.

Mrs. Bernice Bedrick on the roof of the Myles J. McManus School installing a weather station. Mrs. Bedrick worked for NASA earlier in her life. She became a science teacher, was supervisor of science, and was principal of School No. 6.

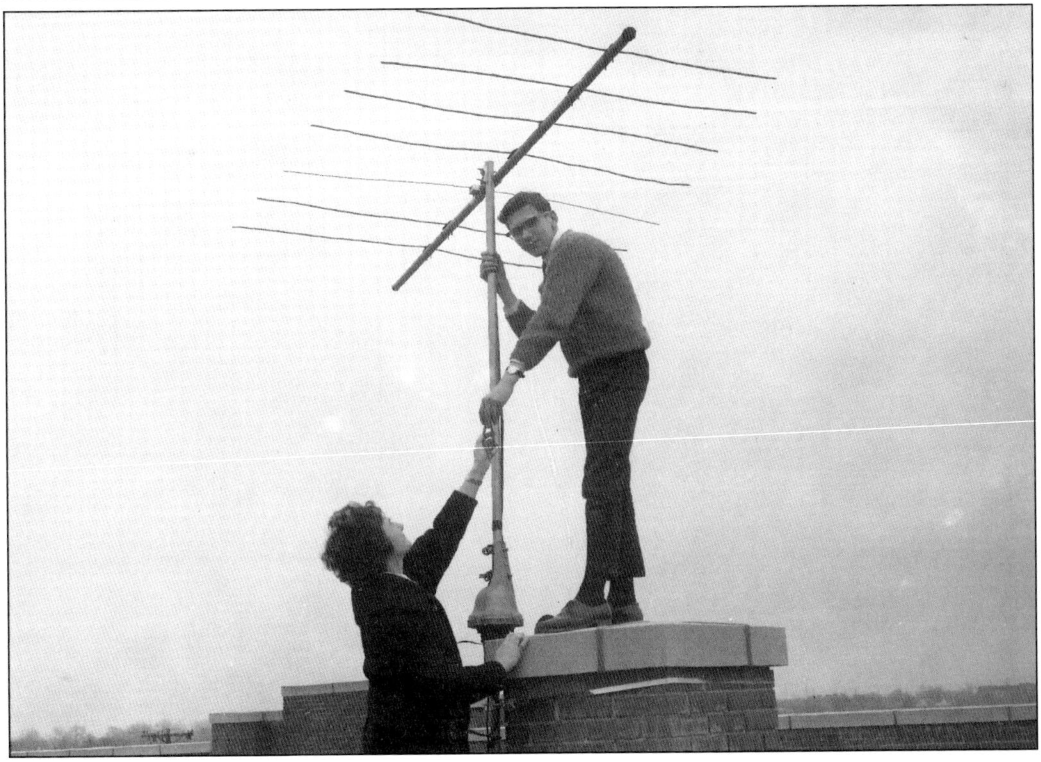

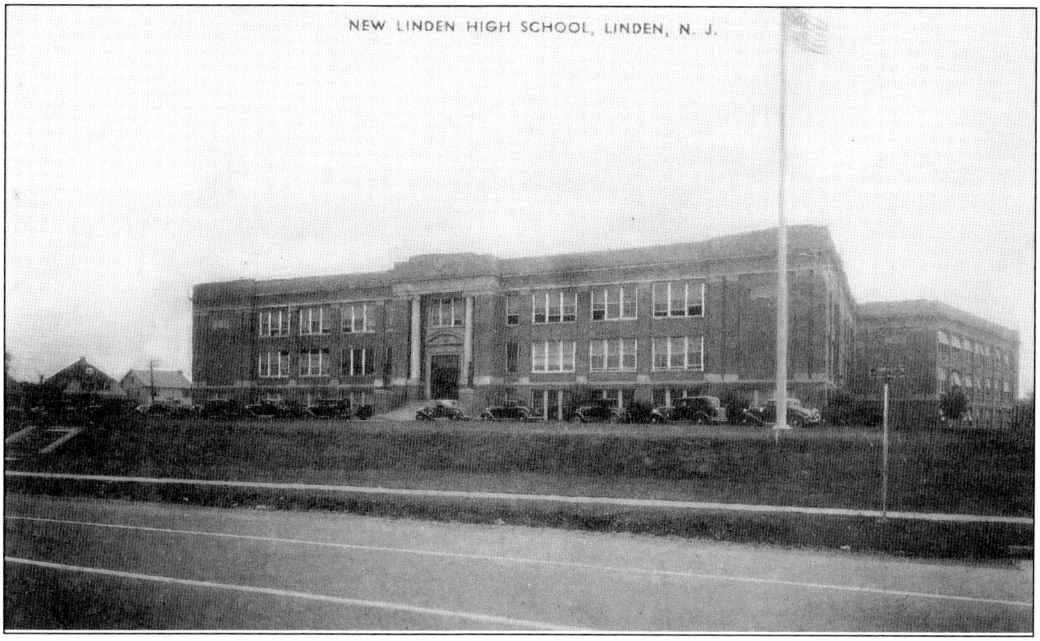

Linden High School, erected in 1925. It is located on St. George Avenue. Two additions to the building came in 1932 and 1961. The Linden Vocational and Technical Building was built across the street in 1971 as part of the high school campus. It is now the Academy of Science.

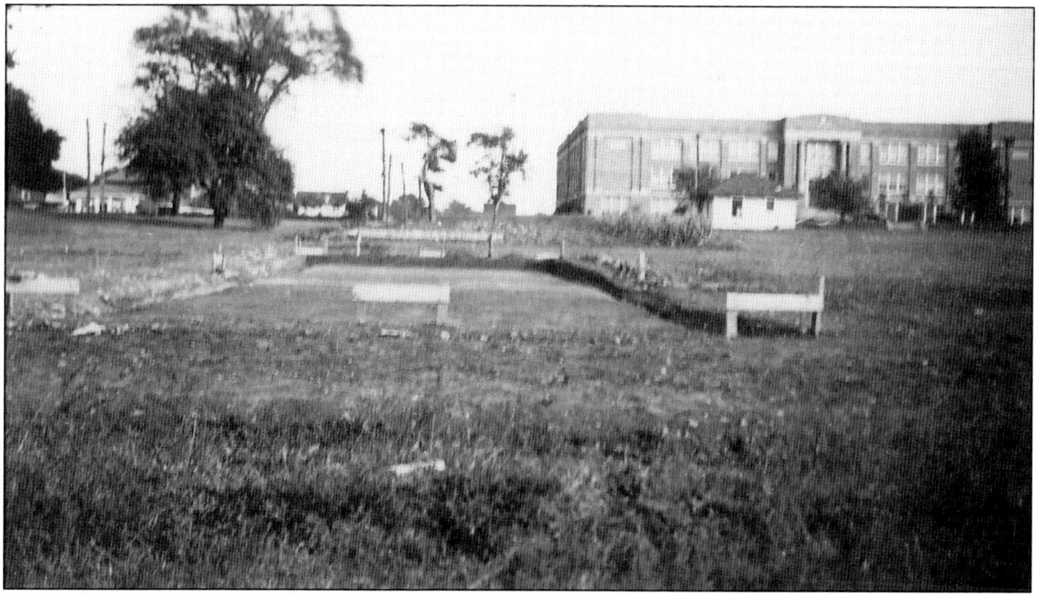

By 1965, the Linden Public School System boasted eleven elementary schools, two junior and one senior high schools. George McGillvray Sr. had dairy farm on St. George Avenue that began from Wood Avenue to DeWitt and as far back as Raritan Road. The Linden Board of Education purchased the homestead property located across from the high school. This image depicts the area before Linden Vocational and Technical School was built in 1971. The property surrounding it is Wilson Park, where the basketball courts are under construction.

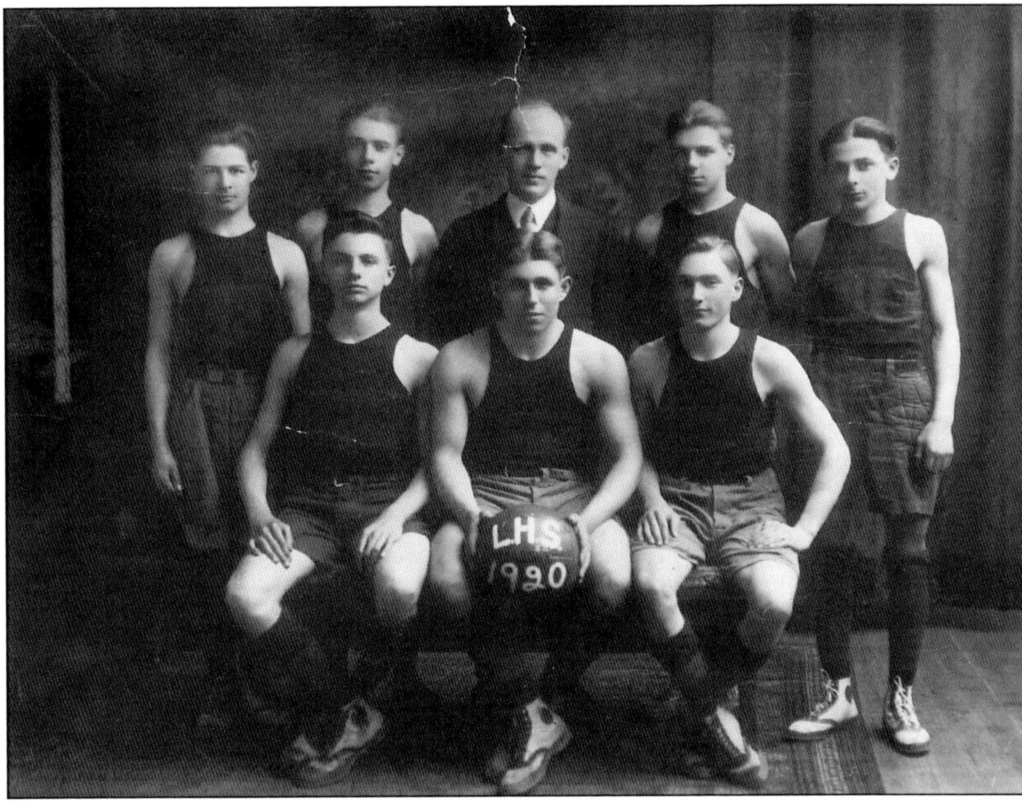

The 1920 Linden High School Basketball Team.

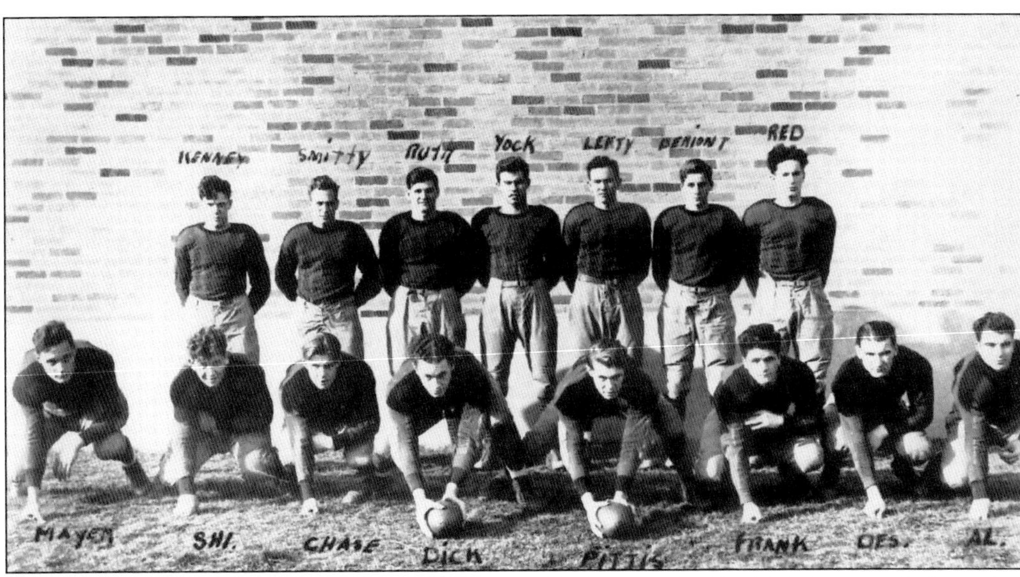

Linden High School's undefeated football team of 1934, coached by Ted Cooper. Ted coached them to an undefeated, not-scored-on, and untied season. Ted Cooper Field was named after him in 1967.

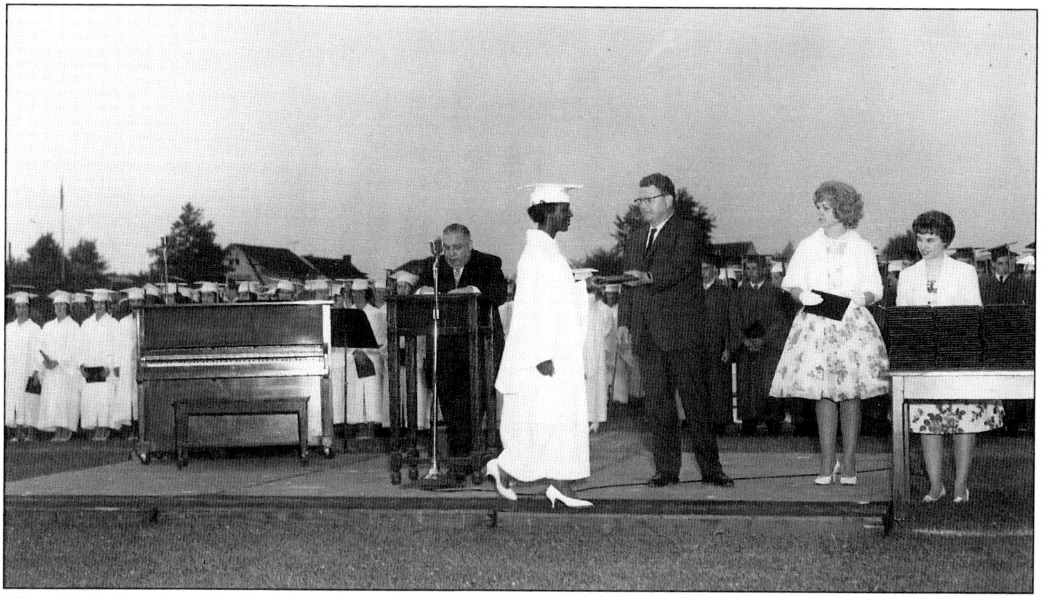

The 1962 Linden High School graduation. Ceremonies were held at the athletic field, which was named Ted Cooper Field in 1967.

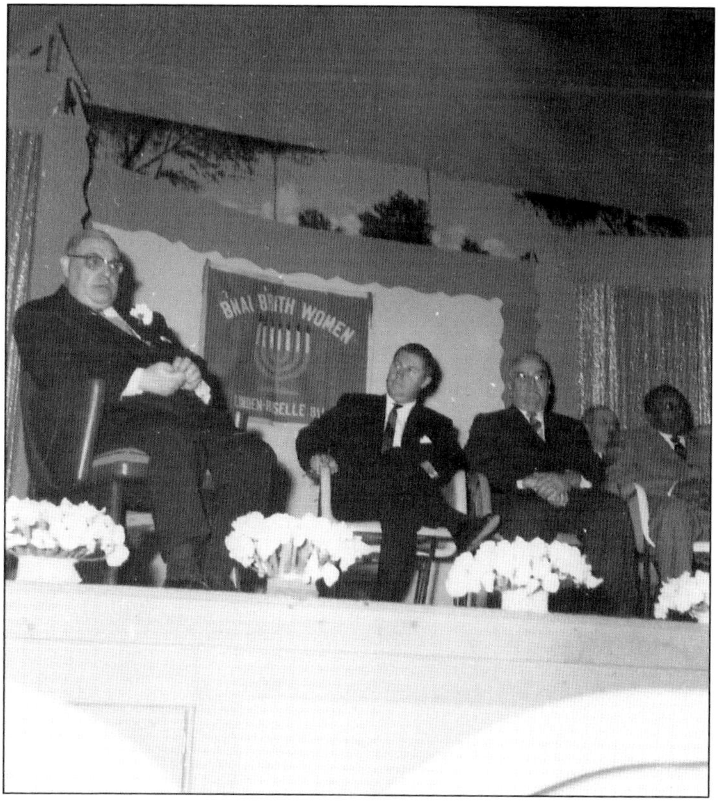

The B'nai Brith Americanism Award, 1959. From left to right are Emanuel Bedrick, James J. O'Brien, Dr. Paul R. Brown, Tom Teagle, and Sam Milberger (at the rear).

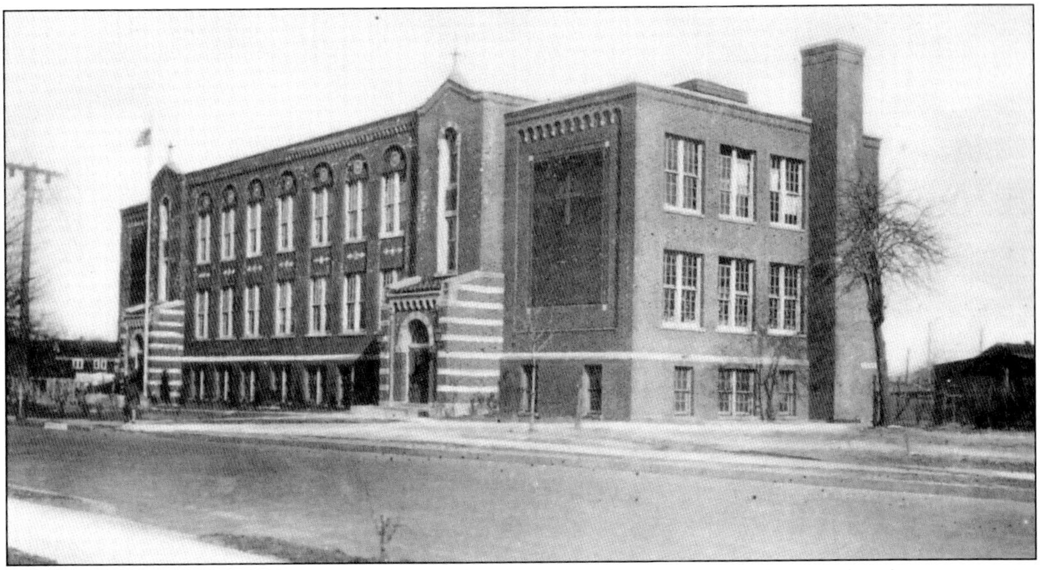

There were three accredited Parochial Schools in Linden, but St. John's School is unique in that the building incorporates the parish church which has its address in Clark. This vintage postcard depicts St. Elizabeth's Parochial School which opened in 1927. It was the brainstorm of Fr. Meinrad Hettinger. Its first teachers were Nuns from the Dominican Order.

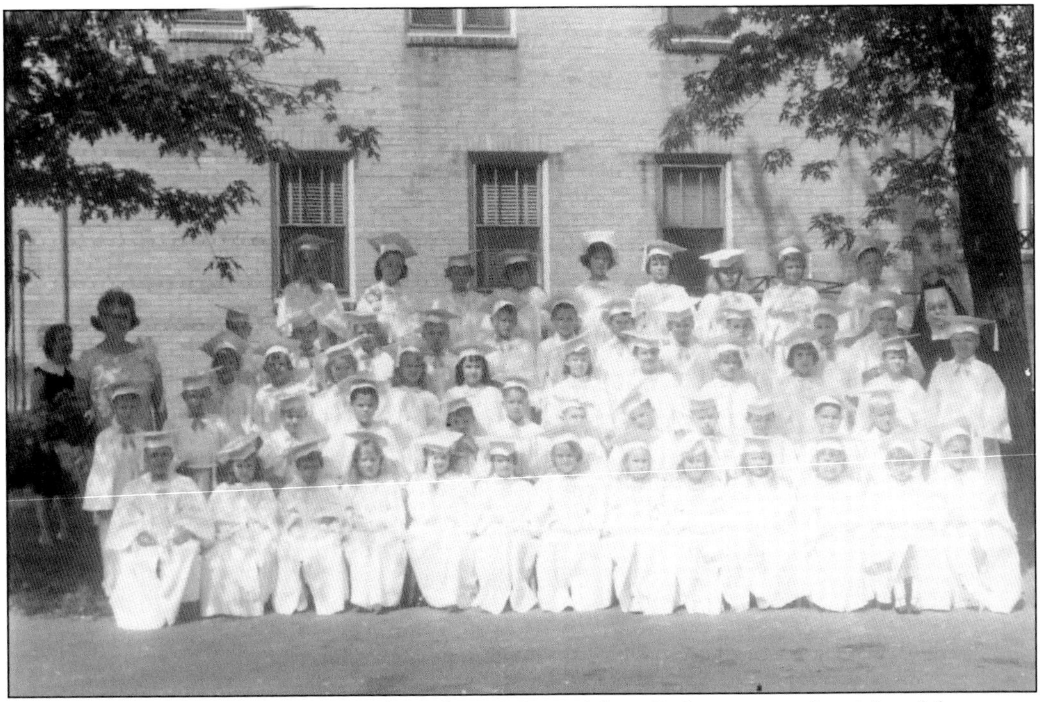

St. Theresa's School kindergarten class of 1966. Sister Mary Gadiouse is to the right of the group. Mrs. Mary Stachowiak, teacher of the fifty-six students, is on the left. The school conducted a full-day program with one teacher.

Seven

Houses of Worship

The original settlers in our area were almost all Puritans. People of many religious denominations immigrated to the new nation of the United States from around the world. As in most ares, people would gather at one anothers homes of for services at first. As the population of each group grew, buildings to hold the large crowds became a necessity.

Each house of worship has its own unique history. This chapter will show some of the many religious groups that are in existence in Linden today.

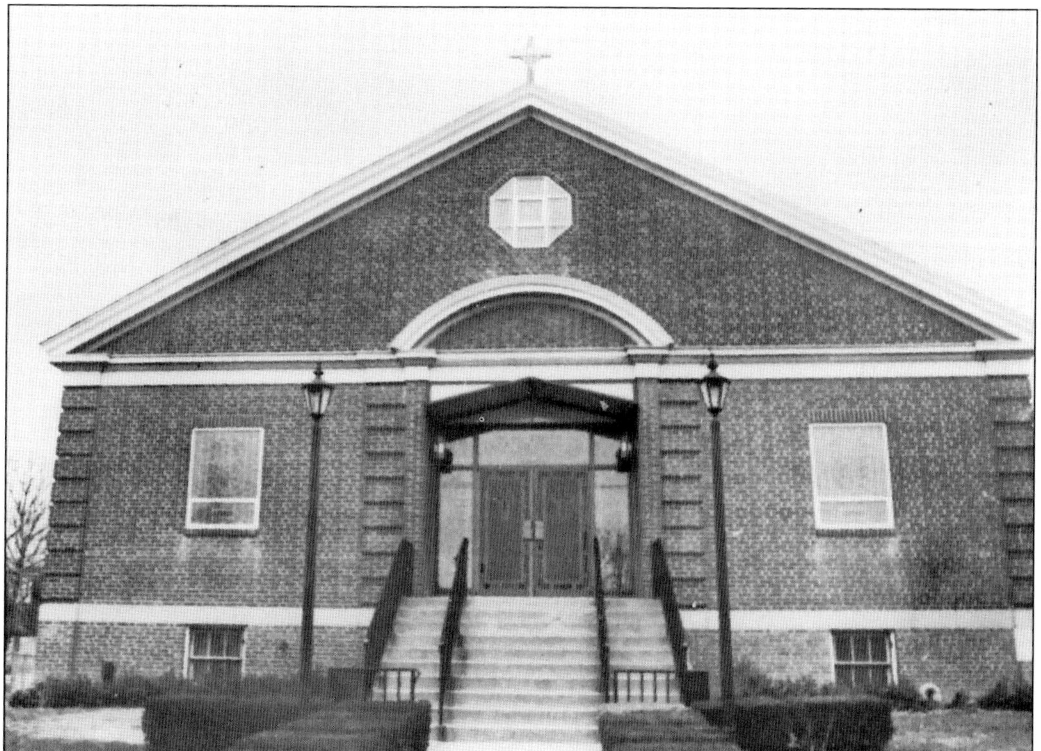

Prior to 1940, the parish of Holy Family Roman Catholic Church began having mass said by a priest from St. Joseph's in Elizabeth, in the community building then owned by DuPont. The church pictured was erected as a community center at Monroe and Parkway Streets. It became a mission church of St. Joseph's. In 1955, Fr. Komar came to Holy Family full time and made renovations so it more resembled a church. In 1956, the church was incorporated. In 1958, the parish bought the community building from DuPont. It is now named for Fr. Komar.

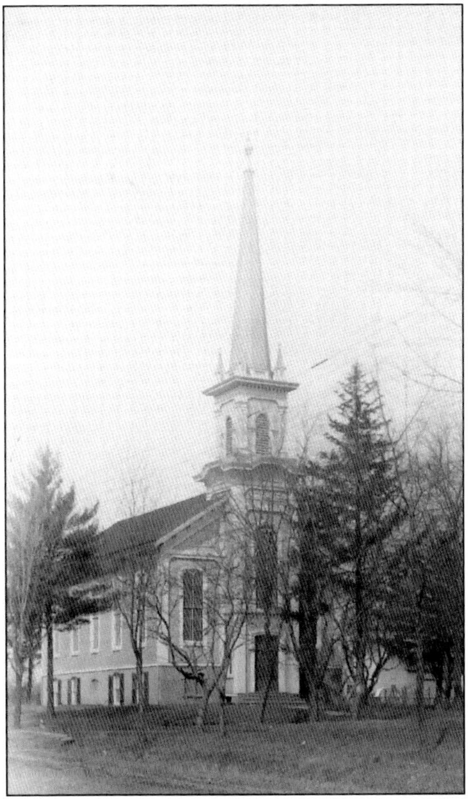

The Reformed Church of Linden is the oldest church building currently being used in the city. The cornerstone was laid in 1871 on land deeded to the congregation by Ferdinand Blancke.

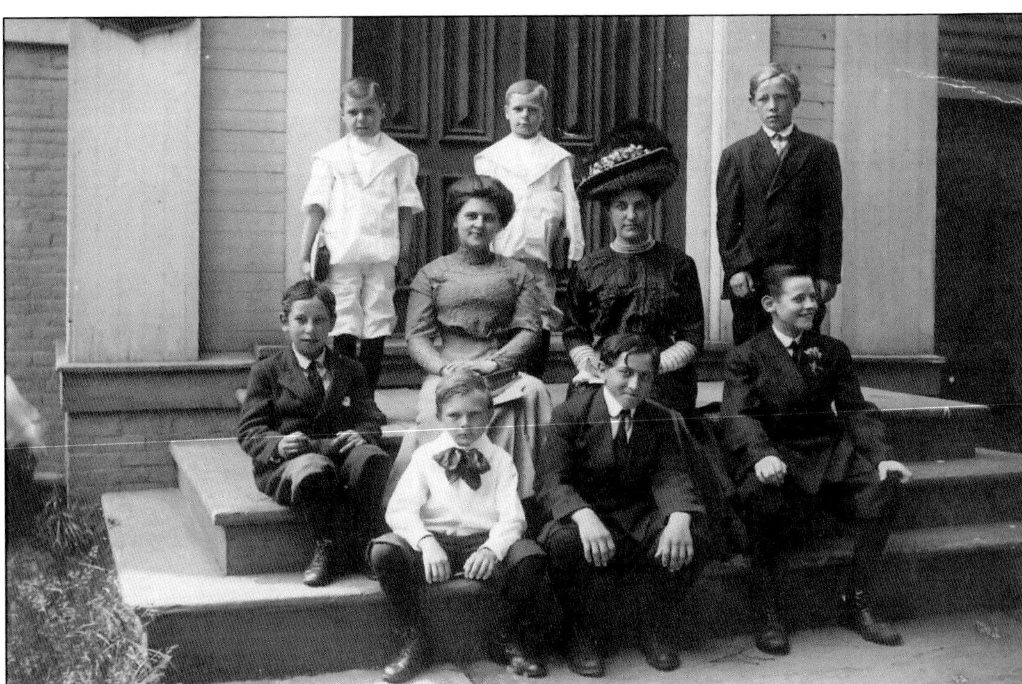

The Reformed Church of Linden, Sunday, June 7, 1912.

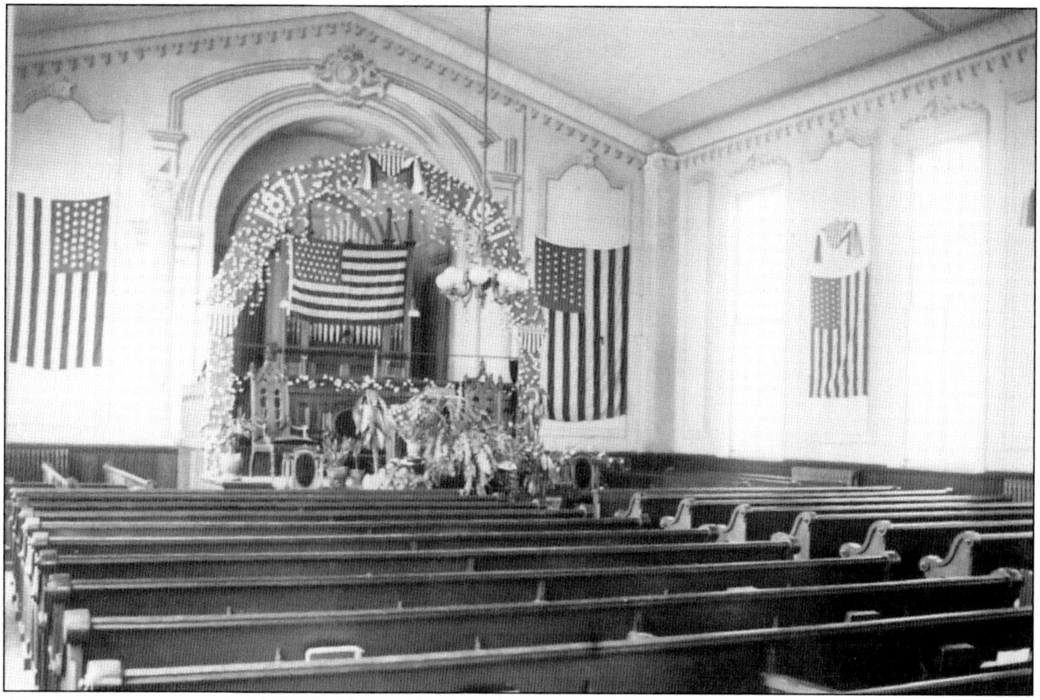

The 40th anniversary of the Reformed Church of Linden in 1911.

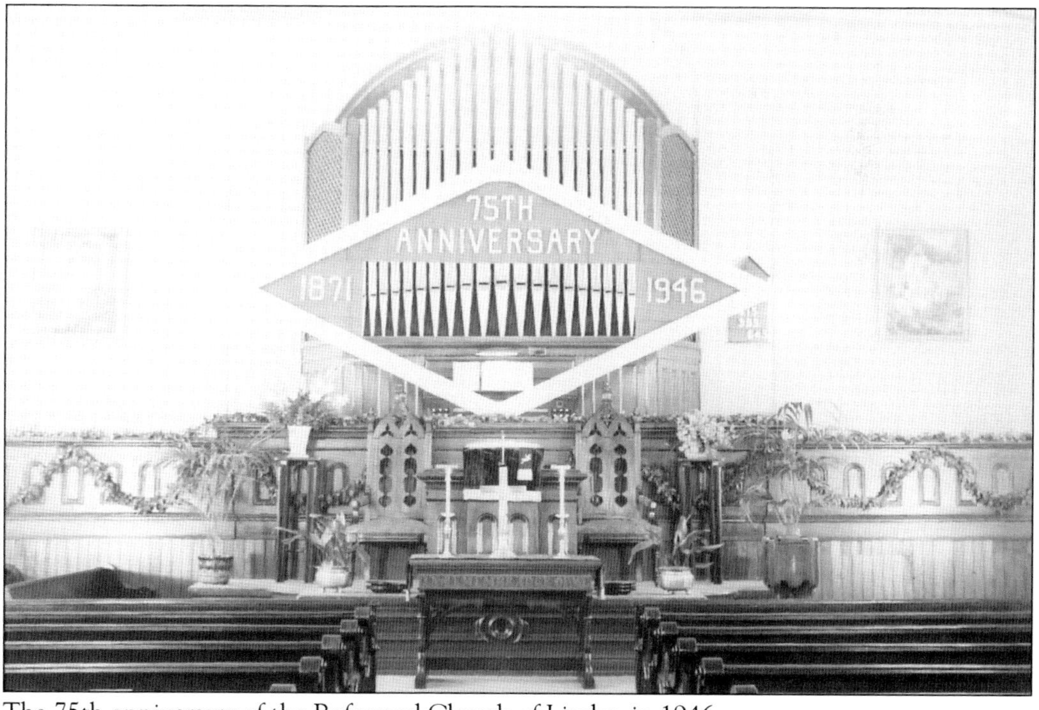

The 75th anniversary of the Reformed Church of Linden in 1946.

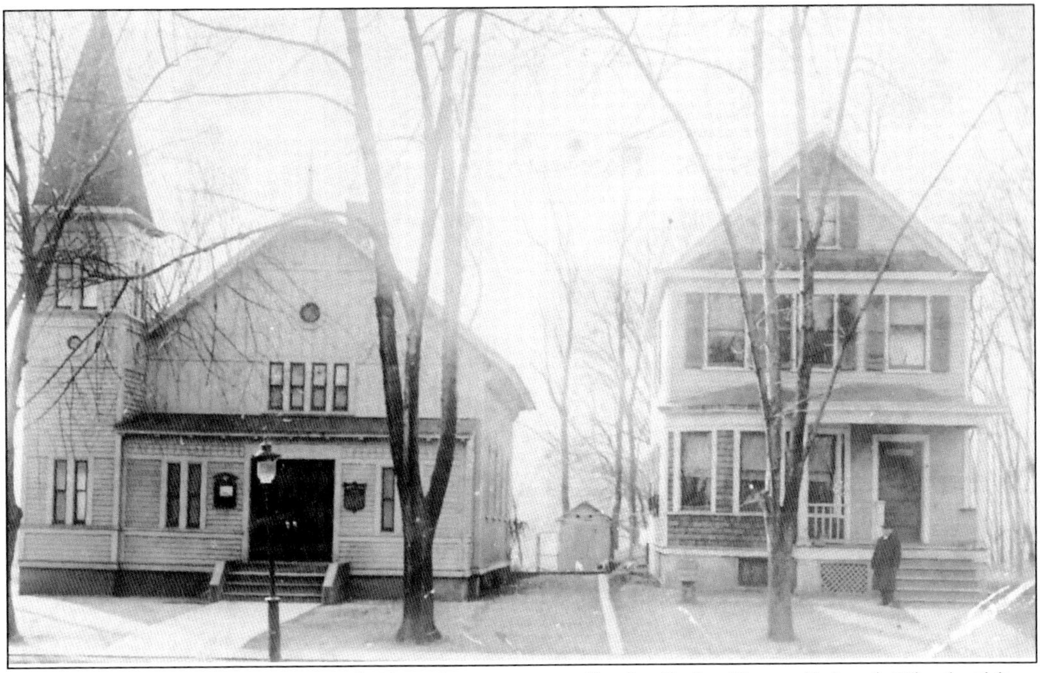

The Linden Methodist Episcopal Church was originally the Stiles Street School. The building was dedicated on April 3, 1870.

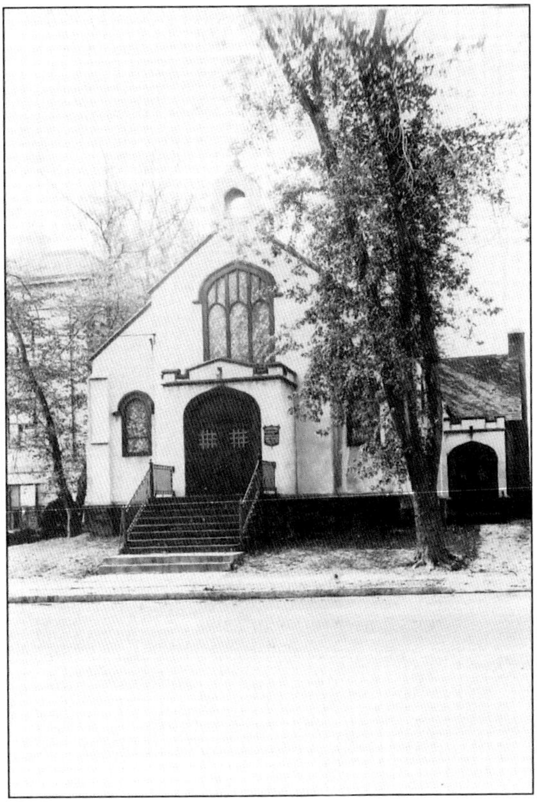

The Linden Methodist Church. The congregation is the oldest religious group in the city, established in 1866. They purchased the old schoolhouse on North Stiles Street from Mr. Blancke and dedicated it in 1874. It was known as the Linden Methodist Episcopal Church. This is the Linden United Methodist Church, presently located at 321 North Wood Avenue.

The Grace Episcopal Church, Washington and Elm Streets. The first marriage to take place in the church was that of Fred Blancke and Isabel Langley. The building was razed in 1967. The current home of the church is on DeWitt Terrace.

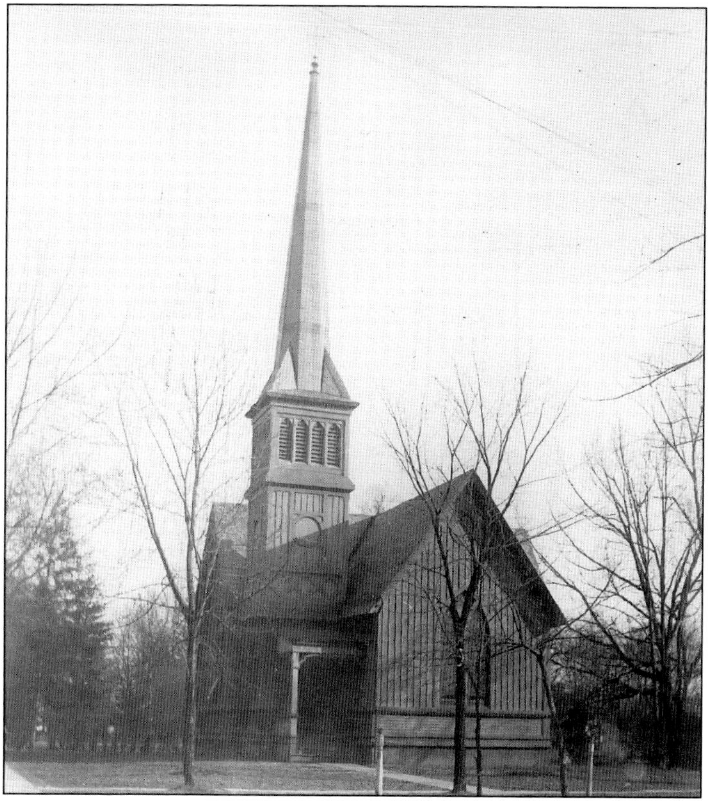

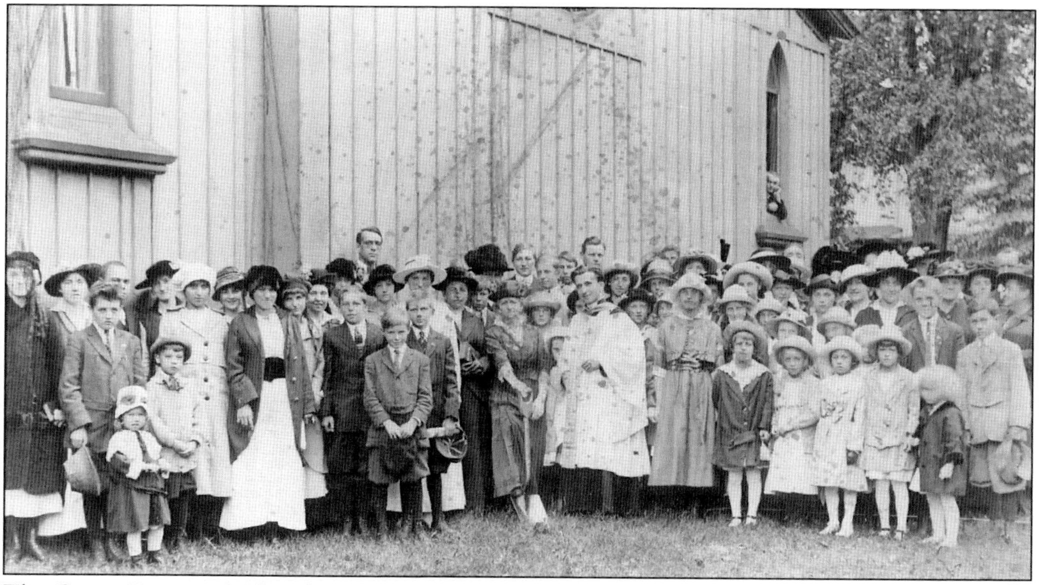

The Grace Episcopal Church traces back to 1870. This building was on West Linden Avenue. It was moved to the corner of East Elm Street and Washington Avenue in 1887.

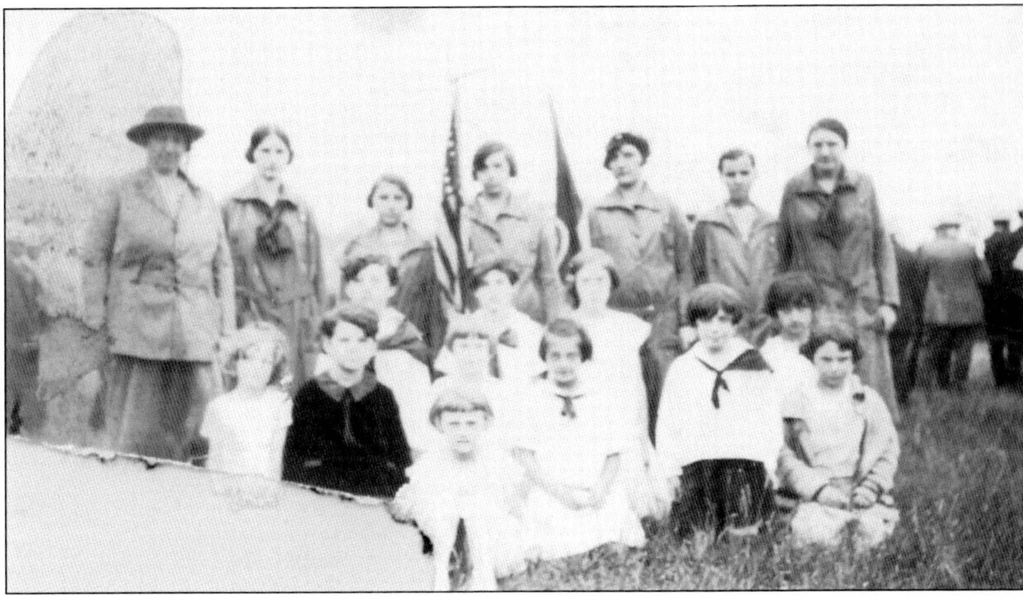

The first Pansy Girl Scout Troop, c. 1920. Eleanor Rogers, Mable Rogers, Ruth Miska, Christina Hauswald, Adelaid De Page, Madeline Page, and Aurore Frank are shown here. The young ladies met at the Methodist Episcopalian Church.

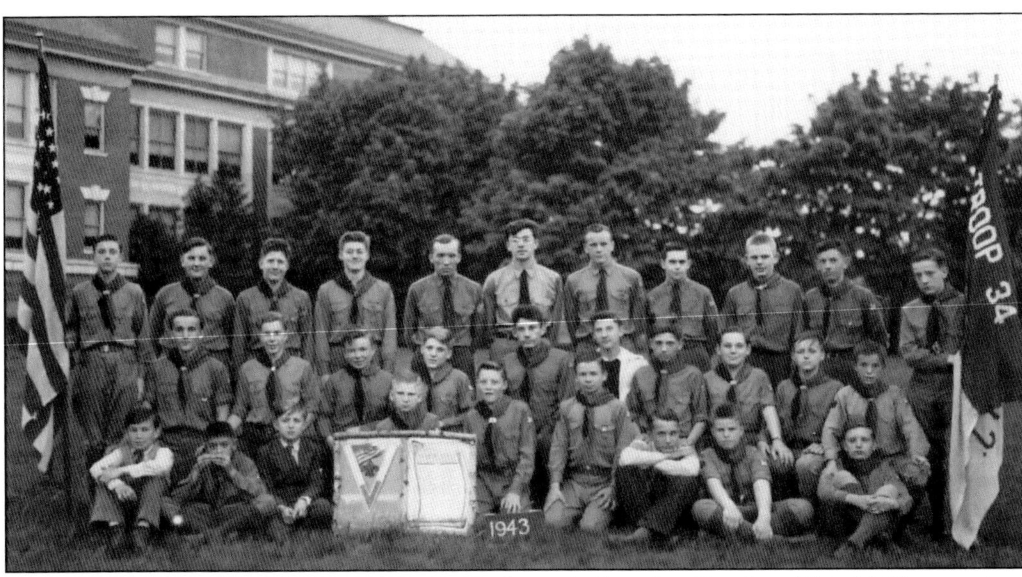

Boy Scout Troop No. 34, sponsored by the Reformed Church of Linden. This 1943 group is on the lawn of School No. 1.

From left to right are (front row) Charles Kehrer and Frank Amon; (back row) Anton Amon, William Kovacs, unknown, Mike Hubert, and Louis Hergert.

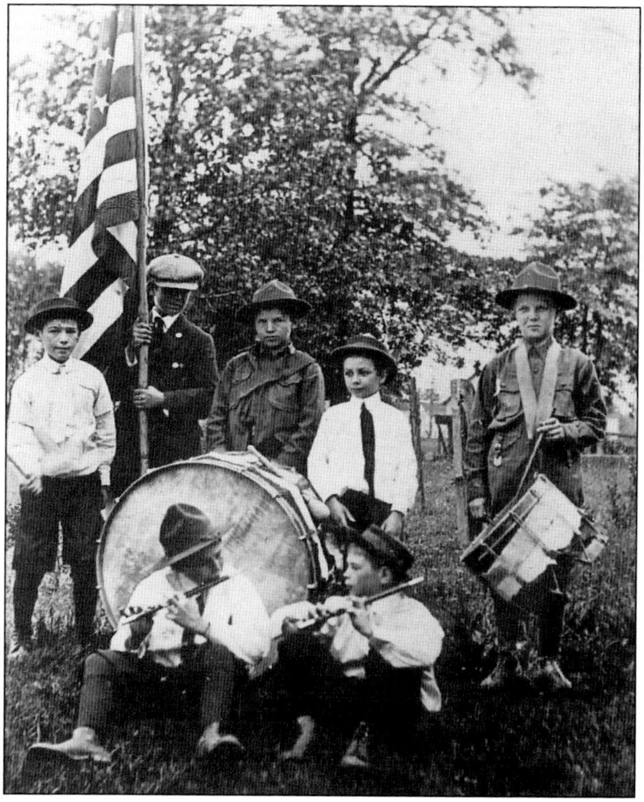

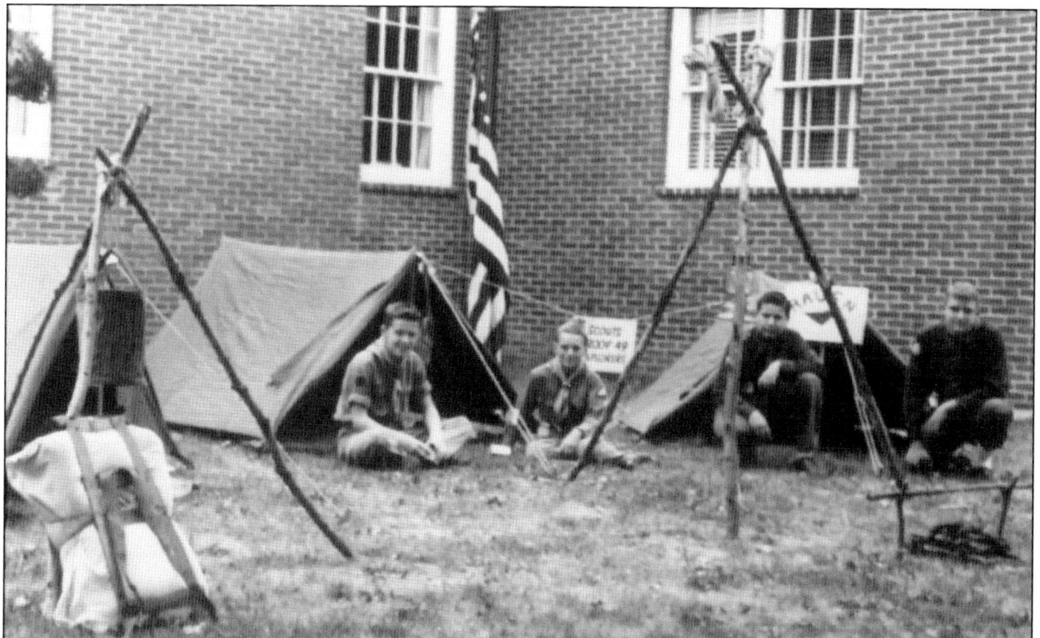

The Linden Presbyterian Church Boy Scout Troop No. 49 camping outdoors.

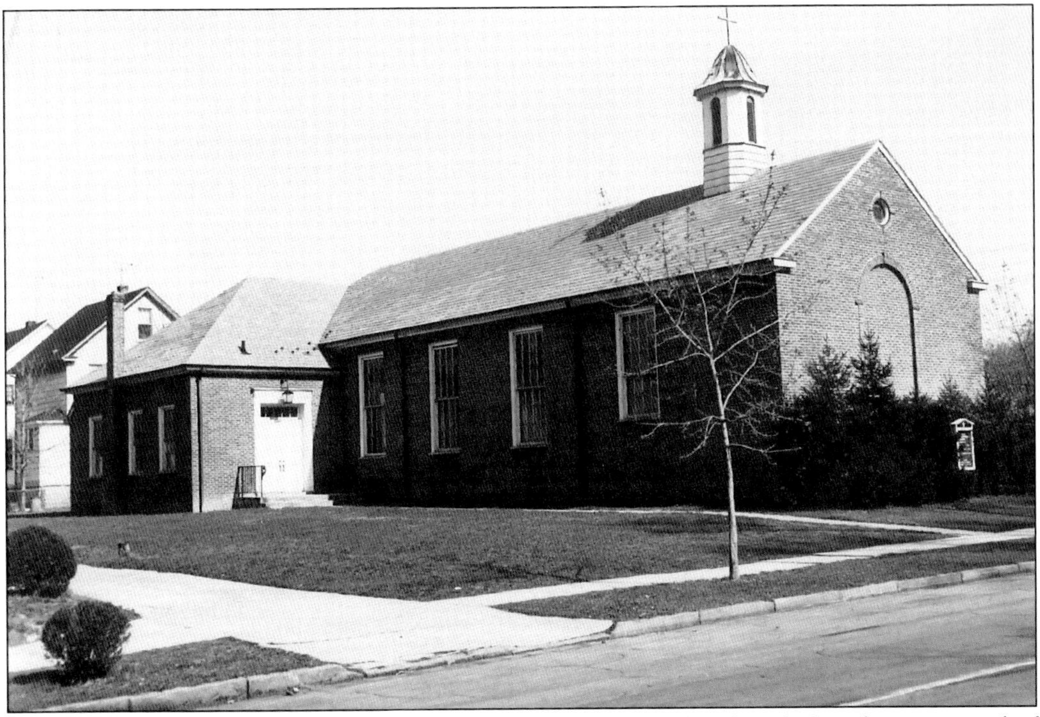

St. Paul's Evangelical Lutheran Church, organized in 1928. The church founders consisted of members of twenty primarily German families. The church building was erected in 1938 on the corner of East Elm Street and Moore Place.

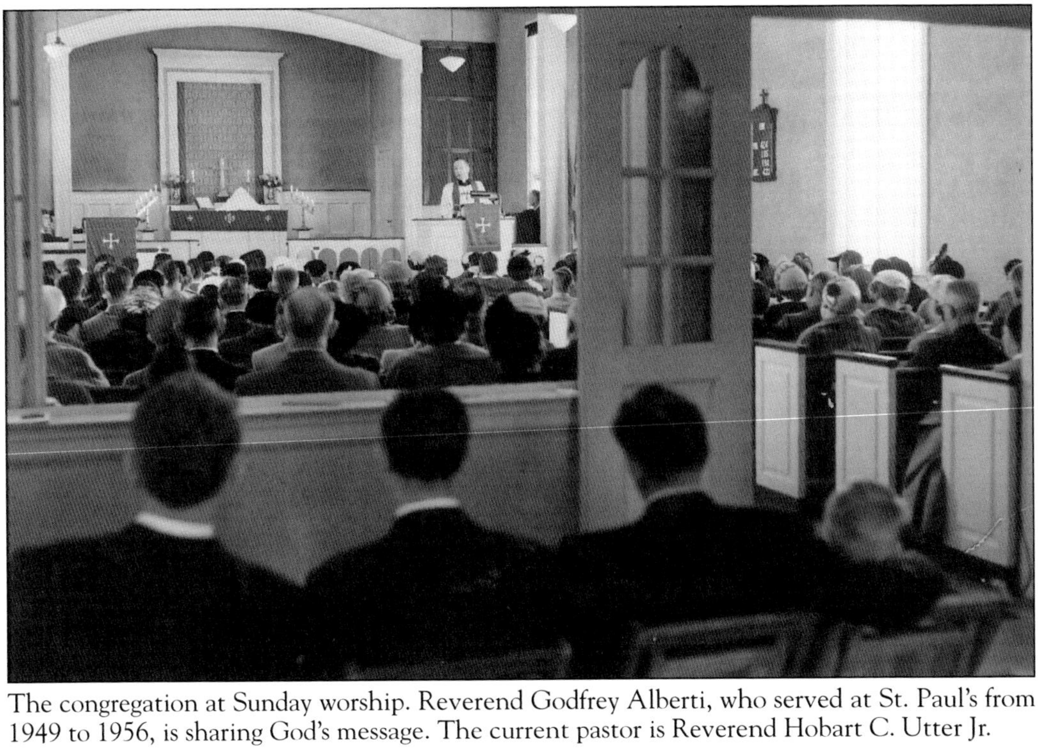

The congregation at Sunday worship. Reverend Godfrey Alberti, who served at St. Paul's from 1949 to 1956, is sharing God's message. The current pastor is Reverend Hobart C. Utter Jr.

The parish of St. Elizabeth's began in a storefront in 1909 on West Blancke Street. The original St. Elizabeth's Church was a wooden structure and was dedicated in 1912. It then housed the church CYO activities. It was located on the site of the current parking lot for the new church (pictured here). This church was built in 1952 and is located on East Blancke Street.

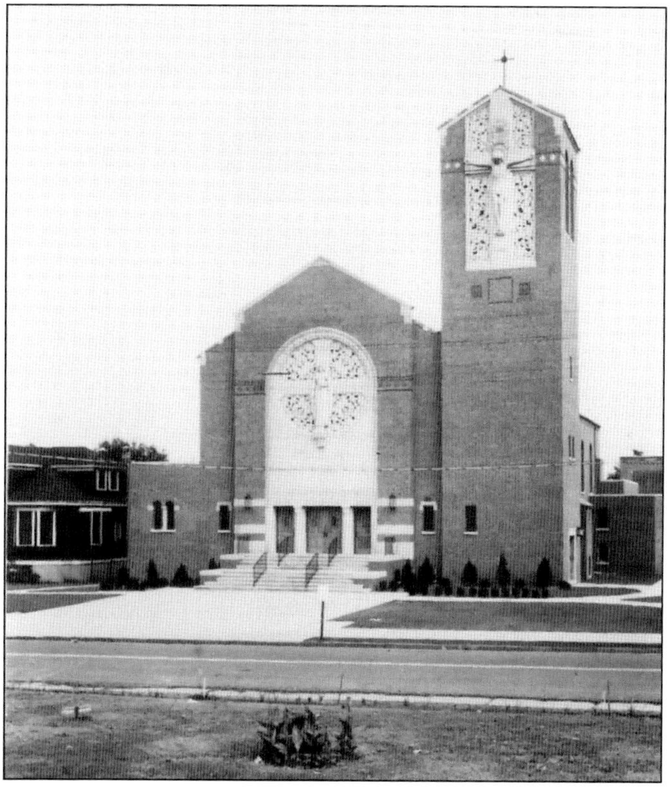

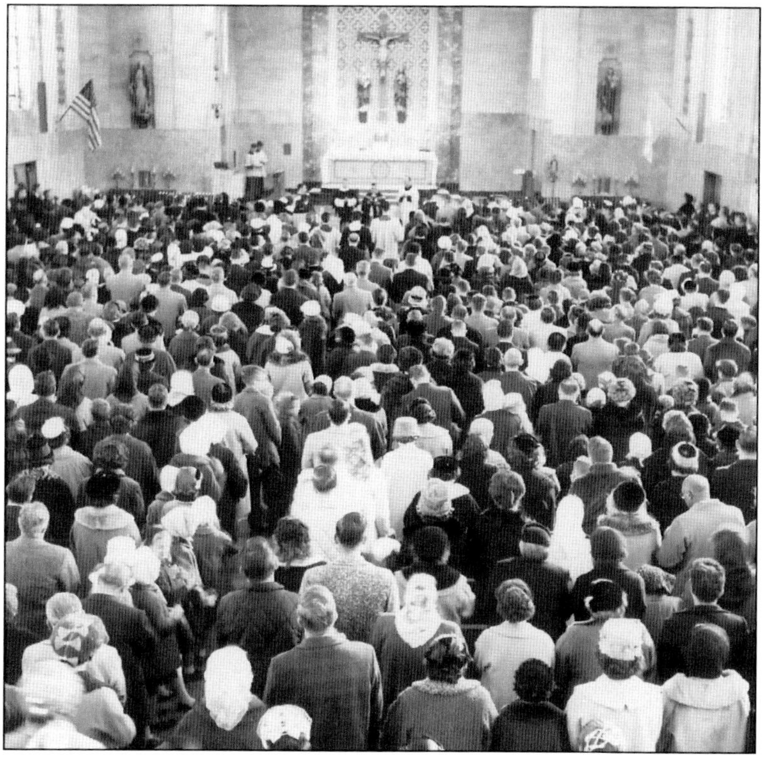

A Mass at St. Elizabeth's Church mourning the death of President John Fitzgerald Kennedy. It was a very sad time for Americans. Many looked for spiritual comfort at this memorial from Linden.

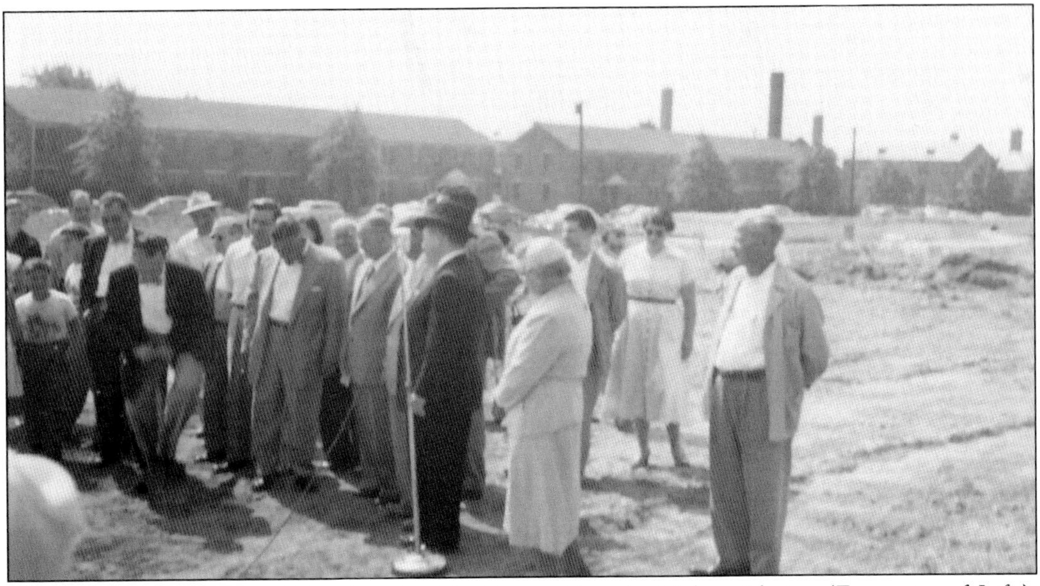

Groundbreaking for the Suburban Jewish Center-Temple Mekor Chaim (Fountain of Life), August 23, 1953.

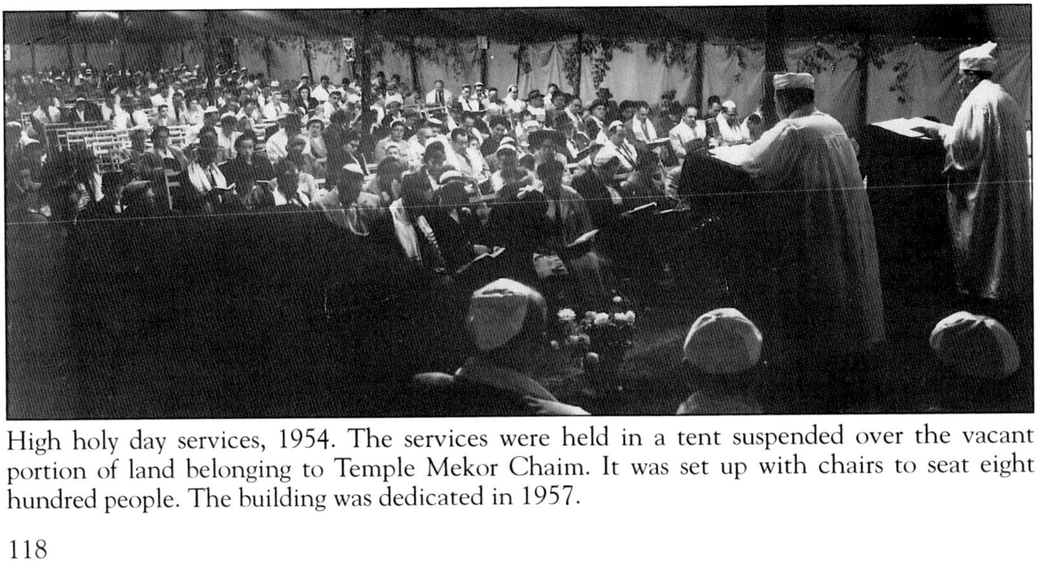

High holy day services, 1954. The services were held in a tent suspended over the vacant portion of land belonging to Temple Mekor Chaim. It was set up with chairs to seat eight hundred people. The building was dedicated in 1957.

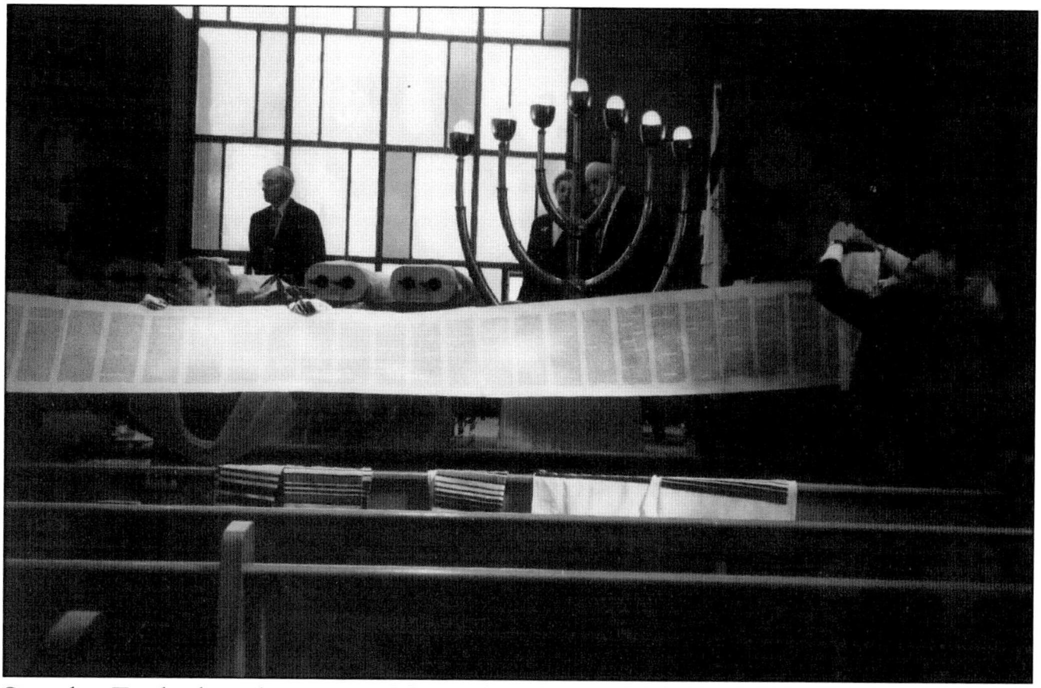

Siamchas Torah, the culmination of the reading of the Torah.

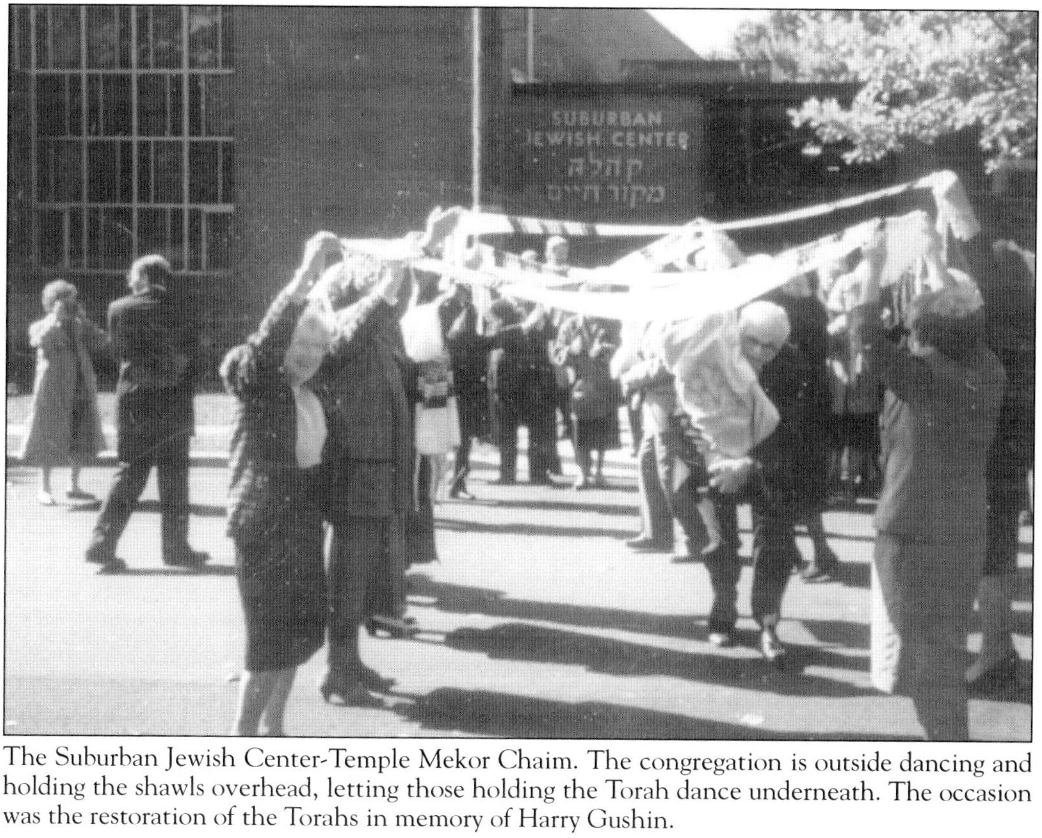

The Suburban Jewish Center-Temple Mekor Chaim. The congregation is outside dancing and holding the shawls overhead, letting those holding the Torah dance underneath. The occasion was the restoration of the Torahs in memory of Harry Gushin.

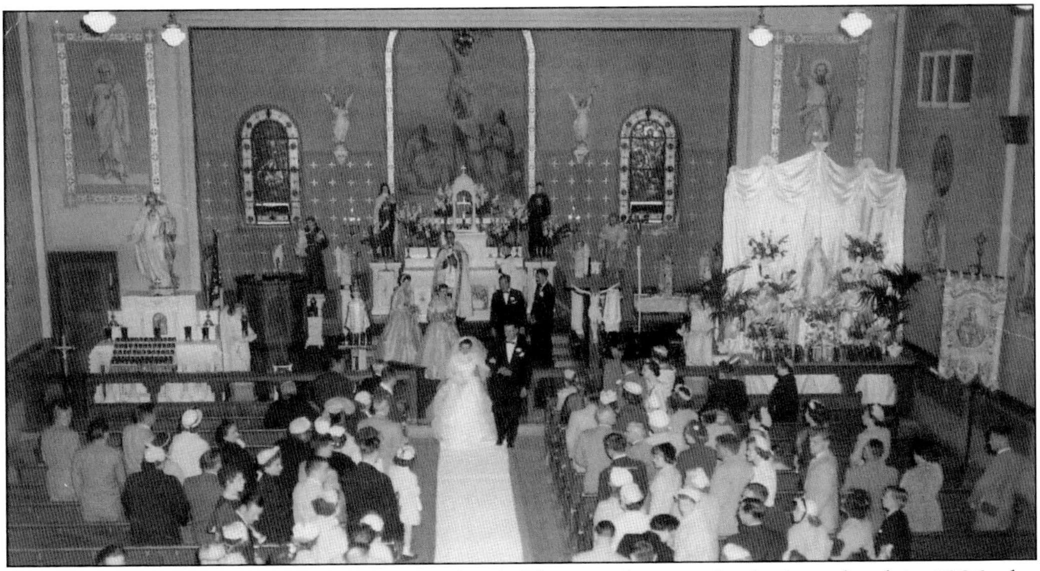

The Saint Theresa of the Child Jesus School. The parishioners built the school in 1926; the church was housed in what is now the school auditorium. The cornerstone of the present church was laid in 1954. This photograph was taken on May 8, 1955, at the wedding of Mary and Joseph Bodek Sr. Bridesmaids are Theresa Kowalski and Viola Bodek. Groomsmen are Joseph Pavelek and Joseph Zaremba. Father Miller was officiating.

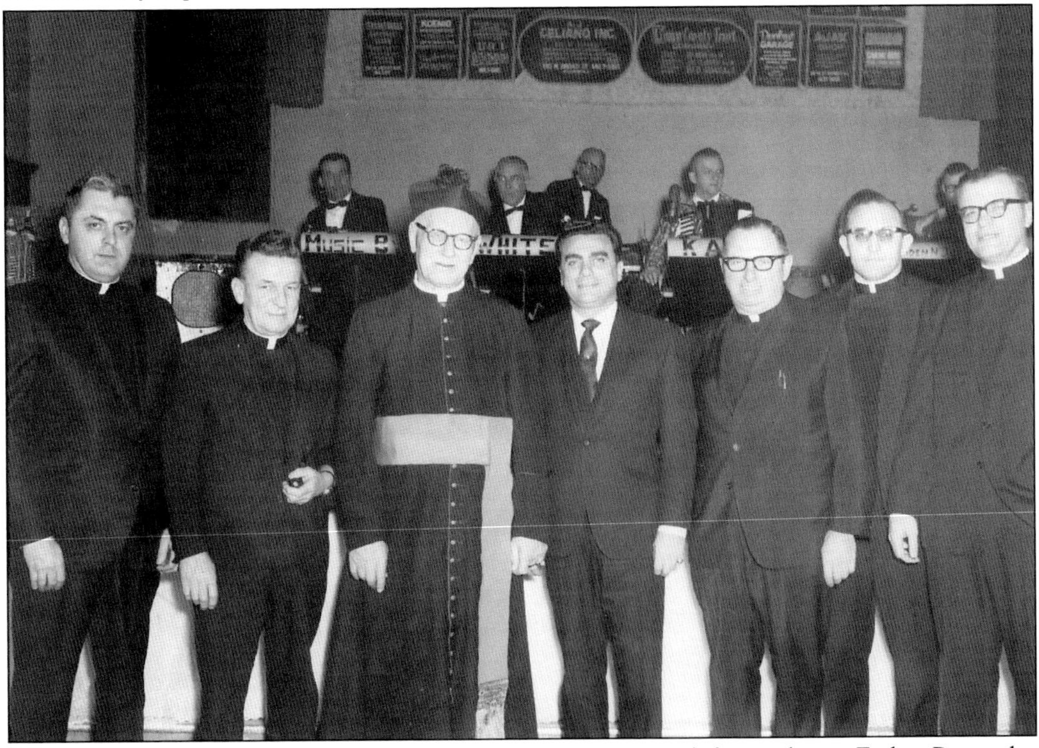

A time of celebration at St. Theresa's School Auditorium. From left to right are Father Piacinski, Father Chester Midowski, Monsignor Stanislans Stachowiak, Mayor John T. Gregorio, Father Fred Miller, Father John Smith, and Father Lukenda.

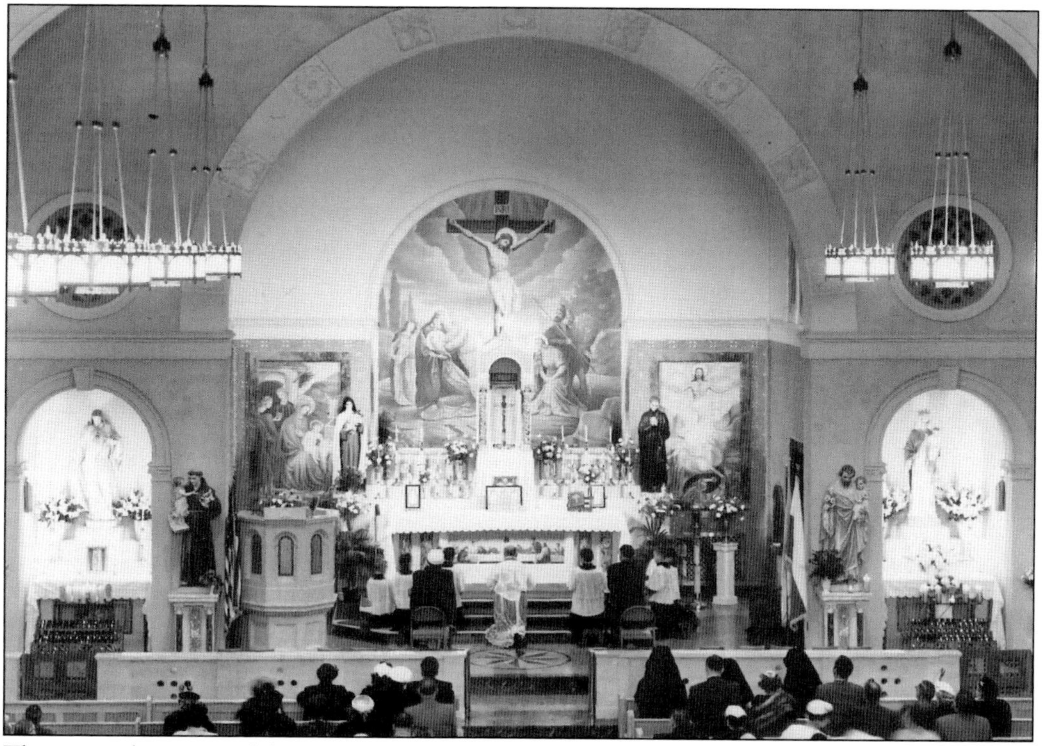

The original interior of the Saint Theresa of the Child Jesus Church, 1959.

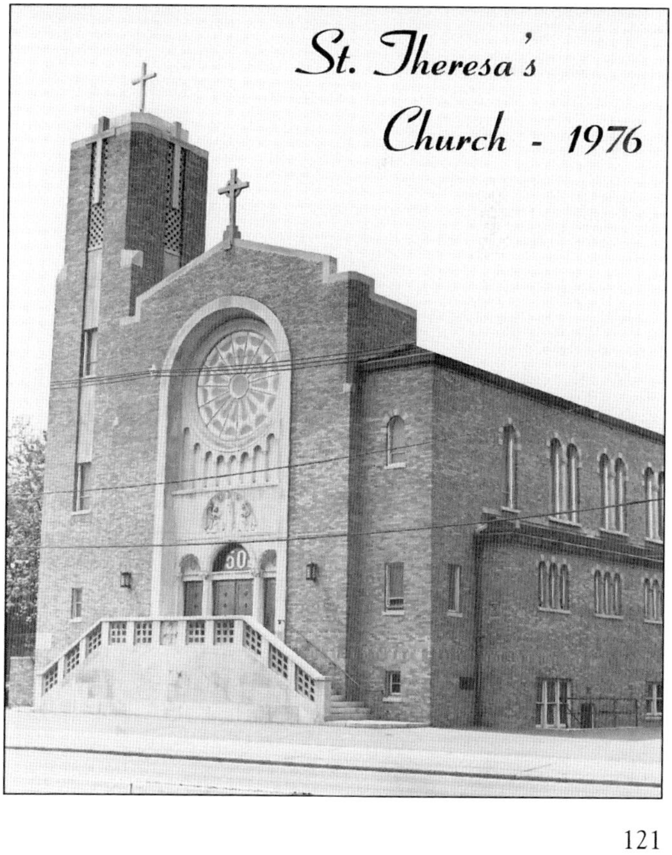

St. Theresa's Church. The cornerstone for the building was set in 1954, and it was completed in 1955. The building has seen many changes to date. This is the original exterior of the church.

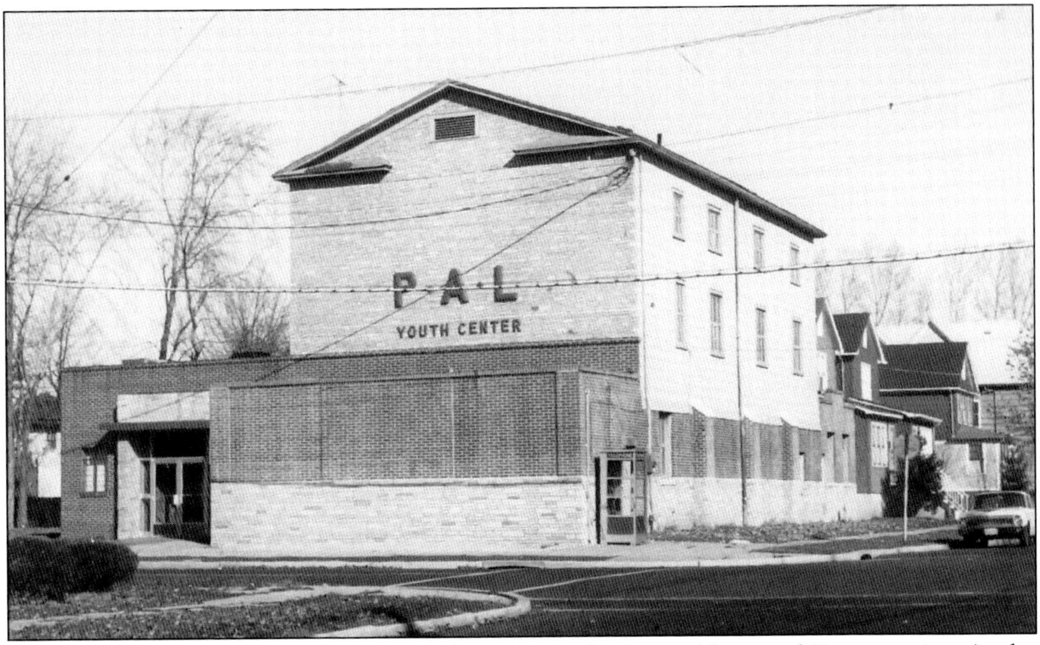

The Linden Police Athletic League Building. It was the original home of Congregation Anshe Chesed. It was constructed in 1921 at the corner of Maple Avenue and Blancke Street.

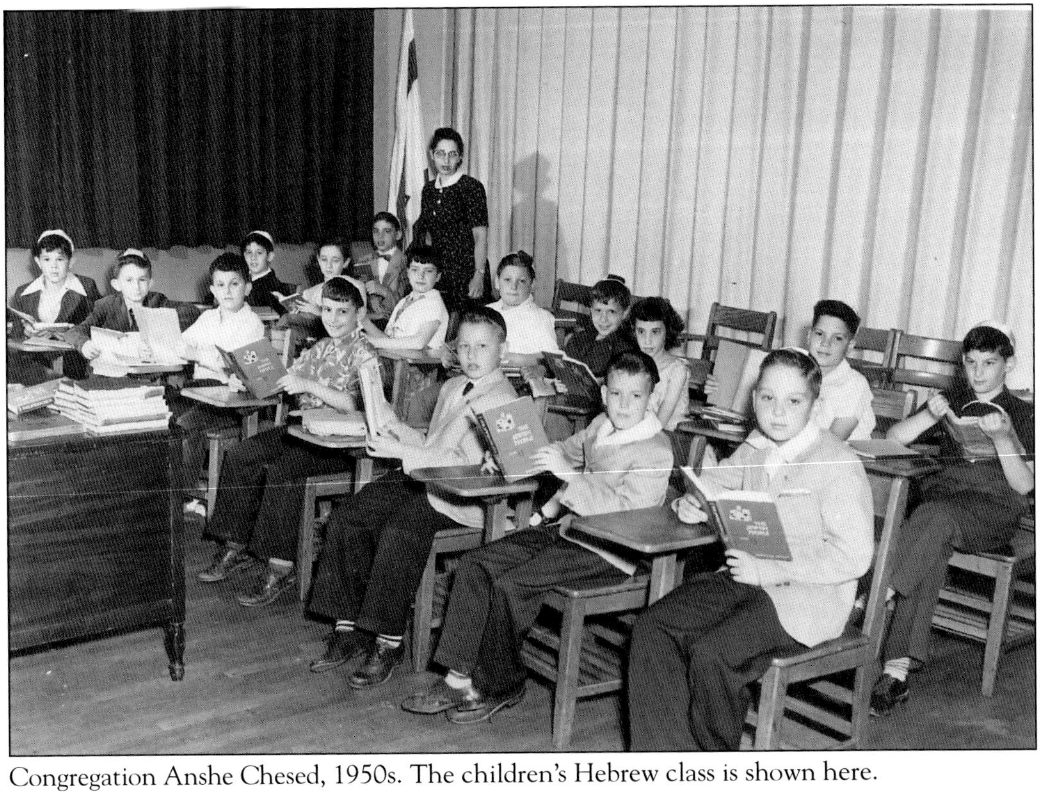

Congregation Anshe Chesed, 1950s. The children's Hebrew class is shown here.

Congregation Anshe Chesed. Rabbi Aaron Shapiro and Rabbi Morris Baikofsky are in front of the beautiful stained-glass windows.

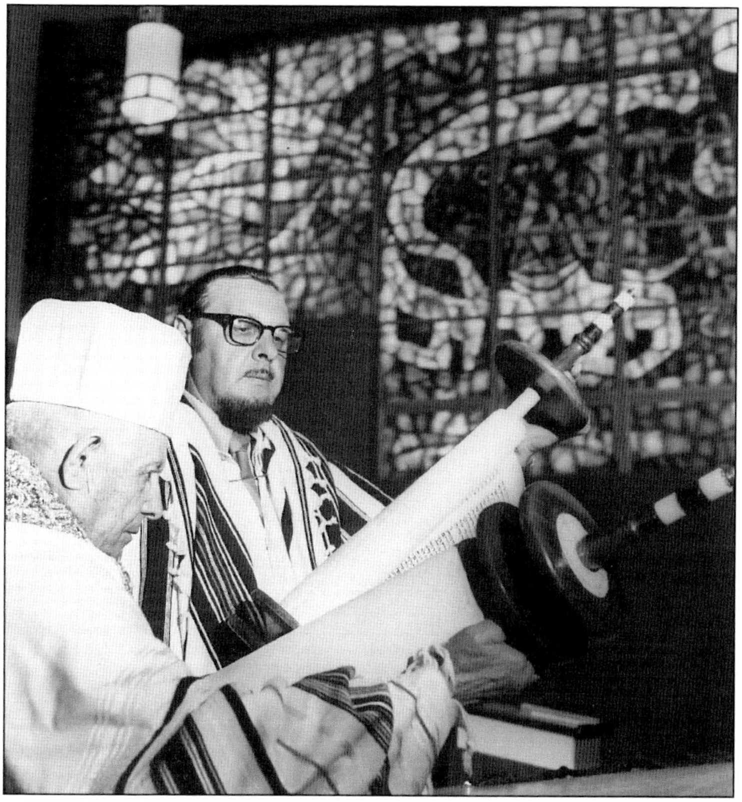

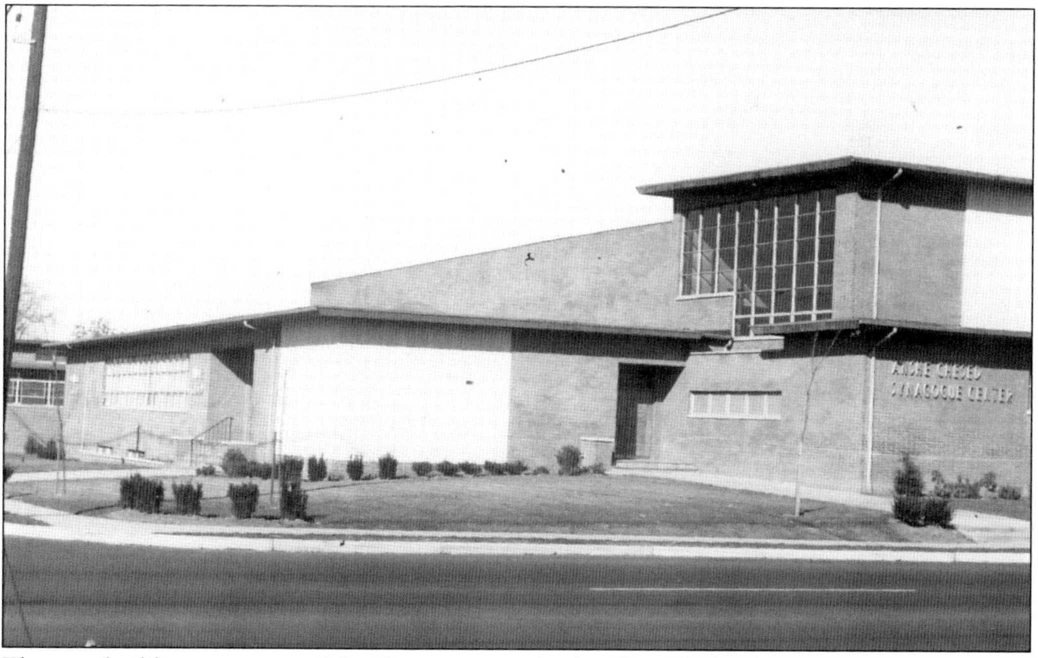

The new building constructed for Congregation Anshe Chesed. At the time, it was considered to be the largest and most complete traditional orthodox facility in the state. It is located at the corner of Orchard Terrace and St. George Avenue.

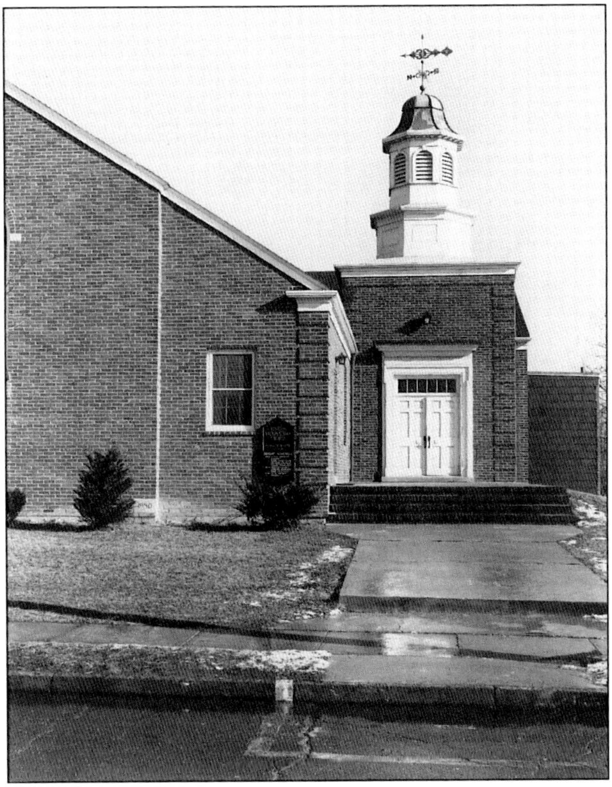

The Linden Presbyterian Church is located at the corner of Princeton Road and Orchard Terrace. The front door of the church is shown here prior to the groundbreaking of its church school, which would be to the right of the door and the wheelchair access ramp at the stairway. The hall in the education wing was dedicated to Reverend Kenneth E. Walter. The current pastor is Reverend Dr. William Weaver.

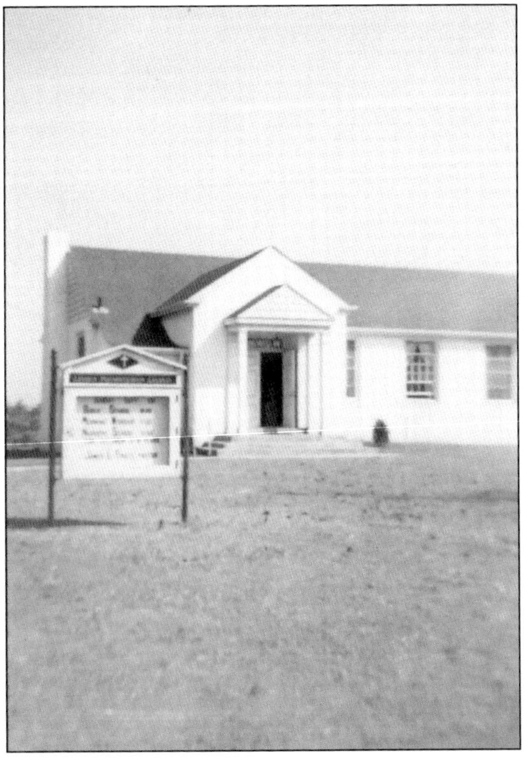

The congregation of the Linden Presbyterian Church held their first meetings of worship in the small community house at Wilson Park, and then moved to the present location. This photograph was taken in 1941, before the addition of the new Sanctuary. It was dedicated to Reverend James Ewalt, the first pastor of the church.

The St. George Byzantine Catholic Church at McCandless and Blancke Streets. The church was built in 1923 and was razed in 1959. On the same land, the new St. George Church was built in 1960.

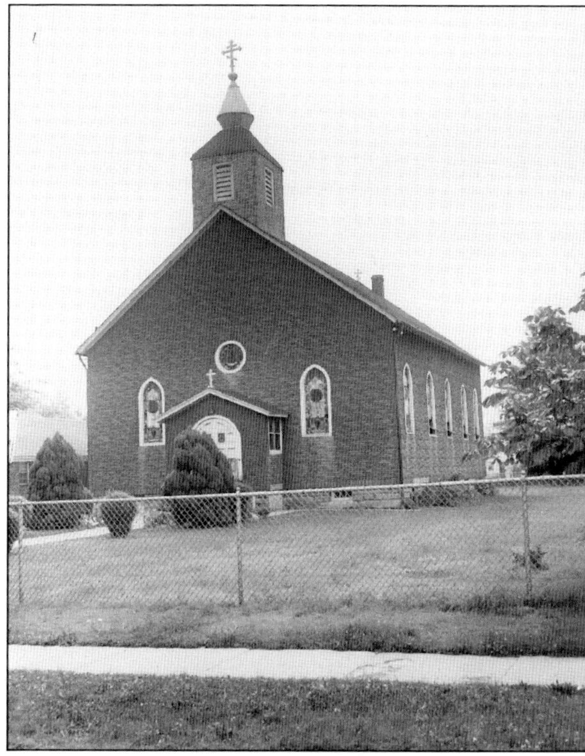

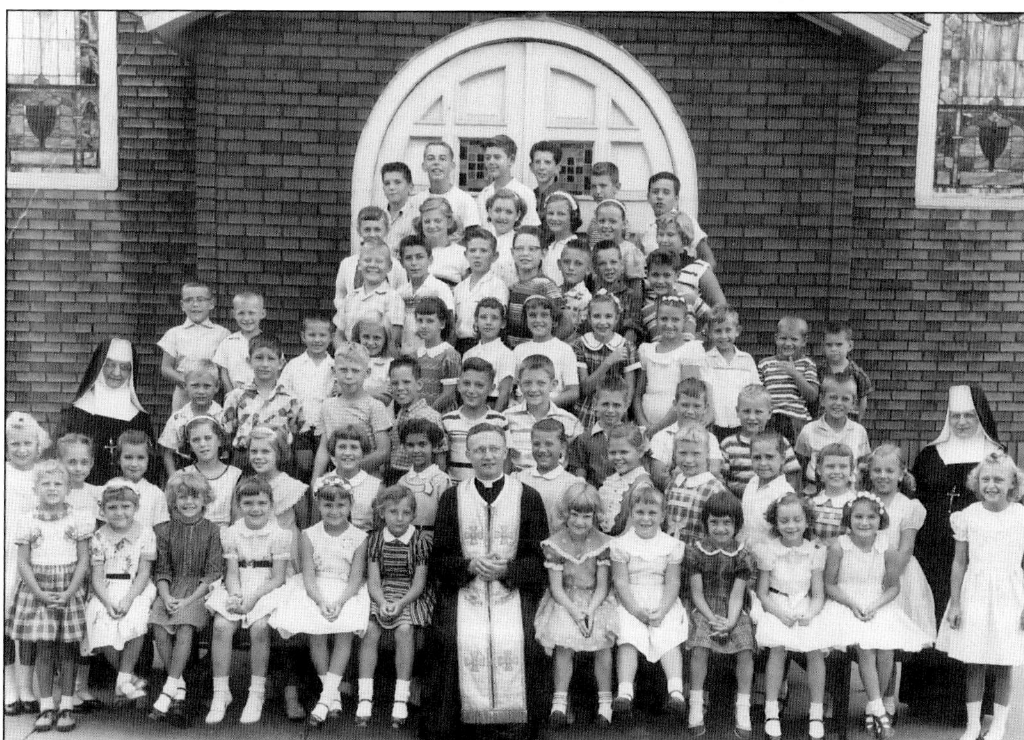

Father George Billy sitting among the Sunday school classes of 1957.

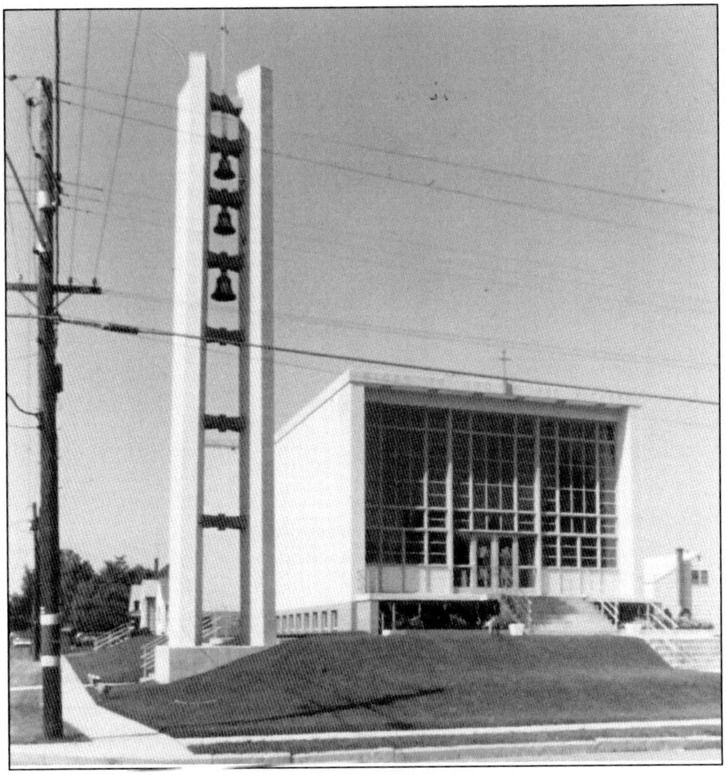

The new St. George Byzantine Church, built in 1960. It is still standing at the present location of Blancke and McCandless Streets.

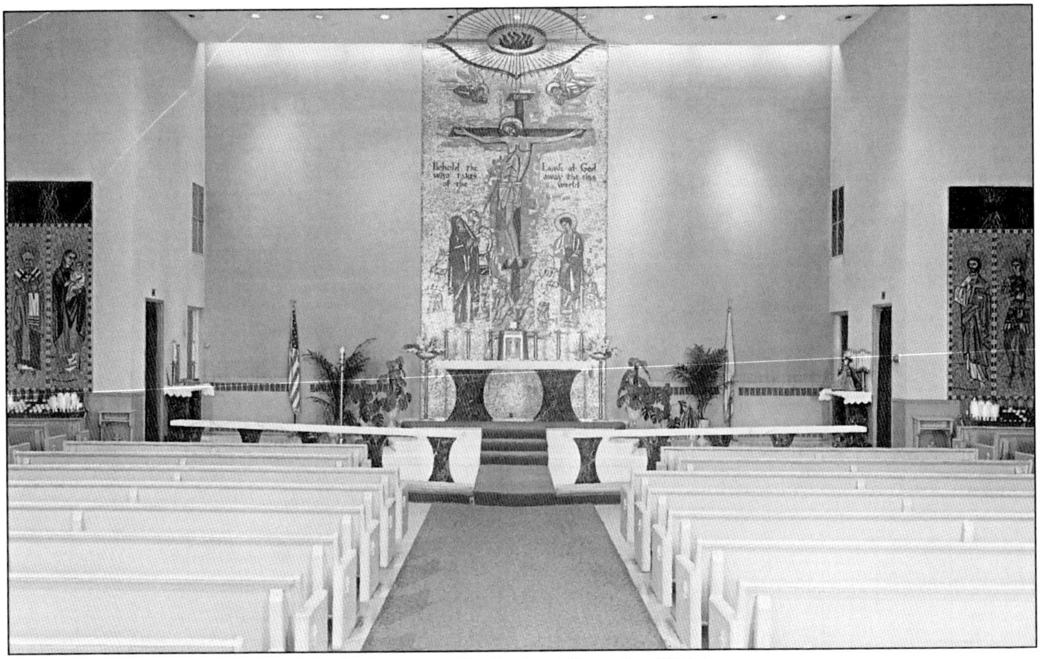

The interior of the St. George Byzantine Catholic Church, 1960.

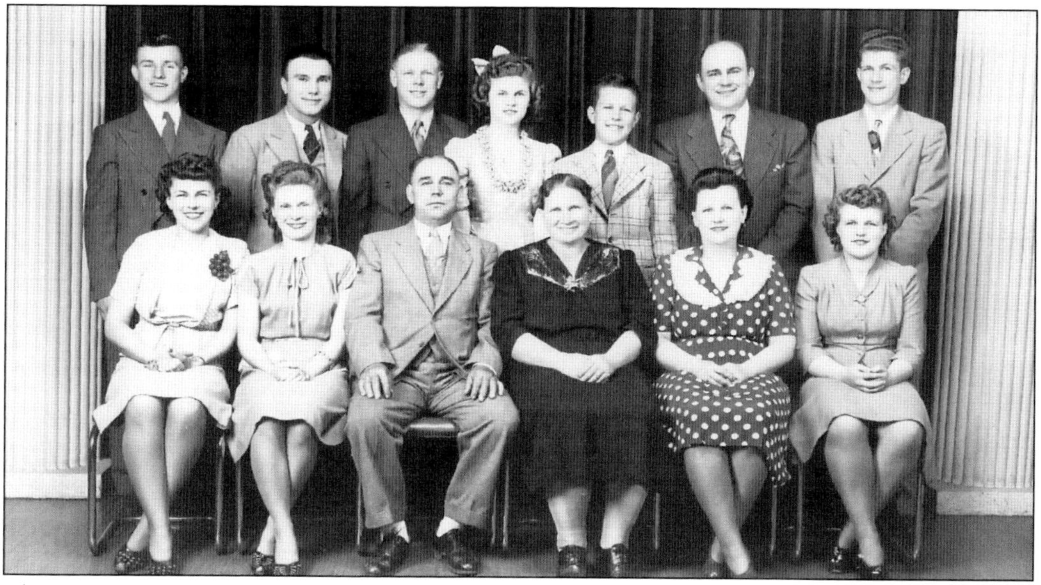

The Pancurak family. Joseph Pancurak and Anna Hutnyan came from Austria, Hungary. Joseph married Anna in 1908 in Yonkers, and moved to Mahoney City, P.A., where he became a butcher. The couple had two sons, Joseph and George. Anna died in 1913. Joseph married her sister Julia, and they had nine children. By 1942, the family moved to 31 West Sixteenth Street. Joseph Sr. was a blacksmith, butcher, and landscaper in Linden. He was the patriarch of eleven children, twenty-eight grandchildren, forty-seven great-grandchildren, and six great-great-grandchildren. From left to right are (front row) Betty Wade, Ann Ondek, parents Joseph Sr. and Julia, Mary Stetts, and Olga Tyburczy; (back row) Steve, George Pencer, Andy, Ronnie Bakunas, Emil, Joe Jr., and Michael.

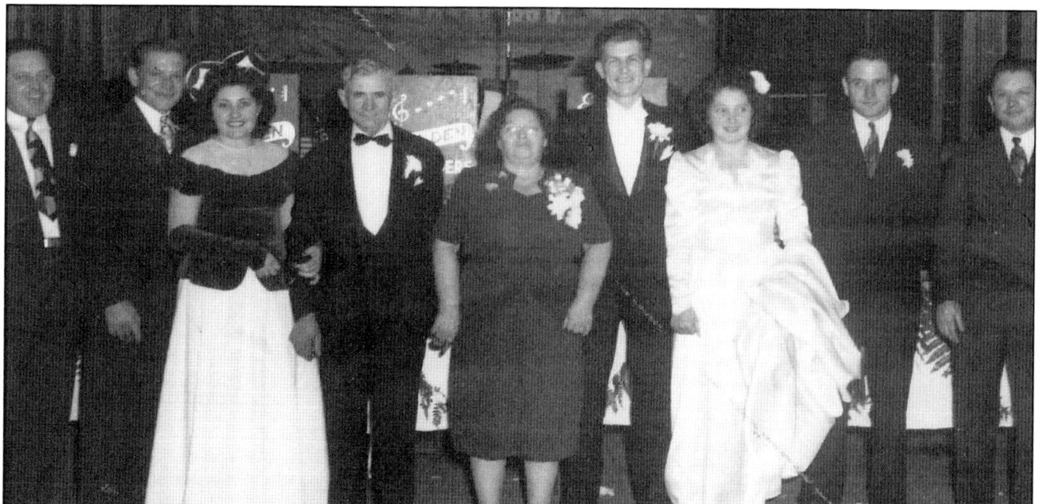

The Gorecki family. John Gorecki and Amelia Kozakiewicz came from Poland and were married in 1910 in Bayonne. As the head of the family they had six children, eight grandchildren, twenty great-grandchildren, and four great-great-grandchildren. This is a wedding photograph of Irene Gorecki and Michael Pancurak taken on November 15, 1947. Pictured are, from left to right, Raymond, Henry, Cecilia (later Baldwin), parents John and Amelia, Michael and Irene Pancurak, Stanley, and Joseph.

Bibliography

Cunningham, John T. *New Jersey: A Mirror on America.* Afton Publishers: Florham Park, 1978.
Honeyman, A. Van Doren. *History of Union County* (3 vols.). Lewis Historical Publishing, 1923.
Lawrence, Grace F. and Sara Light. *History of the Schools of Linden*. Linden: Linden Board of Education, 1961.
League of Women Voters. *This is Linden*. Linden, 1961.
"Looking back to Look Ahead: The Story of 100 Years of Vigorous Growth, City of Linden, NJ." 1961.
Shippey, Melda. *The Winans Family*. Family History Publishers: Bountiful, UT, 1990.
Weisbrot, William and Isabelle Newmark. *The History of Linden*. Linden: WPA project, 1938.

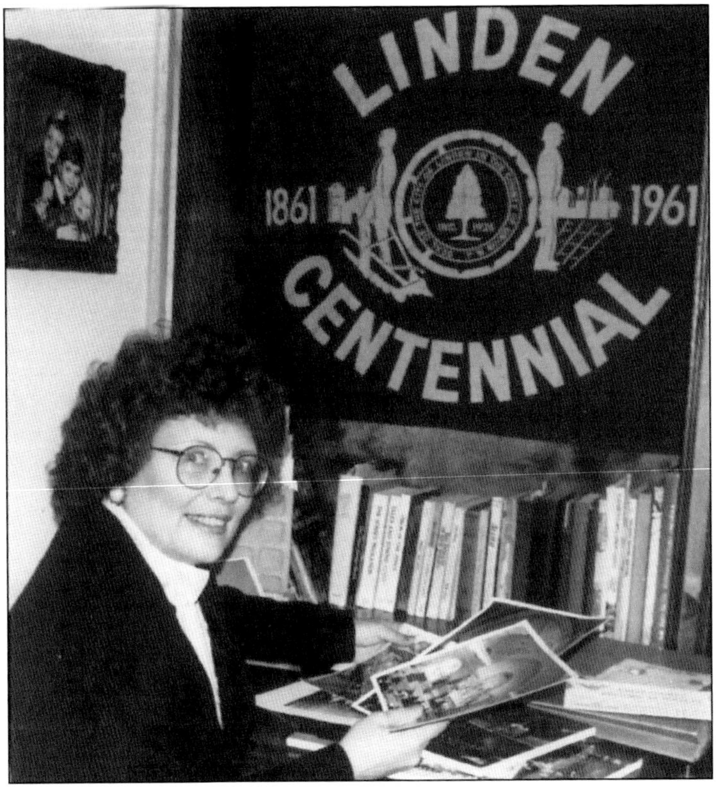

Lauren Pancurak Yeats.